IMAGINING AND REIMAGINING THE RESTORATION

IMAGINING AND REIMAGINING THE RESTORATION

ROBERT A. REES

GREG KOFFORD BOOKS
SALT LAKE CITY

Copyright © 2025 Robert A. Rees.
Cover design copyright © 2025 Greg Kofford Books, Inc.
Cover design by Loyd Isao Ericson.
Cover image imagined by Robert A. Rees using Chat GPT.

Published in the USA.

All rights reserved. No part of this volume may be reproduced in any form without written permission from the publisher, Greg Kofford Books. The views expressed herein are the responsibility of the author and do not necessarily represent the position of Greg Kofford Books.

ISBN: 978-1-58958-824-0 (paperback)
Also available in ebook.

Greg Kofford Books
P. O. Box 1362
Draper, UT 84020
www.gregkofford.com
facebook.com/gkbooks
twitter.com/gkbooks

Library of Congress Control Number: 2025934401

This book is dedicated to two women
with remarkable gifts of imagination—
Ruth Stanfield Rees and
Gloria Gardner Rees—
whose love, patience, and inspiration have greatly
deepened, enriched, and enlarged my own imagination,
and to all women who use their gifts of imagination
to bless God's children, beginning with Eve
who imagined glorious possibilities beyond the Garden.

A special debt of gratitude to two angels disguised as gifted editors:
Dawn Hall Anderson and Dlora Hall Dalton.

Contents

Foreword: The Perils and Possibilities of Imagination,   ix
        by Philip Barlow

Introduction: The Gift and Power of the Imagination,   1

1. The Imagination and Christ,   7
2. Imagining the Restoration: Joseph Smith and the Face of Christ,   17

        Interlude 1A: Somewhere Near Palmyra,   27
        Interlude 1B: Emma in Sunlight,   29

3. Searching for Heavenly Mother: Toward an Imaginative Latter-day Saint Theology,   33

        Interlude 2A: A Mother Here,   45
        Interlude 2B: Her,   47
        Interlude 2C: Birdsong/Eve's Song,   49
        Interlude 2D: A Final Gift of Grace,   51

4. Imagining Mary, Mother of the Messiah,   53

        Interlude 3: Mothers,   61

5. *Tikkun K'nessiah*: Repairing the Church,   63
6. Imagining "All Are Alike unto God": Lester Bush's Gift of Revelation to the Restoration,   75
7. Toward a Feminine Mormon Midrash: Mormon Women and the Imaginative Reading of Scripture,   81

        Interlude 4A: The Prodigal Daughter,   95
        Interlude 4B: Abish,   101

8. All In the Family: Opening Our Hearts, Homes, and Chapels to Our LGBTQ Members,   105

9. Imagining a Holier Holy Week,   121

      Interlude 5A: Calvary,   127
      Interlude 5B: The Empty Tomb,   129

10. Imagining a Whole and Healthy Planet: Earth Stewardship in Light of Matthew 25,   133

11. Forgiving the Church and Loving the Saints: Spiritual Evolution and the Kingdom of God,   141

12. Why the Imagination is Essential for the Ultimate Flowering of Mormonism,   159

A Final Word on the Imagination and Love,   173

Acknowledgments, 175

Bibliography,   177

Index,   187

FOREWORD

The Perils and Possibilities of Imagination

Philip Barlow

Senior Research Scholar, Neal A. Maxwell Institute for Religious Scholarship

> Imagine there's no heaven
> It's easy if you try
> No hell below us
> Above us, only sky . . .
>
> Imagine there's no countries
> It isn't hard to do
> Nothing to kill or die for
> And no religion, too . . .
>
> You may say I'm a dreamer
> But I'm not the only one
> I hope someday you'll join us
> And the world will be as one.

I've long been a sucker for the best of John Lennon's creations. His 1971 song "Imagine" ranks among them—an anthem for the generation that dreamt it, a nostalgic hymn of hope for others who followed. Among the dangers of the ballad's siren lure, however, is that in our swooning we may overlook the several *layers* of imagining into which "the thinking man's Beatle" beckons us. We are invited to imagine a world free of a heaven, which in turn is imagined, Marxist style, as a place of pipe dreams and fears, a place that anesthetizes and distracts us from the realities of the here and now on earth. In the song's imaginary, heaven and countries and religion are the sources of illusion, possessiveness, and conflict. If we can rid ourselves of the former, we will free ourselves of the latter too. The world will then be free to share the world in bliss.

Lennon does have a point. Religion, religion's heavens, and nationalism have indeed engendered illusion, greed, and strife across history. But then so also have the vain imaginings of secular folk.[1] These threats are

---

1. We need only glance back at an earlier and Russian Vladimir Lenin, who similarly and through violent means imagined the disappearance of all governing states. The asterisk to this beatific vision was that, until such time as the populace was prepared to actually live without legal oversight, "caretakers" such as himself—with absolute and merciless power—were required.

not inherently a religious problem, but rather a human problem that may assume a religious guise. We imagine too far if we construe these ills as inevitable whenever people gather in religious devotion or political alliance. Groups and institutions can accomplish much, for good *or* ill, that is beyond the means of any individual.

In the essays that follow, Robert "Bob" Rees—John Lennon's peer as an engine of creativity—does not ask us to imagine religion into oblivion. To the contrary, he asks us to imagine a specific religion, his own Church of Jesus Christ of Latter-day Saints, for which his passion runs deep, as living into its potential. Living in openness, that is, to new visions and an expanding apprehension of the Restoration's potency for lifting humans to a more godly state of being, and of being together. Line upon line, precept upon precept, wonder upon wonder.

Of course, to read of "imagination" in connection to the gospel of the Restoration may strike some as self-indulgent. If we are somber-browed disciples, the prospect may even offend our piety. Real religion, after all, is a serious and time-consuming affair. What is at stake is how we are to construe our lives, and how we are to spend them, before God. We may clutch at a simple gospel: that old-time religion precisely as we fancy our forebears to have understood it. The infrequent mention of "imagination" in scripture, in fact, tends to rail against it as a source of self-deception, vanity, foolish meanderings, and devious plots.

We might mistake this book's topic as self-indulgent for a second reason, for ours is an era of peril and urgency. The poor and the wounded languish within our reach. Stranger, friend, and family require our ministering. Aspiring Saints have scripture to study and lessons to prepare, to say nothing of dinner. Domestic and professional tasks swallow our days. Everything is more expensive than it was yesterday, so we must work harder if we are to afford it. Our democracy frays and our world warms. Fret and stress are default modes for many of us. Under such conditions, we cannot help but daydream or night dream here and there, glazing over. But who has time to deliberately surrender to the playful whims of imagining, let alone to *read* of imagining?

Those of us who are framed by such sensibilities as these, especially we who live in technologized prosperity, with its attendant sense of *hurry*, would do well to examine our sense of time. If in our hustle we find no space for imagination, for the play and work of it, especially in our apprehension and application of our magnificently expansive gospel, it may be time to purchase *fanatic insurance*. That is to say, if our imaginations fail us while we flail amid the competing tugs in our daily lives, we are at risk of becoming fanatics: people who double their speed when they have lost their way. Common symptoms of this brand of fanaticism are fatigue without fulfillment, submersion in trivial diversions, excess confidence that our static understandings of the gospel constitute the gospel's apex, and a countervailing undercurrent to this overconfidence that plays out as anxiety or malaise (in our children if not in ourselves). The distinguishing character of this malaise is that it is unaware of being itself until it metastasizes, at last becoming despair. Without an active imagination enlarging our understanding, we may wake one day to find our passion for the gospel has paled. We may find ourselves bored, when in fact the boringness lies in us.

Like courage and time,[2] imagination is in fact a principle of the gospel without being widely recognized as such. We can scarcely ponder a precept or phenomenon until we have named it. But "imagination" lurks everywhere in our gospel. It can be discerned in scriptural and pulpit urgings to "ponder." It is inherent in the Lord's declaration that we are amiss ("damned," in fact, or spiritually blocked) if we wait to be commanded in all things (D&C 58:26–29). It is latent in diverse accounts that tell of prophets and witnesses seeing with their "spiritual eyes" and noting that all things were created spiritually before they were created physically upon the earth. It is there in the close scriptural association twixt "dream" and "vision." The Restoration's founding prophet displayed the import of imagination through a thousand experimental actions and through visions and even explicitly through his words: "Thy mind, O man! if thou wilt lead a soul unto salvation, must stretch as high as the utmost heavens, and search into and contemplate the darkest abyss, and the broad expanse of eternity—thou must commune with God."[3]

While our imaginations might be unleashed by contemplation of the creations of our Creator and by the implications of the Restoration midwifed into the world through the Prophet Joseph Smith, it may help us also to consider more proximate examples of faithful master imaginers. The life and writings of Robert Rees, including the creative poetic and midrashic compositions of his own imagination that punctuate this volume,

---

2. For an explanation, see Philip L. Barlow, *Time: Themes in the Doctrine and Covenants* (Maxwell Institute and Deseret Book, 2024).

3. "History, 1838–1856, volume C-1 [2 November 1838–31 July 1842]," The Joseph Smith Papers, https://www.josephsmithpapers.org/paper-summary/history-1838-1856-volume-c-1-2-november-1838-31-july-1842/86.

comprise a striking case study. He is an uncommon person who has lived an uncommon life and has written with uncommon reach and imagination. There is scarcely a significant aspect of the Restoration on which he has not made creative public comment, often in print. Yet more rare, he has, in the pages that follow, contemplated imagination itself: a provocation to me and, I hope, to you.

Better to grasp what Rees hath wrought in this collection, imagine a strand in the life of the ingenious John Lennon, who endured a tough childhood in the rough quarters of England's Liverpool and Woolton. He acted out that inheritance as he grew, frightening the parents of his mates. According to his later reflections and those of Paul McCartney, this background was not irrelevant to his sometimes edgy creativity. Lennon could not abide tedium and was impatient with societal as well as musical conventions. His resulting musical success was historic. However, his personal life, though episodically flashing courage in admirable causes, was laced with alienation, cruelty, violence, drugs, and despair.

The ingenious Bob Rees endured a childhood rather more grim than Lennon's. Because these early years somehow did not crush him, Rees's origins may provide clues to his extraordinary later life, which brims with the opposite of alienation and despair. Despite its rawness and because of its bearing on our topic, a glimpse at his beginnings is thus warranted. His childhood and teen years were chaotic, dispiriting, and violent.

His parents themselves had difficult childhoods, beset by the Great Depression. From a young age, his mother was sexually abused, serially, by her father, which left her broken and vulnerable. Like most of the adults in Bob's life, she became an alcoholic. When she became pregnant with her second child, Bob, she was severely depressed and attempted to abort him. The child survived, but while still an infant and while his father was away looking for work, Bob's mother was seduced and impregnated by a predatory friend who persuaded her to run away with him, thus abandoning Bob and his brother. What followed was a series of marriages, divorces, abuses, addictions, and additional abandonments. Bob's mother never fully escaped the lacerations of her own childhood. Members of Bob's family experienced physical, sexual, and emotional abuse; prostitution; incest; a variety of addictions; murder; prison; and chronic homelessness. Bob's father struggled with related problems, including a lifelong battle with alcoholism. His conversion to The Church of Jesus Christ of Latter-day Saints when Bob was ten, however, led to periods of relative stability until the boy left home for college at age seventeen.

Having found a safe and nurturing home in the Church, if not consistently in his own home, Bob developed a deep-seated faith and constructive way of making sense of the world. That led to a life-changing patriarchal blessing at fifteen, college at BYU, and a mission at nineteen. Following his mission and his graduation from BYU, Bob won a Woodrow Wilson national fellowship to graduate school (at the University of Wisconsin), married and started a family, completed his PhD, and began his teaching career at UCLA in 1966.

While at BYU, Bob developed an early interest in Latter-day Saint/Mormon studies under the tutelage of such scholars as Hugh Nibley, Robert Thomas, and Truman Madsen. This led to his teaching at an LDS Institute of Religion at UW and his appointment as the second editor of *Dialogue: A Journal of Mormon Thought* early in his career at UCLA. His long involvement in Mormon studies led him, after retirement, to establish, direct, and teach Mormon/Latter-day Saint studies at the Graduate Theological Union in Berkeley (2010–2022) and to teach a class on Mormonism at UC Berkeley.

Rees's religious imagination has expanded beyond the intellectual realms of teaching and scholarship. It has achieved hands-on expression in his cofounding and fostering a series of enterprises focused on bettering and saving the lives of thousands. These initiatives include:

- The non-profit Lithuanian foundation, "Šeima" ("Family"), when he served in the presidency of the Baltic States Mission in 1994–1996.
- The Bountiful Children's Foundation, which provides nutritional supplementation to pregnant women, nursing mothers, and malnourished children for the first one thousand days of life (crucial to brain and body development) and which teaches health and cognitive development skills to families in underserved areas of the globe.
- Artsreach, a program that takes arts and humanities programs into California juvenile and prison facilities. (Bob and his wife, Gloria, are presently part of the Latter-day Saint prison ministry at San Quentin.)
- The FastForward for the Planet Foundation, which supports members of the world's faiths and others of goodwill to collectively address issues relating to the health and well-being of the earth, its people, and all its living things by raising funds saved through a regular fast or through other modest sacrifices for the future of the planet. This

spreads among others the Restoration idea of charitable fasting, while for Latter-day Saints it means an invitation to fast a second time each month. Currently FastForward is working with other organizations to save the Great Salt Lake.

One may or may not concur with every scenario Rees proffers in *Imagining and Reimagining* for our consideration of a more imaginative discipleship. Whatever our individual judgments may be, I would judge it a mistake to ignore this voice and the topics of its rumination. When Jesus washed the feet of his disciples, it was an act of divine humility, an act of love, an act of instruction. *It was also an act of the imagination.* And an invitation to go and do likewise.

Every facet of the Restoration and every principle of the gospel requires the organic, imaginative effort to grasp and enact it. Our imaginations are, in fact, ever at work whether or not we are aware of it. We all have to "image"—to make sense of—all that we hear or see, all that we embrace or reject. And as we live into what we imagine, we may as well make our effort generous, beautiful, thoughtful, and deliberate. When joined to love, faith, wisdom, and effort, imagination is of the essence. It just may be that Bob Rees, like poet Mary Oliver, is onto something:

> I have refused to live
> locked in the orderly house of
>   reasons and proofs.
> The world I live in and believe in
> is wider than that. And anyway,
>   what's wrong with *Maybe*?
>
> You wouldn't believe what once or
> twice I have seen. I'll just
>   tell you this:
> only if there are angels in your head will you
>   ever, possibly, see one.[4]

---

4. Mary Oliver, "The World I Live In," in *Felicity: Poems* (Penguin Books, 2017), 11.

INTRODUCTION

The Gift and Power of the Imagination

"Perhaps the imagination is the true teleological organ in our evolution, directing all change."

—Ihab Hassan[1]

The imagination is one of the greatest gifts of God and might be considered the greatest unused gift of the Spirit. Genesis suggests that before God (or in Latter-day Saint cosmology, the Gods) created anything, They first imagined it. We know that God and the prophets want us to use our imaginations; otherwise, so much of our sacred texts would not have been written in poetic language. Sixty percent of the Old Testament is presented to us in poetry. Moreover, much of sacred writ relies on such poetic devices as symbolism, imagery, metaphor, allusion, and other devices alongside story, parable, myth, allegory, and other genres—elements and styles that convey meaning that lies beyond the surface of the text. Some scriptural texts (e.g., Psalms, Isaiah, and John's amazing Revelation) cannot be opened to our understanding without the alertness of our eyes and ears as well as our hearts and minds—and even our bodies, as when we experience awe in the presence of certain passages. In other words, the function of scripture is to appeal to our entire beings—our wholeness. Thus, if, as Johannes Kepler posited, the purpose of science is to think God's thoughts after Him, one might say that one of the purposes of scripture is to imagine God's imaginings after Him. One might even imagine God saying, "Come, let us imagine together!"

The Oxford English Dictionary defines imagination as "the creative faculty of the mind in its highest aspect; the power of framing new and striking . . . conceptions."[2] Imagination reveals not what is, but what is possible. I am aware of the negative ways in which the term "imagination"

---

1. Ihab Hassan, "Fiction and Future: An Extravaganza for Voices and Tape," 179.
2. Oxford English Dictionary, s.v. "Imagination." The following more detailed definition, also from the OED, may be helpful in considering the various ways in which the imagination is discussed and explored in the chapters of this collection: "The power or capacity to form internal images or ideas of objects and situations not actually present to the senses, including remembered objects and situations, and those constructed by mentally combining or projecting images of previously experienced qualities, objects, and situations.

is sometimes qualified in scripture with such adjectives as *vain, evil, wicked,* and *foolish.* Imagination can and sometimes does run in those directions, just as with all human inclinations and capabilities. What I have in mind for the chapters and creative expressions in this book is more in keeping with the promise made to William Law in the Doctrine and Covenants: "He shall mount up in the imagination of his thoughts as upon eagles' wings" (D&C 124:99). God reveals to prophets (and others) what He imagines is possible (both in this life and in the eternities) and what He wants them and us to imagine and then do. Such is reflected in the following translation of Hosea 12:10 where God says, "In the hands of the prophets shall I imagine."[3]

The astonishing revelations that began when Joseph Smith went into the woods to pray came about because he imagined some kind of an answer, although he could not possibly have imagined the answer he received nor the dramatic, even startling, way it was presented to him. That vision expanded his imagination exponentially and emboldened him both to seek additional revelations and to awaken his imagination as to their meaning and possibilities. What flowed from those seminal revelations was the beginning of what Latter-day Saints call the Restoration. According to Harold Bloom, former distinguished professor of religion and humanities at New York and Yale Universities, Joseph Smith "was an authentic religious genius and surpassed all Americans, before or since, in the possession and expression of the religion-making imagination. . . . There had to be an immense power of the myth-making imagination at work to sustain so astonishing an innovation" as the Restoration.[4]

The promises of that restoration are found in Smith's personal history and in the new scriptures he introduced to the world. According to Kathleen Flake, then a professor of religion at Vanderbilt University, "Smith's narrative history of human and divine interaction was ultimately oriented *to a future time that served as a basis for acting in the present.* It provided a world of meaning by which his believing readers understood themselves existentially, including their future and not merely their past." This is precisely what I am proposing—that we orient ourselves to a

---

Also (especially in modern philosophy): the power or capacity by which the mind integrates sensory data in the process of perception."

3. Rachael Gordon, "The Power of Imagination: A Kabbalistic Understanding." Unless noted, all biblical quotations are from the King James Version.

4. Harold Bloom, *The American Religion: The Emergence of the Post-Christian Nation,* 91–92.

reimagined future by drawing upon the past and acting in the present. Flake adds, "Most fundamentally, Smith's writings give his believing readers a different sense of what was and what will be"—which, I contend, is one of the main functions of our imagination.[5]

According to Bloom, Smith did not live to see the full flowering of his visionary imagination. What is more, Bloom does not believe Smith's modern and contemporary followers have completely fulfilled or continued the promise and possibilities of the Prophet's religion-making imagination. No less an authority than B. H. Roberts came to the same conclusion at the end of the nineteenth century. Roberts distinguished between what he calls "disciples pure and simple . . . whose whole intellectual life . . . consists of their partisanship . . . and mere repetition" of religious formulas and those disciples who "bring to the new teaching, from the first, *their own personal contribution* . . . [and] help lead the thought that they accept to a truer expression. They force it beyond its earlier and cruder stages of development."[6] Note Roberts's use of the word "force," by which, in this context, I think he intended "[to] bring about by unusual effort."[7] Roberts added (and this is the part of his essay most relevant to reimagining the Restoration) that Mormonism "calls for thoughtful [and I believe he also intended *imaginative*] disciples who will not be content with merely repeating some of its truths, but will develop its truths; and enlarge . . . [Mormonism] by that development." Then he states this astonishing idea: "Not half—not one-hundredth part—not a thousandth part of that which Joseph Smith revealed to the Church has yet been unfolded, *either to the Church* or to the world."

Pause a minute to consider the profound implications of such a statement. Most Latter-day Saints would readily agree that the truths revealed to the Prophet have yet to be unfolded to the world but would likely have difficulty agreeing with Roberts that they have not been unfolded in their fullness to the Church. I contend that his statement should excite our imaginations rather than provoke our doubts, because they encourage our active participation in that very unfolding. Roberts continues, "The work of the expounder has scarcely begun. The Prophet planted by teaching the germ-truths of the great dispensation of the

---

5. Kathleen Flake, "Translating Time: The Nature and Function of Joseph Smith's Narrative Canon," 524–25 (emphasis added).

6. B. H. Roberts, "Two Kinds of Disciples," 712–13 (emphasis added).

7. Online Etymology Dictionary, s.v. "force." The entry is listed under the etymology of force as a verb.

fullness of times. The watering and the weeding [are] going on, and God is giving the increase, *and will give it more abundantly in the future as more intelligent* [and, one might add, *more imaginative*] *discipleship shall obtain.*" Roberts adds, God "will give it more abundantly in the future."[8] To some extent our present is a partial fulfillment of that "more abundant future," but we are also charged with extending the Prophet's vision of the Restoration into an even grander, more abundant future.

What Roberts emphasizes, I believe, is that Mormonism's future requires not a passive waiting for God to reveal those things yet to be revealed, but an active, energetic, imaginative seeking and working for their unfolding. He concludes,

> The disciples of "Mormonism" [which includes contemporary Latter-day Saints], growing discontented with the *necessarily primitive* methods which have hitherto prevailed in sustaining the doctrine, will yet take *profounder and broader* views of the great doctrines committed to the Church; and, departing from mere repetition, *will cast them in new formulas*; cooperating in the works of the Spirit, until they help to give to the truths received a more forceful expression and carry it beyond the earlier and cruder stages of its development.[9]

Roberts's call for "profounder and broader views" and "casting . . . new formulas" is as clear and concise an invitation to imaginative discipleship as I can conceive—or imagine! In the modern Church, we have the choice to transform some of those "primitive methods" into more progressive ones. Such progressive transformation leads to liberation. As Ihab Hassan says, "Liberations come from some strange region where the imagination meets change. . . . We need to reimagine change itself, else we labor to confirm all our errors."[10]

One of Mormonism's unique doctrines is that even though revelation for the Church comes through the prophet, revelation itself is both continuous and scattered—it is democratically available—meaning that all have the opportunity, even the responsibility, to seek for and receive it, although clearly some of us do not realize this principle nor act upon it. The philosopher John O'Donohue stated in a 2007 interview:

> All knowing has an imaginative element in it. We don't see the world as it is at all. Our consciousness always co-creates everything we see. So what you are seeing is not just out there, on its own. You are always seeing it through

---

8. Roberts, "Two Kinds of Disciples," 713 (emphasis added).
9. Roberts, 713 (emphasis added).
10. Ihab Hassan, *Liberations: New Essays on the Humanities in Revolution*, xv.

the lens of your own thinking. Therefore, you are co-creating the world, whether you like it or not.[11]

That was the divine design from the beginning. And so it will continue to be, worlds without end, which should cause us to rejoice.

---

11. Diane Covington, "The Unseen Life that Dreams Us: John O'Donohue on the Secret Landscapes of Imagination and Spirit," 11.

CHAPTER ONE

The Imagination and Christ

At a performance of Bach's wondrous Christmas Oratorio several years ago, I was struck by how significantly and deeply Christ can live in our imaginations—if we truly open our hearts, minds, and spirits to the possibilities that his birth holds for those of us who believe in him and, in a sense, for all the world, including the millions who have little understanding of his influence on creation and on their eternal destinies but who nevertheless are recipients of his love and grace.

The imagination is one of the greatest gifts God has implanted in our hearts, minds, and souls. In his book on the origins of the English imagination, Peter Ackroyd, in citing the seventeenth-century poet Henry Vaughan, speaks of the imagination as being "like a great *Ring* of pure and endless light." Thus, as Ackroyd, states, "it has no beginning and no end; it moves backwards as well as forwards."[1]

In speaking of Christ's miraculous birth in his poem, "The Gift," William Carlos Williams has written,

> . . . the imagination
> knows all stories
>   before they are told
> and knows the truth of this one
>   past all deflection.[2]

There is no story in the annals of human history as this simple story of a baby born in a manger that has so captivated the imagination in story, song, and dance; in sculpture, art, and architecture; and in a wide array of graphic and visual expressions. From the time our ancient ancestors first heard this good news from the mouths of prophets, to the Virgin Mary who heard it from the lips of the angel Gabriel, to the shepherds who heard it from the heavenly hosts that starlit night, and to all who have heard it over the two thousand years since, it has awakened our imaginations as no other story has. And it awakens them anew each Christmas season and will continue to do so as long as there is one person on earth left to reimagine what has come to be known as the greatest story ever told. As the Jewish poetic prayer says, "'Were all the skies parchment, all

---

1. Peter Ackroyd, *Albion: The Origins of the English Imagination*, xxvii.
2. William Carlos Williams, "The Gift."

the reeds quills, all the seas and waters made of ink, and every inhabitant of earth a scribe,' the glories of God still could not be adequately described. Equally impossible, however, to maintain silence."[3] This is why, as we are told, the shepherds ran "with haste" to tell the news when the angel said, "For unto you is born this night in the City of David, a savior who is Christ the Lord" (Luke 1:14). The good news cries out to be imagined and reimagined, told and retold again and again.

Each Christmas we are blessed with magnificent images of this central event in human history. Some, like the simple telling in Luke's gospel, use the power of language to make the story come alive in our hearts and minds. Through Luke's straight forward, matter-of-fact narrative, we picture the events as they were "handed down . . . by those who from the first were eyewitnesses and servants of the word." As a physician, St. Luke is not content to just accept these stories as he has heard them from others but has researched and traced them to their sources: "Therefore since I myself have carefully investigated everything from the beginning," which means, I believe, that he may even have tracked down shepherds who were in the field that glorious night. At any rate, he gives what he calls "an orderly [thorough and accurate] account . . . so that you may know the certainty of the things you have been taught" (Luke 1:1–4, NIV). Note that Luke is writing to "Theophilus," literally "one who loves God."

Another person who loves God is the Book of Mormon prophet Nephi. Having been told of his father's vision, Nephi, not content with seeing through his father's eyes, seeks the clarity and certainty of his own vision so that he can "see, and hear, and know of these things [for himself] by the power of the Holy Ghost" (1 Ne. 10:17). The first thing the angel shows Nephi is a vision of the tree that his father had seen, whose beauty Nephi declares "was far beyond, yea, exceeding of all beauty; and the whiteness thereof did exceed the whiteness of the driven snow" (11:8).

The angel then asks Nephi what he desires, and Nephi responds, "To know the interpretation thereof." In other words, Nephi—recognizing that what he has seen is significant, but, as with what normally happens when people see signs and symbols or images and metaphors, the meaning and significance of which may not be immediately apparent (in other words, beyond the capacity of their imaginations)—wants to know, "What does this mean?"

---

3. As quoted by David Wolpe, *The Healer of Shattered Hearts*, 47.

What is truly beautiful is that in response to Nephi's desire to know what the tree and its fruit mean, the angel doesn't tell him but instead immediately directs his attention to "the great city of Jerusalem . . . and the city of Nazareth" where he sees "a virgin most fair and beautiful above all other virgins." Pause for a moment to consider what it must have meant for Nephi to see the city of his birth, the city he left as a teenager and the one to which he returned, where he was commanded to behead his own relative, and from which he escaped into the desert with the sacred record of his people, a record that included prophecies of this very city. This must have been a profound moment of nostalgia as well as gratitude for him. We can surmise that Nephi knew of Nazareth, perhaps from having visited it when he lived in Jerusalem, but most likely because of its mention in a scripture now lost to the world. In giving Nazareth as the birthplace of the savior, Matthew states, "So was fulfilled what was said through the prophets: he will be called a Nazarene" (Matt. 2:23, NIV).

Seeing Mary and likely recognizing her as the prophesied mother of the promised Messiah, Nephi next observes that she is "carried away in the Spirit for the space of time," after which he sees her "bearing a child in her arms." Perhaps aware that Nephi may not know or is unsure of the meaning of what he is seeing, the angel declares, "Behold the Lamb of God, yea, even the Son of the Eternal Father." Perhaps hoping to awaken Nephi's imagination, he next asks, "Knowest thou the meaning of the tree which thy father saw?" Nephi, showing that he sees the connection between the revelation of the Messiah and the fruit of the tree, immediately exclaims, "Yea, it is the love of God which sheddeth itself abroad in the hearts of the children of men. [In this context, *sheddeth*, from Middle English, means "as a tree sheds its leaves."[4]] Wherefore it is most desirable above all things." Confirming and expanding Nephi's interpretation, the angel says, "Yea, and the most joyous to the soul." (1 Ne. 11:18–24). With this enlightened understanding, the angel knows Nephi is not only prepared for the vision of Christ's life from his birth to Calvary but also his promised visit to the Promised Land and the tragic unfolding of Nephite history.

Our Father in Heaven has blessed some individuals with marvelous, imaginative gifts. Artists like Raphael, Michelangelo, Botticelli, and other masters use rich pigment to give color and shape to the birth of Christ in its marvelous variety of imagined glory and beauty. Composers like Praetorius, Bach, and Handel, all blessed with musical imaginations, use

---

4. Online Etymology Dictionary, s.v. "shed."

sounds and words to tell the story through melody and rhythm so that, with our voices and hearing, we have an experience in which our entire bodies feel the power of the story. But the story is told not only by great narratives of sound and sense and of voices and visions, but also by simple, unlettered folk, by children, and by ordinary believers—like us—in whose hearts, minds, and imaginations the story is always alive. I love the following telling from the Massai:

> We believe that God made good His promise by sending His Son, Jesus Christ, a man in the flesh, a Jew by tribe, born poor in a little village, who left His home and was always on safari doing good, curing people by the power of God, teaching about God and man, showing the meaning of religion is love. He was rejected by his people, tortured and nailed hands and feet to a cross, and died. He lay buried in the grave, but the hyenas did not touch him, and on the third day, He rose from the grave. He ascended to the skies. He is the Lord.[5]

The gift of the imagination that God gives to all his children—marvelously, never two alike in all of creation—is the capacity to imagine His Son in infinite ways and the power to ever make it new. It is with love that God made us in His image, but it was with a special love that He created us to imagine Him as uniquely as each of us is capable of doing. Thus, to each of us He appears as we see Him in our imaginations, in our hearts, and in our minds. As "Rabbi Levi said: God appeared to Israel in infinite images reflecting the appearance of each individual, and all felt personally addressed."[6]

The ways in which we bring the Christ child alive in our hearts and minds is a reflection of both our imaginative abilities and our devotion. Whatever gifts of imagination we are blessed to have, I believe that we each have the capacity to deepen and enrich such gifts. As Rabbi David Wolpe says, "Any description of God's qualities is also a statement about our lives and the way we wish them to be."[7] As we expand and deepen our capacity to experience God's love and feel our own capacity to love expand, I believe our imaginations can expand infinitely and eternally. According to Neville Gardner, "All things exist in the human Imagination. . . . The world of Imagination is infinite and eternal, whereas the world of generation or vegetation is finite and temporal.

---

5. Krista Tippitt, "Transcript for Jaroslav Pelikan—The Need for Creeds."
6. Wolpe, *The Healer*, 47.
7. Wolpe, 47.

There exists in that eternal world the permanent reality of everything we see reflected in this glass of nature."[8]

The scriptures speak of the vain and foolish imaginations of our hearts, which I take to be those that are self-centered rather than Christ- or other-centered. The English writer Eudora Welty has written poems and stories in which she contrasts a person named Cramer (from Gaelic, meaning "strong man"[9]), who has an egocentric imagination, with one whose imagination is centered squarely on Christ. In a poem called "The Nativity," Cramer sees himself, not the Lord, as his "heart's praise" and his "heart's flame." He stands for the soulless, modern person who worships himself rather than, as the Anglican catechism puts it, seeking "to glorify God and enjoy him forever."

In Welty's story "The Seraph and the Zambesi," the nativity is set in Africa with Cramer as a central character who celebrates himself rather than Christ. As he rehearses a Christmas masque or play he has written, in which natives play the various parts of the Nativity story, a real seraph appears. Like the seraphim described in the sixth chapter of Isaiah (which is traditionally believed to allude to the birth of Christ[10]), this seraph has three sets of wings. Cramer, who says he can't imagine this being a real seraph, shouts "Hamba!" or "Go away!" However, the seraph tells Cramer that his nativity masque won't do and must be replaced by the seraph's own nativity play. Here, the seraphim, who, according to *A Dictionary of Angels* "are the angels of love, of light, and of fire,"[11] stand for Christ and his refining, renewing glory.

Christ himself possesses the greatest imagination of all God's children, showing that imagination is one of the characteristics of godhood. In the preexistence, along with the Father and Mother, Jesus participated in imagining the world and all its possibilities and then helped shape it into existence. In the Promised Land of the Book of Mormon, Christ speaks as his mature, divine self on the day he will be born. To the prophet Nephi (the son of Nephi and grandson of Helaman), who had "cried mightily to his God in behalf of his people . . . who were about to be destroyed because

---

8. Neville Goddard Lectures: "All Things Exist in the Human Imagination," Cool Wisdom Books.

9. "The name Cramer originally appeared in Gaelic as 'Mac Threinfir,' from the words 'trean,' which means 'strong,' and 'fear' which means 'man.'" "Cramer History, Family Crest & Coat of Arms."

10. Especially verses 3 and 8.

11. Gustav Davidson, *A Dictionary of Angels: Including the Fallen Angels*, 267.

of their faith" in the prophesies of Christ's birth, Christ says, "Lift up your head and be of good cheer for behold, the time is at hand and on this night shall the sign be given, and on the morrow come I into the world to show unto the world that I will fulfill that which I have caused to be spoken by the mouth of my holy prophets" (3 Ne. 1:11–13). This was followed by a night without darkness in which, just as in the Old World, "a new star did appear" (v. 21).

In the hours between his speaking to the Nephites and being born from Mary's womb, Jesus must have tried to imagine what it would be like to condescend by stepping down from his heavenly throne to become that helpless of all creatures, a human baby. Standing in the heavens on the verge of what must have been—even for him—an inconceivable transformation, beholding the earth, seeing the events unfold toward that dramatic, liminal moment in which he would cross the threshold from the indescribable glories of his heavenly home to the stark simplicity and commonness of a humble manger, he must have imagined what it would be like to surrender his godly power to become that helpless child. Yet, it is likely also true that, not having ever been mortal, he was not capable of imagining or even envisioning all that mortality held for him. We surmise this because thirty-three years later in Gethsemane, he seemed surprised, even astonished at the weight of the burden of our sins, and the next day was so overwhelmed by the excruciating pain of being nailed to the cross that he cried out for deliverance to that same heaven where he had once reigned supreme.

As he grew in measure and stature, so his imagination grew until it could encompass not only the whole world, but all God's creatures in it, which means that he could imagine each one of us; he could imagine the ways in which many of us would reject him, the ways others would try to follow him and fail, and the ways in which the most faithful would follow him regardless of the cost.

Thus, when he understood as a mortal what his full mission entailed—perhaps not fully until that last triumphal but nevertheless fatal week when he rode the donkey into Jerusalem—he knew that he would soon be compelled by his great love to go beyond imagination to the reality of immense suffering. The Book of Mormon teaches us something profound about this realization. There, Alma explains,

> And he [Christ] shall go forth, suffering pains and afflictions and temptations of every kind; and this that the word might be fulfilled which saith he will take upon him the pains and the sicknesses of his people. And he will

take upon him death, that he may loose the bands of death which bind his people; and he will take upon him their infirmities, that his bowels may be filled with mercy, according to the flesh, that he may know according to the flesh how to succor his people according to their infirmities. (Alma 7:11–12)

But consider this: "Now the Spirit knoweth all things [in other words, Jesus could have had some approximate understanding of the suffering he had to endure by revelation or through the power of his imagination]; nevertheless [Alma goes on to say] the Son of God suffereth according to the flesh that he might take upon him the sins of his people, that he might blot out their transgressions according to the power of his deliverance" (v. 13). In other words, Jesus chose, at the ultimate moment, to move beyond imagining what the Atonement would be like to actually experiencing it so that he might make our salvation a reality.

What caused him to choose this ultimate way, I believe, is that he imagined you and me trying to be faithful disciples yet falling short of the mark, doing things that would wound his heart, and therefore making it impossible for us to return with him to the presence of our Heavenly Father and Mother. Imagining our being in such a fallen state awakened all his faculties of godly sorrow, compassion, and imagination. It was, I believe, because he could imagine the world in all its possible tragedy, as well as its possible triumph and glory, that he agreed to be born and to take upon himself our sins, and to imagine that we all had the hope of redemption. And he invites us to join him both in imagining and in reaching our glorified end.

One of the aspects of a refined spiritual imagination is that it compels us to share it. In Marilynn Robinson's wonderful novel *Gilead,* the narrator, an aging minister who is close to death, tells of an experience when he was a boy on a trip with his father, looking for the graveyard where his grandfather is buried. When at last they find the gravestone, the father kneels before it and prays. As he does so, the son looks at the sky and sees "a full moon rising just as the sun was going down. Each of them was standing on its edge, with the most wonderful light between them. It seemed as if you could touch it, as if there were palpable currents of light suspended between them." He adds, "I wanted my father to see it, but I knew I'd have to startle him out of his prayer, and I wanted to do it the best way, so I took his hand and kissed it. And then I said, 'Look at the moon.'" His father looked and said, "I would never have thought this place could be beautiful. I'm glad to know that."[12] This impulse to share the beatific light is why Lehi wanted to share his vision of the tree with his wife and sons, and why, when Nephi saw his father's vision in his mind's eye—that is, in his imagination—he wanted to have his own imagination awakened, his own visionary experience of the Christ child's birth.

Such an imagination also explains Joseph Smith's desire to know Christ in a way that transcended the limited imaginations of the religious thinkers and ministers of his day. It was only such an imagination that could have awakened him to the Christ-centered glories of the Restoration. This is why I believe that, as pointed out earlier, the eminent Yale critic Harold Bloom called the Mormon Prophet an "authentic religious genius [who] surpassed all Americans, before or since, in the possession and expression of what could be called the religion-making imagination."[13]

Where do our imaginations find Christ? In Truman Capote's "A Christmas Memory," the old woman says,

> My, how foolish I am. . . . You know what I've always thought? . . . I've always thought a body would have to be sick and dying before they saw the Lord. And I imagined that when He came it would be like looking at the Baptist window: pretty as colored glass with the sun pouring through, such a shine you don't know it's getting dark. . . . But I'll wager it never happens. I'll wager at the very end a body realizes the Lord has already shown himself. That things as they are . . . just what they've always seen, was seeing him. As for me, I could leave the world with today in my eyes.[14]

As Angelus Silesius has written, "If in your heart you make a manger for his birth, then God will once again become a child on earth."[15] In an essay called "The Bible and Christian Imagination," N. T. Wright quotes Isaiah's prophecy that "the world *will* be filled with the glory of God, as the waters cover the sea." To this, he adds:

> We . . . are called to live between the vision of the world which is already filled with the glory of God, and a world which is yet to be filled with the glory of God, "as the waters cover the seas." It's a fascinating phrase. *How* do the waters cover the sea? They *are* the sea. God intends to flood the world with himself, with his love in fresh ways, in which what we already know of

---

12. Marilynn Robinson, *Gilead*, 14–15.
13. Harold Bloom, *The American Religion: The Emergence of the Post-Christian Nation*, 92.
14. Truman Capote, *The Complete Stories of Truman Capote*, 224–25.
15. Angelus Silesius, "Angelus Silesius Quotes."

the beauty and power and majesty of creation will be taken up and enhanced yet further."[16]

Wallace Stevens speaks of "the imagination's new beginning." I believe that for a Christian, that new beginning takes place each Christmas as we bow before the babe in the manger and adore him as Christ the Lord, *our Lord*, knowing he will, as the scriptures say, learn "obedience by the things which he [will suffer for us]. And being made perfect, he [will become] the author of [our] eternal salvation" (Heb. 5:8) by having the love to go into Gethsemane and the courage and fortitude to be nailed to the cross.

In truth, Christ had the most vibrant, fertile, and expansive imagination of anyone in history. As I read his life and teachings in the gospels, as I contemplate how he has changed my life by inspiring a mighty change of heart that has caused me "to sing the song of redeeming love" (Alma 5:26), I see a great and fecund imagination. It isn't just the inventive language, the subtle irony and humor, or the fresh metaphors and narratives that flowed from his mind and heart that make Jesus of Nazareth such a great imaginer, but his capacity to imagine each of us caught in the snares of sin, lost in temptation's tangled web, and each uniquely in need of his grace, mercy, and love. Beyond this was his godlike capacity to imagine each of us in a glorified state, each of our futures a reflection of his present.

---

16. N. T. Wright, "The Bible and Christian Imagination."

CHAPTER TWO

Imagining the Restoration: Joseph Smith and the Face of Christ

"He will unveil his face to you."
—D&C 88:67–68

"Everything in the realm of nature and human existence is a sign—a manifestation of God's divine names and attributes. . . . As it is said in the Qur'an, 'Wherever you turn, there is the Face of God.'"
—Avideh Shashaani[1]

During a recent fireside, I asked, "What was the most powerful experience Joseph Smith had in the Sacred Grove?" I wanted those in attendance to try and imagine Joseph's visionary experience as if it had happened to them. I asked further, "What did Joseph see that had the most profound influence on him for the rest of his life? What was the most startling realization he had upon seeing the Father and the Son?" After a moment, a woman answered, "He saw that God had a face like his." I said, "Yes! Exactly."

I have heard the Joseph Smith story innumerable times over the course of my life. I have told it myself thousands of times during my six years of full-time missionary service and in countless Sunday School, seminary, Institute, priesthood, and university classes I have taught at UC Berkeley and the Graduate Theological Union. In all that time, I don't remember a single person speaking of Joseph seeing God's and Christ's faces. Usually, our focus is on him seeing *beings* or *personages*, the latter of which is the word he uses in his accounts of that remarkable day, but we don't emphasize the most significant aspect of those sublime personages—their faces.

What Joseph saw, therefore, was not simply an embodied God or Gods (or, as his first recounting says, "the Lord"), not simply beings with bodies similar to his own, but beings with faces he could look into as with all the mortals in his life, faces with their unique glorified physiognomies.

Even though most Christians, Jews, and Muslims do not believe it is possible for humans to literally look upon the face of God, God promises in Ezekiel, "I will no longer hide my face from them when I pour my spirit

---

1. "Islam: Weekly Summary," Center for Action and Contemplation.

on the House of Israel" (Ezek. 39:29). Certainly in 1820 and thereafter, according to Latter-day Saint belief, the Lord was pouring His spirit upon the House of Israel in what is known as the Restoration.

While we may not be able to imagine God's face, we also can't imagine God not having a face any more than we can imagine Him not having a heart. And even if one takes the view that God is too ineffable either to have a face or, having one, allow mortals to behold it, we know that Christ did have a face, one that artists have attempted to visualize and portray for the past two thousand years. As Richard Rohr observes, "In Jesus, God was given a face and a heart. God became someone we could love. While God can be described as a moral force, as consciousness, and as high vibrational energy, the truth is, we don't (or can't?) fall in love with abstractions. So God became a person 'that we could hear, see with our eyes, look at, and touch with our hands' (1 John 1:1)."[2]

What I want to emphasize is how absolutely profound, transcendent, and life-changing seeing the faces of the Father and the Son must have been for Joseph. It was likely the most powerful experience of his truly remarkable life. Perhaps only poetry and scripture are capable of bringing us close to the experience, but only close, for seeing those faces was equivalent to looking into the heart of eternity, illumined by a thousand suns. And I believe that seeing those faces fired Joseph's imagination from that time forward with the *possible* glories of the Restoration. If it was possible to have such a vision, what else might be possible? While I don't believe Joseph could possibly have imagined all that has followed from that spring day, he was ready for the beginning of those "great and glorious" revelations that have continued to this day and will continue until Christ completes the restoration of all things with his second coming.

I believe God's face and heart are always turned to us, as the following story from the Jewish midrash (the Rabbis' imaginative expansion of scripture) illustrates:

> The son of a king was a hundred days' journey away from his father. His friends said to him, "Return to your father." He said, "I can't; I'm too far away." His father sent to him and said, "Go as far as you can and I will come the rest of the way to you." Thus the Holy One, blessed be he, said to Israel, "Return to me, and I will return to you."[3]

---

2. Richard Rohr, "Love Needs a Face."
3. Stephen Mitchell, *The Gospel According to Jesus*, 227.

How delighted God must have been that this young American farm boy was turning to Him at a moment when God needed someone with faith to seek His face, someone to whom God could show His face—and that of His Son—and set in motion the grand restoration of all things, as spoken by the prophets.

The look on God's face would have changed as He turned toward His Son and said to Joseph, "This is My Beloved Son. Hear Him!" That look of unconditional love, pride, and overwhelming gratitude that the Father felt for His Son, we can perhaps obliquely imagine because most of us have had similar experiences of looking into the face of someone we love completely and unconditionally and, equally, of seeing that look on the face of another person who sees us as beloved, the object of his or her unconditional love. We know that look! And Joseph, seeing the Father look toward His Son, could not have withheld his own gaze from that son's face.

What Joseph saw in and on the faces of the Father and the Son were the mystery and majesty of their natures, their beings, their *personalities*. He saw faces filled with love, kindness, generosity, forgiveness, mercy, magnanimity, grace, and benevolence—all those virtues God reveals to us in ten thousand ways and in ten thousand places.

The moment Joseph saw the faces of God and Christ, he knew that much of what he had been taught about deity from creeds and pulpits was false. This was not an invisible, distant God; it was not an angry God, and Joseph was not a despicable creature God was dangling over the fires of hell. Rather, there was the shock of recognition that God was like him and that he was like God. In his book *Mormon Christianity: What Other Christians Can Learn from the Latter-day Saints*, Evangelical scholar Stephen Webb asserts, "If God looks like something (rather than being completely without form), doesn't it stand to reason that he looks like us?"[4] This truth is confirmed by modern revelation: "When the Savior shall appear we shall see him as he is. We shall see that he is a man like ourselves" (D&C 130:1).

Joseph would have recognized that face when he saw it again in a vision he shared with Sidney Rigdon. Joseph reports:

> And while we meditated upon these things, the Lord touched the eyes of our understandings and they were opened, and the glory of the Lord shone round about.
>
> And we beheld the glory of the Son, on the right hand of the Father, and received of his fulness; . . . And now, after the many testimonies which have been

---

4. Stephen Webb, *Mormon Christianity: What Other Christians Can Learn from the Latter-day Saints*, 9.

given of him, this is the testimony, last of all, which we give of him: That he lives! For we saw him, even on the right hand of God; and we heard the voice bearing record that he is the Only Begotten of the Father. (D&C 76:19–23)

One can assume that the "fullness" of which Joseph speaks included seeing Christ's face since in this same revelation he says the Lord was a personage "whom we saw and with whom we conversed in the heavenly vision" (D&C 76:14). This was followed by yet another vision in the Kirtland Temple during Holy Week in 1836, in which Joseph describes the Lord's face in specific detail:

> We saw the Lord standing upon the breastwork of the pulpit, before us: and under his feet was a paved work of pure gold, in color like amber. His eyes were as a flame of fire; the hair of his head was white like the pure snow; his countenance shown above the brightness of the sun; and his voice was as the sound of the rushing of great waters, even the voice of Jehovah. (D&C 110:3–4)

Modern neuroscience is unfolding our understanding of the many hitherto hidden mysteries of our brains. For example, scientists have identified a part of the brain, the sole function of which is face recognition: "The ability to recognize faces is so important in humans that the brain appears to have an area solely devoted to the task: the fusiform gyrus."[5] The fusiform gyrus, located in the temporal lobe of the brain, helps us recognize faces and interpret facial expressions. According to Linda Graham, a psychotherapist specializing in neuroscience and human relations,

> We all rely on the fusiform gyrus in the right hemisphere of the brain to read the facial expressions of another person. The direct eye contact of emphatic, responsive parenting stimulates the development of this structure in the baby's brain; we can strengthen the functioning of this structure through eye contact with other people lifelong. Research has shown that when our right hemisphere reads safety and trust in the facial expressions of another person, the amygdala calms down, and the stress response is reduced.[6]

God knew of the dark terror that had enveloped Joseph just prior to his vision, a terror so threatening that Joseph experienced being on the edge of annihilation. As he describes it, he was captive to "the power of this enemy which had seized upon me, and at the very moment when I was ready to sink into despair and abandon myself to destruction not to

---

5. Elizabeth Norton, "Facial Recognition: Fusiform Gyrus Brain Region 'Solely Devoted' To Faces, Study Suggests."

6. Linda Graham, *Bouncing Back: Rewiring Your Brain for Maximum Resilience and Well-being*, 262–63.

an imaginary ruin, but to the power of some actual being from the unseen world, who had such marvelous power as I had never before felt in any being." It was in this moment when he was about to succumb to total despairing darkness that he cried out for deliverance, "exerting all [his] powers to call upon God to deliver" him (JS—H 1:16).

At this dramatic moment when, one assumes, God has allowed Joseph to experience the full force of demonic power, when he is on the verge of being sucked into the vortex of the very heart of darkness, a pillar of light "above the brightness of the sun" descends. Joseph looked into that light and, seeing the face of God, immediately found himself "delivered from the enemy which held [him bound]" (JS—H 1:17). Again, repeating Linda Graham's observation: "Studies have shown that when one person sees calm in the facial expression of another person, activity in the amygdala—the fear center [of the brain]—in the first person calms down. The functioning of [this structure] is developed through eye contact and mirror neurons, as in relationships of secure attachment and between a true other and a true self."[7]

Consider what Joseph experienced in the Sacred Grove: "The direct eye contact of emphatic, responsive parenting" would have stimulated the development of this structure in his brain. It would also have immediately dispelled the darkness surrounding him, which he described as "some power which entirely overcame me, and had such an astonishing influence over me as to bind my tongue so that I could not speak. Thick darkness gathered around me and [it] seemed to me as if I were doomed to sudden destruction" (JS—H 1:15). Imagine how Joseph must have felt at that moment, looking into the faces of the Father and the Son. It would have been like standing on the earth when "darkness was upon the face of the deep . . . And God said, Let there be light" (Gen. 1:1)—except in this instance it was light combined with abundant, palpable love. I think of the mother who, upon gazing into the eyes of her newborn infant, exclaimed, "I felt like I was beholding the universe." Or, as Elizabeth Bowen says, "To turn from everything to one face is to find oneself face to face with everything."[8] Richard Rohr adds, "Jesus is the one face, we are the interface, and Christ is the Everything."[9]

It is interesting to speculate that as preexistent creatures, however we came into being, the first thing we would have beheld were the faces of

---

7. Graham, 200.
8. Elizabeth Bowen, *The Heat of Day*.
9. Richard Rohr, "The One Face and the Everything."

our Heavenly Mother and Father. That first imprinting on our premortal brains—and souls, our *intelligent* refined-material bodies—would have locked us into love from the very beginning. Our first experience of seeing the eyes and faces of these divine beings is likely embedded somewhere in our subconscious.

One of the things that marked Joseph's trying, at times terrifying, and even tragic life was an amazing confidence that he was on the Lord's errand. Derided, persecuted, brutalized, deserted, and betrayed, he was never defeated. On one occasion he exclaimed, "Never be discouraged. If I were sunk in the lowest pits of Nova Scotia, with the Rocky Mountains piled on me, I would hang on, exercise faith, and keep up good courage, and I would come out on top."[10] Even when he knew he was headed for certain death, he said, "I am going like a lamb to the slaughter; but I am calm as a summer's morning; I have a conscience void of offense towards God, and towards all men" (D&C 135:4).

Many years ago, I published a poem on this subject called "Somewhere Near Palmyra" in which, reflecting on a time when I stood in the Sacred Grove, I tried to imagine Joseph's experience:

> He saw something that morning
> deep among the delicate leaves
> burning against the Eastern sky:
> the sun and suns,
> radiance enfolded
> in oak and elm,
> visages of light
> luminous as seer stones
> rinsing the still grasses;
> personages of fire,
> jasper and carnelian,
> dispersing the morning dew:
> images that bore him
> through dark of night,
> terror of loneliness,
> blood of betrayal,
> the ache of small graves,
> to death from the prison window
> where collapsing
> through the summer air,
> he fell—

---

10. George A. Smith, "History of George Albert Smith by Himself," 49.

It was that holy, glorious visage (or visages) that I believe sustained Joseph throughout his life. It is interesting to speculate that as he crossed the Mississippi on his way to safety, those searing images of God's and Christ's faces that he had seen thirty years earlier were brought into his consciousness. My speculation is spurred by what I consider to be the most significant phrase in Joseph's holograph record of his first vision. After his encounter with deity, he reports, "My soul was filled with love and for many days I could rejoice with great Joy and the Lord was with me but [I] could find none that would believe the hevnly [sic] vision nevertheless I pondered these things in my heart."[11] This seems to me the kind of genuine expression of someone who has had a transcendent experience. It is interesting that Joseph uses the same phrase Mary used in describing her experience when Gabriel heralded the impending birth of the Savior—"ponder in the heart." *Ponder* (from the Latin *ponderare*, "to weigh") means "to wonder, to think of deeply . . . to consider something carefully and thoroughly." That, undoubtedly, is what Joseph did following his theophany and, one would imagine, many times thereafter.

At the same fireside mentioned above, a new convert said, "I also think that when God looked into Joseph's eyes, Joseph saw a reflection of his own face." Of course he would have, just as we who look into our spouses', children's, or grandchildren's eyes see a reflection of our own. It occurred to me not long ago that if we each carry the physical DNA of our earthly parents and other ancestors, why wouldn't our spirits, which are refined matter, carry the DNA of the parents of our spirits? And if this is the case—which it is in the logical conclusion of Latter-day Saint cosmology—then we carry in our refined material souls the indelible imprint of the faces of our heavenly parents.

Their intention from the beginning was that we would be of Their lineage and in Their images, and Their further intention was to reveal this to us. As the midrash states, "It is with love that God made human beings in His image, but it was with a special love that *He let them know that He had made them in His image.*"[12] Why? So that we would understand that on both the material and refined material levels we are deeply, deliberately, literally related, and connected eternally to these our divine sires. As Rabbi David Wolpe observes, "There is only one bond among human

---

11. Dean C. Jessee, *The Personal Writings of Joseph Smith*, 6.
12. Rabbi Akiba, as quoted in David Wolpe, *The Healer of Shattered Hearts*, 71.

beings that cannot be broken, the bond of being a child of God. It can be betrayed, but never erased."[13]

Further, Heavenly Father and Mother intended that *Their* first begotten in the spirit world would be the means for bringing us back to Them by making it possible for us to have his light—the light of Christ with which we are all born—to harmonize with Their light. Gerard Manly Hopkins shows this beautifully in his sonnet "As Kingfishers Catch Fire." Hopkins argues that everything expresses its nature by what it does: the wings of kingfishers and dragonflies catch sunlight, stones ring when dropped down wells, strings of instruments sing when plucked, and bells ring when pealed—all sounding their inner essence by outwardly manifesting it. As with creatures and inanimate things, he adds,

> Each mortal thing does one thing and the same:
> . . . speaks and spells [its being],
> Crying *Whát I dó is me: for that I came.*

He then argues that it is through Christ that we are capable of doing more than this, more than what we can do by ourselves:

> I say móre: the just man [Christ] justices . . .

That is, Christ, as our advocate, justifies us to God, pleading our individual cases, in spite of our sins and failings, as worthy of redemption.

The last three lines of the poem tie all this marvelously rich imagery together and bring us back to Joseph's powerful experience. Hopkins says,

> —For Christ plays in ten thousand places,
> Lovely in limbs, and lovely in eyes not his
> To the Father through the features of men's [and women's] faces.[14]

Christ plays our part before the Father as if he were an actor, making us lovely—lovelier and more lovable than we deserve—by showing our faces, lightened by his light, to the Father (and, presumably, hopefully, to our Mother).

I think of Joseph that fateful day in Carthage, his premonition of death about to become a reality. He had to be thinking of Christ because he and his brother Hyrum requested their friend, and future prophet, John Taylor sing "A Poor Wayfaring Man of Grief," an English hymn that Taylor had recently included in both the Manchester and general Church hymnals. That hymn, based on chapter 25 of Matthew, epitomizes Christ's

---

13. Wolpe, 67.
14. Gerard Manley Hopkins, "As Kingfishers Catch Fire."

gospel and is particularly poignant in relation to the theme of this chapter since it seems to invite all of us to look into the face of anyone who is poor, hungry, thirsty, naked, imprisoned, or destitute in any way and see the face of Christ himself.

It is not difficult to imagine that during those last fateful moments at Carthage as Joseph fell to his death from the prison window, he saw again the face of Christ as he had seen it in that light-blessed woods when he was fourteen, later in the Kirtland Temple, and at other times during his brief life, including in "The Vision" described in section 76 of the Doctrine and Covenants.

It was likely the first face he saw when he passed through the veil.

I imagine all of us having that experience, looking into the faces of Christ and our heavenly parents, rejoicing as we see ourselves reflected in their faces.

Martin Schaling's lovely hymn text "Herzlich lieb hab ich dich, O Herr" ("Lord, Thee I love with all my heart"), which Bach used as the final chorale for his magnificent *Passion According to St. John*, expresses that ultimate promise:

> Lord, let at last Thine angels come,
> To Abram's bosom bear me home,
> That I may die unfearing;
> And in its narrow chamber keep
> My body safe in peaceful sleep
> Until Thy reappearing.

Schaling then imagines us being awakened by Christ, perhaps in the way a loving parent awakens a sleeping child:

> And then from death awaken me
> That these mine eyes with joy may see,
> O Son of God, Thy glorious face,
> My Savior and my fount of grace . . .

INTERLUDE 1A

Somewhere Near Palmyra

"The glory of the City was the temple of the sun."
—Will Durant

He saw something that morning
deep among the delicate leaves
burning against the Eastern sky:
The sun and suns,
radiance enfolded
in oak and elm,
visages of light
luminous as seer stones
rinsing the still grasses,
personages of fire,
jasper and carnelian,
dispersing the morning dew:
images that bore him
through dark of night,
terror of loneliness,
blood of betrayal,
the ache of small graves,
to death from the prison window
where, wings collapsing
through the summer air,
he fell—
And I know, kneeling
among the secret trees
this winter morning
where no birdsong rings
among the barren bush
and no leaves spring green,
where darkness thickens and gathers
among the withered weeds

and my tongue is a fish
under the river's roof,
that I, too, see what he saw—
sun, light, fire—
images of glory
flashing through the
morning mist.

INTERLUDE 1B

Emma in Sunlight

I

Even before they met
she had heard the stories—
spirits, treasure, salamanders—
and the warning of her father's voice:
"shiftless," "visionary."

The night they ran away to be married
was the first time she heard it
in his telling.
Lying in a field
looking into heaven,
her body bathed in moonlight,
wonder in her eyes,
any story
was believable.

At first she thought
it must have been a dream—
the way he told it,
as if he were awakening
in a vortex of darkness:
he stopped, stuttered, his breath quick.
A ghost story
to frighten her?
She shuddered
as she grasped his hand.
Then It was too fantastic—
angels, light, the sun,
his heart a seer stone.
Who was this man
her father so feared
who could tell such tales,
who had seen the inside of the sun?

II

Later, one morning at his parents' farm
while he was away,
life growing in her,
she walked to the forest
beyond the farm
searching for the place
he had scribed in her mind:
a large beech with a white stone
tangled among the roots.

Finding it, she looked up at the trees
and then the sky,
hoping to see
what he had seen.
Suddenly, a chorus of birdsong:
black-throated warblers, scarlet tanagers, purple finches—
She closed her eyes and listened:
indigo bunting? . . . hermit thrush? . . .
There were too many to name.
She listened . . .
The wind on leaves?
Angels' wings?
She opened her eyes to the sun lighting her face
and knew.
When he came back the next night,
she asked for the story again
as they embraced in moonlight
prismed through the window.

III

Years later, after Missouri, after
the temple overlooking the great river,
after the rumors
that froze her heart,
the night before they took him away,
she said, "Tell it to me again."
"Which part?"

"All of it, from the beginning."
He paused, took a deep breath, and began,
"A devouring darkness overclouded my mind,
flooded my heart with
blackened blood like the rivers of hell."
She felt him flinch.
"My tongue was bound,
a whirlpool pulled me
down and down . . .
and then the sun opened its heart
and I was ablaze in brightness."
"I know," she said,
"I saw it too."
They held each other
until dawn
when they took him to Carthage.

IV

Years after the wagons had rolled over
the ice-covered river,
after the abandonment
by the Usurper,
after all the questions about
wives and lovers,
after all the entreaties
to go to the Great Basin,
the night before she died
she dreamed
"The Lord of light"
and said,
"Joseph! Yes, yes,
I'm coming."

CHAPTER THREE

Searching for Heavenly Mother: Toward an Imaginative Latter-day Saint Theology

(co-authored with Gloria G. Rees)

"Surely some revelation is at hand!"
—William Butler Yeats

"Heavenly Mother's emergence out of obscurity changes everything. Profoundly."
—Terryl and Fiona Givens[1]

I

It is important to say this at the outset: the truth that we have a Heavenly Mother is one of the most glorious and revolutionary revelations of the Restoration. The fact that we know so little about this feminine goddess and make so little of Her divine position as the co-equal partner of the Father is, at the very least, a mystery and, at the most, something of a scandal! If She is a feminine being who became exalted through the same process by which Heavenly Father did, then She is equal with Him in every significant way—in intelligence, power, and glory—and especially in love and holiness. The big question: being so, how could She not be equally known, equally powerful, and equally *present* and involved in the lives of Her mortal children? What explains Her absence, Her silence, Her apparent abandonment of Her children for millennia? And, further, isn't it somehow inexplicable that Her identity could have been revealed to the Prophet Joseph Smith only to leave us waiting, for nearly two hundred years, for more knowledge, more understanding, and more revelations about Her?

Something is wrong with this picture! As a co-equal partner with God the Father, isn't She deserving of being in the godhead? And, as her children, are we not deserving of having Her be so? Some have speculated that the Holy Ghost, seen in some texts and traditions as feminine, is in

---

1. Terryl Givens and Fiona Givens, *All Things New: Sin, Salvation, and Everything In Between*, 25.

fact Heavenly Mother.[2] If She isn't the Holy Ghost but a silent, invisible member of the godhead, then, to borrow a term from Walt Whitman, might She not be included in a sort of "Square Deific"? If She is not in the godhead, where is She? If, as we are told, the Father knows of our loneliness and longing, and He sorrows over our broken hearts and weeps over our broken world, wouldn't She (*doesn't She?*) at least equally do the same? If faith and reason tell us we have a mother there, then both faith and reason, our hearts and our minds, should tell us we should also have Her *here*, and *now*, when we need Her so much. What in heaven's name are the heavens waiting for?

If it is true that we have a divine mother and that an increasing number of us long for Her, the reasons we give and the stories we tell about why She isn't intimately and urgently present in our lives don't make sense. As the Divine Being at least partially responsible for our existence, why would She not insist on being here? Or is Her absence during the long "eons of amnesia"[3] proof of Her emotional distance—or nonexistence? This is a question explored by Emily Dickinson in relation to God the Father. Consider the first two stanzas of her poem "I Know that He Exists" (with a simple change in pronouns):

> I know that She exists.
> Somewhere—in silence—
> She has hid her rare life
> From our gross eyes.
>
> 'Tis an instant's play—
> 'Tis a fond Ambush—
> Just to make Bliss
> Earn her own surprise!

That is, Dickinson speculates, like a father playing hide-and-seek with a child, Heavenly Father is hiding and silent because He is going to make a sudden, dramatic appearance that will be so welcome it can only increase our surprise and bliss.

But, this wry poet asks, what if God never comes? With characteristic irony, Dickinson poses that possibility in asking the disturbing, ultimate question:

---

2. Janice Allred, "Toward a Mormon Theology of God the Mother." While the word for Holy Spirit in Greek is masculine, in Hebrew and in Aramaic—the language Jesus spoke—it is feminine.

3. Ann Gardner Stone, "Mother." Hereafter, *Dove Song*.

> But—should the play
> Prove piercing earnest—
> Should the glee—glaze—
> In Death's—stiff—stare—

What if when we die, there is no God (no Heavenly Father)?

> Would not the fun
> Look too expensive!
> Would not the jest—
> Have crawled too far!⁴

That is, adapting Dickinson's logic in terms of Latter-day Saint theology, what if Heavenly Mother is a shadowy fiction in our theology, a ghost in our mythology? What if the paucity of information we have about Her has a darker implication than the arguments we tend to hear; for example, that, like a Victorian matron, She is too sensitive to hear Her name taken in vain, too tenderhearted to witness the blood and horror of mortality; or that such a doctrine would be offensive to other Christians and would therefore be a stumbling block to conversion—although that seems not to have impeded our telling them of our other, and likely more scandalous, doctrines of the godhead, polygamy, and the plurality of gods! In other words, so our various arguments seem to suggest, She must be shielded from the darker, harsher realities of this world, and therefore, other believers must be shielded from one of the most glorious revelations of the Restoration. Such logic might make Dickinson's "crawled" (from the Old English *creulen,* meaning to move slowly across the ground, like a crab) connote her more subtle, intentional meaning of having one's flesh crawl.

II

"Great indeed, we confess, is the mystery of godliness." (1 Tim. 3:16)

Is God the Father our sole divine parent willing to be present in our lives, the only parent apparently willing (or capable) of speaking to us, of identifying the Savior as *His* son and us as *His* sons and daughters? The thought makes not only reason stare, but sense, both common and uncommon, protest. In the modern Church, at least until recently, not only has our reason been staring in relation to our Heavenly Mother, but it essentially has also been struck dumb. As Peggy Fletcher Stack states, "Though she has been acknowledged by Mormon prophets and celebrated in LDS

---

4. Emily Dickinson, *The Complete Poems of Emily Dickinson*, 160.

hymns, Mother in Heaven is absent from missionary materials, religious manuals, youth programs, and, for the most part, scriptural texts."[5] And, one might add, She is also almost entirely absent from our handbooks, our sacrament and conference addresses, and even our ordinances and temples.

In spite of Her apparent absence and silence, an increasing number of Latter-day Saints insist that She does exist. Some—speculating that knowledge of Her, along with other "plain and precious" truths, has been excised from scripture—have excavated our sacred texts to resurrect this divine goddess. Others, not content with occasionally singing a hymn about Her or hearing Her alluded to in the phrase "heavenly parents," have been searching our history for evidence that She resided in the hearts and minds of earlier generations of Latter-day Saints who sought Her, although, echoing Paul's assertion in Acts, She "is not far from each one of us" (Acts 17:27).

In spite of what we understand were revelations to Joseph Smith, Eliza R. Snow, and others in both the early and modern Church, in the contemporary Church we have accepted Heavenly Mother as the feminine *deus absconditus* (the hidden god), the mother who is removed (has removed Herself?) from our consciousness, our presence, our world. But for an increasing number of Latter-day Saints, She has only been awaiting our poor eyes to see Her. How tragic that this divine being, this Goddess of Light and Love, should have been kept in darkness. How sad that this voice of sun, moon, and stars, of universes and eternities, should be so silent, so voiceless, so *absent*. And yet She is present in the interstices of our history, in the white spaces of our texts, in our myths and legends, in our private dreams and visions, and, surprisingly, in even more of our declarations and revelations than we generally are aware. As David L. Poulsen and Martin Pulido summarize in their *BYU Studies* article "'A Mother There': A Survey of Historical Teachings about Mother in Heaven," She has been here all along, hiding in plain sight:

> The Heavenly Mother portrayed in the teachings we have examined is a procreator and parent, a divine person, a co-creator, a co-framer of the plan of salvation, and is involved in this life and the next. Certainly, consideration of these points reinforces several unquestionably important LDS doctrines: divine embodiment, eternal families, divine relationality, the deification of women, the eternal nature and value of gender, and the shared lineage of Gods and humans.[6]

---

5. Peggy Fletcher Stack, "A Mormon Mystery Returns: Who Is Heavenly Mother?"
6. David L. Poulsen and Martin Pulido, "'A Mother There': A Survey of Historical Teachings about Mother in Heaven," 71–97.

Consider the following from their study:

- "God is a married being, has a wife. . . . We are the offspring of Him and His wife." (George Q. Cannon, 1884)
- "All men and women are in the similitude of the universal Father and Mother and are literally the sons and daughters of Deity." (The First Presidency, 1909)
- Regarding the formation of Abraham's character, "our great heavenly Mother was the greater molder." (Susa Young Gates, 1891)
- ". . . the divine Mother, side by side with the divine Father, [has] the equal sharing of equal rights, privileges and responsibilities." (Susa Young Gates, 1920)
- "The glorious vision of life hereafter . . . is given radiant warmth by the thought that . . . [we have] a mother who possesses the attributes of Godhood." (John A. Widtsoe, 1928)
- "On a particularly difficult day . . . what would this world's inhabitants pay to know that heavenly parents are reaching across those same streams and mountains and deserts, anxious to hold them close?" (Jeffrey R. Holland, 1985)[7]

This is our doctrine! This is what we believe! And yet how many in the contemporary Church are hearing such expressions for the first time?

III

> . . . *Remember,*
> *in me also you live*
> *and move and have*
> *your being*—my *being*
> our *being. Remember*
> *you are.*
> We *are.*
> *I am.*[8]

The most profound realization we have as human beings is that we have being—that we exist, *that we are someone*. The second most profound awareness happens when, upon awakening from the spaceship of

---

7. All of the bulleted quotes in this section are cited with full documentation in Poulson and Pulido, "A Mother There."

8. Robert A. Rees, "Mother," 175–76.

the womb, we look into the eyes of our earthly mother, into the face of love, and see a reflection of ourselves, that mystical connection reflected in our mother's face—in the seer stones of her eyes!—a mirror of ourselves. Looking into the love inscribed on the face of that being from whose body our bodies have come, our awareness, however primitive and limited, is that we are part of her, of the universe of her being, and are somehow deeply connected by an indelible affirmation of love. In some mysterious way, that awareness that we will forever be inarticulate to fully express stems from our prenatal awareness of being nurtured in her womb for nine long months, fed physically through the umbilical connection between our bodies and spiritually through her spirit, including the words she has spoken and the lullabies she has sung to us. However little we may understand, we know by the profound experience of a newborn looking into his or her mother's eyes that our being is affirmed by her being, by the mystical but nevertheless real interconnected bonding of unconditional love across a liminal space no larger than several feet yet as expansive as eternity.

Latter-day Saint theology leads us to imagine that the kind of experience we have as newborn infants gazing into the face of our earthly mother is a mirror of similar experiences we had in the preexistent world with our Heavenly Mother. That is, it stands to reason that however we were begotten or came to be the eternal beings we are, in the preexistent world one of our first experiences was looking into the faces of those who "organized," engendered, or somehow brought us into being, and having our first indelible experience of being loved. We speculate that such experiences were frequent in that world before our world and that somewhere in our deepest subconsciousness we hold memories of those gazes between us and our Heavenly Mother. We further speculate that, in a pattern repeated in this world when we leave our earthly parents to go to college, serve a mission, or start lives on our own, when it was time for us to cross the veil between the worlds, Heavenly Father and Mother called us into Their presence, blessed and embraced us, and promised Their love would be with us—a farewell which Orson F. Whitney and Harold B. Lee referred to as "a bittersweet occasion."[9] Such memories are also part of our history, even if we can't recall them.

---

9. Poulson and Pulido, "A Mother There."

IV

"When the last days come, I will give my Spirit to everyone. Your sons and daughters will prophesy. Your young men [and young women] will see visions, and your old men [and old women] will have dreams." (Acts 2:17, NIV)

Latter-day Saints believe in continuing revelation. Since the Restoration is a process and not an event or series of events that took place in nineteenth-century America, we can rejoice in our radical theology of the heavens being always open. We know from scripture and church history that such revelation is both vertical and horizontal, that it is given to and received by ordinary saints as well as by prophets, seers, and revelators, and that it flows both from prophets to ordinary saints and sometimes the other way around. Joseph Smith welcomed both kinds of revelation and in fact welcomed all truth, no matter its source. There seems to be no other way to explain why Latter-day Saint men and women have had dreams, visions, intuitions, impressions, and intimations of immortality related to our Heavenly Mother almost from the beginning of the Restoration.

Emily Dickinson suggested that the absence of revelation is not revelation of absence, that lack of communication is not due to God's parsimoniousness, but rather our unreadiness to receive it: "Not 'Revelation'—tis—that waits / But our unfurnished eyes."[10] "Unfurnished" as in *unprepared*.

It is interesting to contemplate that an increasing number of Latter-day Saints have had dreams and even auditory and visionary visitations from our Heavenly Mother. Here is one example from Maxine Hanks:

> My encounter with the divine feminine began in dreams, when I was a teen; yet, a sense of Her was there before, in the love of my mother and the lyrics of my favorite Primary song: "our lilac tree" and "butterfly wings" and "the magical sound of things," resonated Her presence. My first dream of Her came in 1972; a female figure led me to our Chapel, where a crystal bowl of pristine water waited on the sacrament table, for me to partake.[11]

After recounting other dreams, intuitions, impressions, and unfoldings, Hanks concludes, "She was there long before I knew Her, before I could even conceive of Her. And She abides with us today, whether we see Her or not. She simply IS, so She waits, to be seen and known."[12]

---

10. Dickinson, *The Complete Poems of Emily Dickinson*, 339.
11. Maxine Hanks, "Heavenly Mother's Day: Dreaming of the Divine Feminine."
12. Hanks.

In her *Women in Authority: Reemerging Mormon Feminism*, Hanks chronicles the experiences of a number of modern Latter-day Saint women who have had revelatory experiences with our Heavenly Mother. Speaking of the opening of such experiences in her "Finding Our Bodies, Hearts, Voices—A Three-Part Invention," Martha Dickey Esplin writes:

> Possibly my finding and accepting the Mother came about because of a small tear in the veil . . . the tear has become a rending. Maybe all of the earnest striving for the feminine in the divine results from glimmerings through the opening in the veil, from rays of light shining and reflecting on those souls who have felt the pull that now is the time to open the veil enough to let the Mother through. . . . Maybe the time has come for men—the patriarchs—to accommodate the feminine power, to be ready to work together to save our planet, our church, maybe even our souls.[13]

If we were to "furnish" our eyes and ears, our hearts and minds, we might be surprised not only by revelation, but also by joy.

V

> *"As women now are, Heavenly Mother once was;*
> *As Heavenly Mother now is, women may become."*
>
> —Variation on a revelation to Lorenzo Snow

Our official theology informs us that not only do we have a divine mother *there*, but that She, the mother of all creation as we know it, was also once *here* (or some similar world), as a mortal woman. According to Orson F. Whitney, "There was a time when that being whom we now worship . . . our eternal Father and Mother were once man and woman in mortality."[14] If Heavenly Father passed through a mortal probation similar to ours, then His eternal companion had to have done the same. Understanding the implications and extensions of our theology, unraveling the promises and possibilities of our revealed religion, we see Heavenly Mother in an eternal context. Looking back far enough, peeling back the layers of time and eternity, we see Her first as unorganized intelligence and then as a spirit daughter of *Her* heavenly parents. Next, we see Her as participant in a premortal council, raising Her hand in support

---

13. Martha Dickey Esplin, "Finding Our Bodies, Hearts, Voices—A Three-Part Invention," 261–62.

14. Orson F. Whitney, "Bishop O. F. Whitney," as cited by Poulson and Pulido, "A Mother There."

of venturing into the treacherous terrain of mortality and later actually passing through the veil into the mortal world as a newborn infant sired of mortal parents who were charged with loving and nurturing Her in the same way we love and nurture our children.

In this mortal sphere, She would have lived in a particular place—a desert, a plain, a land of lakes and forests or mountains and rivers. She may have come of age in a village or a large city. Her parents may have been peasants or professionals. She likely had siblings and a large extended family. As a child, She would have learned songs, perhaps played the lute, and read scrolls or books. From Her mother She may have learned how to weave and cook, how to study scripture and to tell stories, how to care for others, and how to negotiate a world dominated by men. From her father She may have learned self-reliance, independence, and how to navigate the world outside Her home by knowing and valuing Herself and by setting boundaries. Undoubtedly, like most young girls, She dreamed of a world beyond Her own.

Next, we imagine Her blossoming into young womanhood, passing through adolescence, experiencing all the natural processes of mortal maturing, developing physically, emotionally, and spiritually, evolving through the redemptive process toward holiness similar to that known to us. Looking into the future before our future, we see Her as an exalted, glorified woman, beautiful beyond all telling and lovely beyond all singing. Eons later, we see Her in partnership with our Heavenly Father, organizing us out of intelligence and making it possible for us to follow the same path She has traversed from intelligence to mortality to the glory of godhood.

Although She is essentially absent from the pages of our sacred history, we imagine Her participating in the creation of the world Her children would inhabit and then being concerned about them throughout the period of their mortal probation.

Taking the bare bones of what has been revealed, the shards of allusion and light, the fragments of scripture and story, the particles of poetry and prophesy, we exclaim, "I have a Mother there—and here!"

VI

> *I would like to suggest that as individuals and as a church we open our hearts and minds, awaken our imaginations to the possibilities that our Heavenly Mother holds for us. Let us celebrate her elevated place in our theology and teach others about her. Surely many men and women in this godless world might find their way back to the light through this goddess of all the worlds.*
> —Robert A. Rees[15]

We posit that imagination constitutes a kind of revelation, one that opens our views not only through an opening in the veil, but through an expansive opening into the heavens through the imagination's exploration, inventiveness, and fecundity. Imagination is thus one of the greatest gifts and endowments given us by deity. We know that before anything came into being, including our individual beings and the entire world as we know it, the Gods—Heavenly Father *and* Heavenly Mother—*together*, first imagined, then created and finally revealed to us, Their children, what They had done, so that such revelations could inspire *our* imaginations, and in turn our imaginations could call forth new revelations. Nothing else makes sense, even though we pretend it does.

It is through the imagination that contemporary Latter-day Saints are clothing the Divine Mother in the richness She deserves, in the silks and velvets, the jacquards and brocades; in the blues and golds, the purples and greens; in the diamonds and diadems, the sapphires and pearls of Her queenly status.

Consider the marvelous flood of light and delight that has inspired such works as Carol Lynn Pearson's *Mother Wove the Morning* (1989) and her more recent *Finding Mother God* (2020); Rachael Hunt Steenblick's *Mother's Milk: Poems in Search of Heavenly Mother* (2017); the cornucopia of *Dove Song: Heavenly Mother in Mormon Poetry* (2018), an anthology of poetic renderings spanning 175 years of Latter-day Saint creative expression; Kathryn Knight Sonntag's *The Mother Tree: Discovering the Love and Wisdom of Our Divine Mother* (2022); and a multitude of other compositions appearing in a variety of publications and internet sites during the first two decades of the twenty-first century. The following are illustrative of how contemporary Latter-day Saint poets yearn for and are celebrating the awakening of this divine goddess.

---

15. Robert A. Rees, "Our Mother in Heaven," 49–51.

"I thought I was a Motherless child
 in an always motherless house
 and then your little surprises began to come."
    —Carol Lynn Pearson

"I sit a queen lost in the wilderness of men's hearts.
 When will 'shh' become 'She?'"
    —S. E. Page

"But when nothing is known
 The human mind scatters seeds
 Of speculation and gardens of stories
 Crop up to fill our emptiness
 And heal our loneliness."
    —Will Reger

"Wherever we are
 she is what
 is missing."
    —Terresa Wellborn

"A mother's pain
 needs a Mother's comfort."
    —Taylor Rouanzion

"I need you . . .
 . . . to reveal your ways
 . . . to guide my light
 When I am lost."
    —Lisa Bolin Hawkins

"I want to know you, mother.
 I want to know you Mother.
 I want to see your face."
    —Janice Allred

"She who has no name
 looks just like you remember her."
    —Joanna Brooks

"Yet, you were there all along, I recall the night my soul
 awoke inside a dream. . . .
 You were here the whole time."
    —Maxine Hanks

"What if that Holy Heav'nly Three
 Is Godly Him and Him and She?"
    —Jonathon Penny

"She is your face in the mirror."
—Melody Newly Johnson

"O you who no one names . . .
The earth is yours and every living thing says your name."
—Emma Jay

"These are windows through which shines her grace."
—Martin Pulido

"The Mother woke at every sound . . .
I hear Her everywhere."
—Rachael Hunt Steenblik

"I think of her in a place of dreaming . . .
I offer the stone of my heart to her touch."
—Tara Timpson

"O my daughters, my sons
how often would I have gathered you as an eagle
feeds her fledglings."
—Susan Elizabeth Howe

"Her thousand branches adorning the long climb
into the milky stars . . .
hosts and hosts and hosts and hosts."
—Kathryn Knight Sonntag

INTERLUDE 2A
A Mother Here

Here,
not there
or there
or where?
Now,
not if
or then
or when?
This present
not the past
or an imagined
future.
This life,
not a preor
post-life.
Here, known,
not there unknown
or hoped for.
This habitation,
which together
we make holy,
today,
not yesterday
or tomorrow.
This mortal childhood
not one primeval
or promised.
Here,
now
where your spirit
resides.

Touch
your heart,
feel it beating.
Press deeper—
feel mine beating,
here.

INTERLUDE 2B

Her

For some reason
he kept wondering
what She looked like,
how She spoke,
how She carried
Herself.
He thought of his mother,
a raven-haired, porcelain-skinned
beauty.
Perhaps there was something
of her.
Then he remembered his wife,
dead now
but still alive
in his heart,
and surmised that at least some
of her
might reveal traces—
haloed hair,
blue eyes,
grace and generosity
without measure,
and a voice that echoed
heaven.
Next, he thought of his daughters,
bright and beautiful,
dignified, alive,
and his granddaughter,
who unraveled
light and color
from rivers and stars.
Yes, he thought,
some of her too was in
Her as well,
as was some of

Eve
and Mary
and even
Bathsheba
and the Magdalene.

Perhaps when She helped
shape the
first woman,
encoding some of Herself
in her hair,
in her eyes,
in her beautiful mouth
and rounded breasts,
planting seeds of Herself
deep down,
under her skin,
in her heart,
in dendritic cells
and genes,
so that
down the ages,
some trace of Her
survived
in every woman
on earth,
and watching them,
seeing them,
delighting in them,
even loving them,
was how he could
imagine Her.

INTERLUDE 2C
Birdsong/Eve's Song

Birdsong brings relief
to my longing...
Please, universal soul, practice
some song ... through me!
—Rumi

Never again would birds' song be the same,
And to do that to birds is why she came.
—Robert Frost

On the way to Tennessee Beach,
hearing a meadowlark singing,
ringing through the reeds,
she thought of Eve
and wondered:
Who sang first
and who first listened
with wonder
there in the marvelous garden?
Perhaps neither,
but both, to the First Singer Herself
who sang melodies as She fashioned feathers
and hummed tunes as She shaped
tiny throats and tongues—
of the red-winged blackbird,
the indigo bunting,
the scarlet tanager,
the nightingale—
so that when they flew from Her hands
and swam in wind,
they blazoned to all the garden round Her singing
Her songs.

And when She shaped Eve's from moist clay,
Her hand delicately forming the slight hollow
of her throat,
making her voice different from all the birds'
and from Adam's as well,
She breathed the breath of life into her voice,
into her heart,
and with it her own treasure trove of song,
the music of stars and spheres,
of suns and deep darkness,
of all creation,
so that she and all her daughters
could hear back
the notes of Her singing,
accompanied by
all the birds—
a rapture of praise
ringing through the world.

INTERLUDE 2D

A Final Gift of Grace

*"The glory of the telestial . . .
surpasses all understanding."*
—D&C 76:89

What mother would not visit a child in prison?
What mother would not go into a dark forest
to save a child from wolves?
What mother having given birth
would not rescue a prodigal child?
What mother, starlight in her heart,
would not
carry a candle into the night
for a child who has lost her way—
or forget a child
born in light
who chose to risk the world?

And so She will go down,
descending from sun
to moon
to stars,
her luminous love
overflowing
to heal hearts
burdened and broken,
bind wounds
self- and other-inflicted,
erase guilt and shame
carried like stones.
She will be there
in that kingdom,
telling stories,
teaching poetry,
singing lullabies,
opening her heart
forever
beyond moons and suns.

CHAPTER FOUR

Imagining Mary, Mother of the Messiah

"[I beheld] A virgin, most beautiful and fair above all other virgins. . . . [who] was carried away in the Spirit. And I looked and beheld the virgin again, bearing a child in her arms."
—1 Nephi 11:15–19

I believe that women may see the Messiah and the expansive conceptualizations of a Messiah through a different lens than men do. That lens is made particularly powerful because of the experience of Mary, the mother of the Messiah. Her story, told over the ages through the uniqueness and richness of story, poetry, film, and art, reveals that these imaginative ways of seeing her have the power to awaken and enrich our imaginations.

The most powerful scriptural predictions of the Messiah were that he was to be born of a divine father and an earthly mother. Christians, including Latter-day Saints, tend to emphasize Jesus's paternal inheritance over his maternal inheritance, which is understandable—after all, who wouldn't favor a divine father over an earthly mother? But the fact is, both were equally essential in creating the figure who became the Messiah; that is, Jesus could not have become the Messiah without their combined divine and mortal genetic influence and their unique gifts and personalities influencing and informing his development, growth, and maturation. The truth is, Jesus could not have become the Christ without his mother's profound influence, an influence so deep and indelible that its feminine characteristics can be seen in the teachings, behaviors, and relationships that both shaped and were reflected in his divine mission and ministry.

According to Latter-day Saint theology, as the first begotten in the spirit world, Jesus had a unique, preordained mission in mortality. It is certain that Mary did as well; that is, her valor in the preexistent heaven meant that she was among those whom Abraham saw as the "noble and great" ones chosen by God for special assignment in the mortal world. Thus, God sent Mary's spirit to inhabit the mortal body created by her parents, who undoubtedly had also been specially chosen to give birth to and raise such a noble soul. With the veil drawn over their remembrances, none of these figures were aware of the miraculous events that were to transpire in their lives when Gabriel announced to their daughter the fulfillment of the prophecy for which all Israel awaited.

We can see this in Mary's response as we imagine Gabriel appearing before her and speaking words that frighten, astonish, and puzzle her: "Hail, you who are highly favored of God, the Lord is with you: blessed are you among women." His words "deeply trouble" Mary as she ponders their possible meaning. Noticing her understandable response, Gabriel assures her by naming her and her primary emotion: "Do not be afraid, Mary, for you have found favor with God!" It is obvious that the full import of Gabriel's greeting is still winding its way through her young heart and mind. Anticipating her confusion and yet eager to avoid any ambiguity, Gabriel says, "God has been gracious to you; Behold, you will conceive in your womb and give birth to a son whom you will name Jesus." In other words, he is telling her that this is something that will happen in her body, not her imagination. Whether she fully hears the rest of Gabriel's annunciation is perhaps doubtful because she is arrested by those words "conceive," "womb," and "give birth to," words whose meaning she knows but has scarcely ever considered in relation to herself.

Perhaps Gabriel pauses to give her time to absorb the full import of his words, and then continues, saying that this child to be born to her "shall be great, and shall be called the Son of the Highest: and the Lord God shall give unto him the throne of his father David: And he will be king over Israel and his reign shall never end." As these words—"Son of the highest," "throne of his father David," "king over Israel," which must have hung in the air between her and the angel, finally become fully imprinted on her heart and mind—she suddenly realizes that of all the daughters of Israel, she alone has been chosen to fulfill Isaiah's prophecy of a young woman of no distinction or status from a family of low estate, and yet *how* what she has just heard is going to happen continues to puzzle her: "How is this possible, seeing I am a virgin?" Gabriel's response sets her head spinning once more: "The Holy Spirit will come upon you, and the power of the Most High will overshadow you. Therefore, the child to be born to you will be holy; he will be called the Son of God."

At last, fully understanding that this will happen even if she doesn't comprehend how, she responds as the boy Samuel did—with certain yet humble affirmation, "Yes, I am a servant of the Lord; let this happen to me according to your word." When the angel is gone away, perhaps she walks alone among the hills near her home or sits by the ancient well from which she has often drawn water, trying to order her feelings, rehearsing over and over not only Gabriel's words but the care and tenderness with which he spoke them, pondering and puzzling their deeper import, whose meaning continues to unfold in her thoughts and dreams over the next days. Alone in her room at night, she reads and rereads the words of the prophets about the Messiah, committing them to heart and hoping they will help prepare her for whatever awaits her.

A few days later she goes to the synagogue to ask questions of the rabbi, although she doesn't tell him of Gabriel's visit. She thinks especially of what will happen when, as promised, the Holy Spirit comes upon her and what it will feel like when she is overshadowed by the power of God. "What can these words mean?" she wonders. As hard as she tries, she can't imagine how it will happen, and then one night when there is no moon and the world lies in darkness, as she rises from prayers it does happen, taking her by glorious surprise. So much light floods into her that she feels as if the sun itself is inside her and she is inside the sun, her heart an orb of glory, wings of fire enfolding her gently in holiness. Later, as the first rays of dawn enter her room, she luxuriates in the luminosity of it all, the blue flame under her skin so alive it seems eternal. She knows she will never forget this night, although she cannot find words to name or describe it. Her entire self, her body, her being, her every cell holds the holiness in blissful wonder. Later, she will say simply, "He that is mighty has done to me great things; and holy is his name." Two thousand years later, a twenty-first-century poet named Marie Howe will find words for her:

> Even if I don't see it again—nor ever feel it
> I know it is—and that if once it hailed me
> it ever does—
> And so it is myself I want to turn in that direction
> not as towards a place, but it was a tilting
> within myself,
> as one turns a mirror to flash the light to where
> it isn't—I was blinded like that—and swam
> in what shone at me
> only able to endure it by being no one and so
> specifically myself I thought I'd die
> from being loved like that.[1]

As the divine seed planted in her womb begins to grow, it causes dramatic changes in her young body, changes that are both mysterious and thrilling. Knowing that rumors will soon begin circulating in Nazareth, she has an urgent need to talk to someone—to another woman. She begins making plans to visit her cousin Elizabeth, who herself has had a

---

1. Marie Howe, *The Kingdom of Ordinary Time*, 11.

miraculous conception following a divine visitation and promise of a son who "will be filled with the Holy Ghost" in her womb.

Elizabeth lives in the hill country some distance from Nazareth, so Mary sets out alone to see her, a long and dangerous journey for a young woman of her time. When Elizabeth sees Mary coming, she cries out, "God's blessing is on you above all women, and on the fruit of your womb." Mary's response, eloquent and majestic (and the longest expression by a woman in the New Testament), begins with these exultant words: "Tell out, tell out my soul, the greatness of the Lord, rejoice, rejoice, my spirit, in God my savior. My soul now magnifies the Father because my soul has been rejoicing in his son whose holiness I am nurturing in my womb."

Mary's song is praise, prophecy, and poetry. Barry Taylor speaks of Mary as a prophet: "a prophet of the highest order. . . . She becomes the threshold [of history], that moment when time stands still . . . when the heavens shift and shake. . . . She becomes the threshold between what God has done in the past and the radically new day God promises to do in and through her . . . for the world."[2]

When she prophesies, she speaks of things that characterized her son's premortal role in Israel under the Old Covenant and that will characterize it under the New Covenant he will one day usher in: mercy, strength, and justice that will "scatter the proud in the imagination of their hearts," "put down the mighty from their seats," "exalt them of low degree," "fill the hungry with good things," and send the rich "empty away." In other words, Mary seems to see in vision her Son's mission and his kingdom come. And she sees her special role as a woman in teaching him those virtues that will mark him as the most radical and revolutionary teacher in history.

Given the understanding in Israel of the Messiah's triumphant victory over Israel's enemies, it is doubtful that Mary has any premonition of how cataclysmically her heart will break when her son is delivered into the hands of those who will betray and crucify him. The euphoria of being such a chosen one has undoubtedly caused her to disassociate other messianic utterances from her experience—that her son would be despised and rejected, mocked and scourged, enclosed in the assembly of the wicked, and scorned and beaten with stripes; that he would be wounded in the house of his friends; and that his hands and feet would be pierced and his soul poured out unto death. All of that will soon enough overwhelm her

---

2. Barry Taylor, "Mary the Apocalypse."

to the point that she, too, may feel forsaken by God, but for now, all she sees is her son's promise and her special role in its fulfillment.

What Luke tells us and what artists and poets throughout history have done opens our imaginations to wonder at Mary's gradual physical, emotional, and spiritual transformation over the nine months of gestation. (What must it feel like to have God literally inside you?!) Imagine feeling the promised Messiah of the world kicking inside your womb! Or feeling his heart beating with yours. Imagine how careful you would be eating, walking, doing your chores—and how mindful you would be of your thoughts and words. (Would you worry if you were impatient or angry?)

We can imagine that it is from his mother that Jesus first learned to be merciful, kind, and just and, perhaps especially, how to care for the poor, the hungry, the downtrodden, and the dispossessed—the kind of tenderheartedness we tend to associate more with the feminine than the masculine. We imagine that she exemplified the virtues of womanhood and motherhood by nurturing her son, singing lullabies to him when she rocked him to sleep, giving him a coin for the blind beggar when she took him to market, baking bread for him to take to a sick neighbor, and brushing tears from his eyes when he fell and hurt himself. Later, when Jesus had brothers and sisters, she taught him generosity, kindness, and forgiveness.

As with Timothy, who was taught the scriptures by his mother and grandmother, so we imagine that Mary read the scriptures to Jesus and asked him questions about their meaning. Always, she was modeling and teaching, nurturing her child as conscientiously as any mother in history, teaching him limits and responsibilities as well as humor and grace and introducing him to the expansive worlds of the imagination. It is easy to imagine that at some point, when he was old enough to begin understanding who he really was, she told him about Gabriel's miraculous visit and of the great and holy things that transformed her from a maiden into a mother and how in bearing him, she had indeed come to feel blessed above all of the daughters of Eve.

We know very little of Jesus's life during the eighteen years between the time he discoursed with the elders in the temple when he was twelve and when he began his ministry, but is it likely that even as an adult he lived for long periods of time at home or nearby under the shadow of Mary's mothering wings.

Mary is the most venerated woman in history, and deservedly so. No woman has been portrayed in art as much as Mary and no mother more than Mary as mother of Christ.

The world's greatest artists, writers, and musicians have tried to capture her beauty, her intelligence, and her devotion, but nothing tells us who she is more than the words she speaks to Gabriel and to Elizabeth. She represents that liminal moment when heaven and earth came together to produce the greatest gift the world has ever known.

Sandro Botticelli's "The Virgin Adoring the Sleeping Christ Child" illustrates the feminine beauty, grace, and adoration of Mary.[3]

There is something marvelously feminine in this painting. I call attention especially to the feminine colors, the blues, crimsons, and pinks traditionally associated with the Virgin, her tunic and robe flowing down and under the sleeping child whom she has tenderly laid down to rest. Her flowing hair and "diaphanous head-dress," and her finely rendered face and hands with their delicacy and grace portray a feminine power as beautiful as it is mysterious. Of special note is the bower of thornless pink roses that surround Mary and Jesus, echoed not only in Mary's tunic but in her lips as well. The allusion to the bride in the Song of Solomon recalls all of the feminine images of that great poem, many of which have been associated with Mary in folklore and song. The other flowers, strawberries and sweet violets, that surround the bottom of the painting and seem almost woven into the hem of her garment reinforce the delicacy and beauty of this Queen of Heaven.

That all the feminine qualities associated with Mary influenced Jesus in his role as Messiah there can be no doubt. We see this in the many women with whom he associated, including those with whom he had particularly close and intimate relationships. Jesus's stories and parables are replete with feminine figures—the woman who loses a coin, the woman at the well, the virgins who wait for the bridegroom, the woman taken in adultery, and the one who touches the hem of his garment.

Women in Palestine during Jesus's time clearly were not considered equal with men. They were regarded as the property of their fathers or their husbands, had clearly defined, generally subservient roles, and were restricted in many ways. Perhaps reflective of their general status was the prayer of Rabbi Juda ben Elai (150 AD). There are three Benedictions which one must say every day: "Blessed be He who did not make me a Gentile"; "Blessed be He who did not make me an uneducated man"; and "Blessed be He who did not make me a woman." Wives had to obey their husbands (who were considered their masters), had to surrender

---

3. Readers can see the full-color painting at the National Galleries Scotland website: https://www.nationalgalleries.org/art-and-artists/57676.

Sandro Botticelli, "The Virgin Adoring the Sleeping Christ Child."

anything they found to their husbands, and could not attend the temple or ritual festivals during the part of the month they were considered ritually unclean.

From what he has learned from his mother's teachings and example, as soon as he begins his ministry, Jesus challenges and overturns these repressive, constrictive ideas about women, and he begins teaching a more enlightened idea of their place in his kingdom—a place equal to that of men, with entitlement to all the gifts and blessings he bestows.

In his poem "The Blessed Virgin Compared to the Air We Breathe," Gerard Manly Hopkins says that in giving birth to Jesus, Mary, though

> Merely a woman, yet
> Whose presence, power is
> Great as no goddess's . . .
> Let all God's glory through,
> God's glory which would go
> Through her and from her flow . . .[4]

Flow, indeed, from the heavens and through her into our hearts.

Imagine that!

---

4. Taylor, "Mary the Apocalypse."

INTERLUDE 3

Mothers

*"Before I formed you in the womb I knew you,
before you were born, I set you apart;
I anointed you as [the earthly mother of* Our Son*]."*
—After Jeremiah

She arranged
the darkness that brightens
the stars,
making the room
at the edge of the desert
where Her daughter knelt
dark
so that only beauty and innocence
brightened
the angel's appearing,
infusing light with light,
magnifying the glory as his appearance,
enveloping her heart
in holiness:

"Hail!
favored daughter,
blessed is the fruit of your womb

. . . the fruit of my womb."

CHAPTER FIVE

Tikkun K'nessiah: Repairing the Church

"I believe 'Mormonism'... calls for thoughtful disciples who will not be content with merely repeating some of its truths, but will develop its truths; and enlarge it by that development. Not half—not one-hundredth part—not a thousandth part of that which Joseph Smith revealed to the Church has yet been unfolded, either to the Church or to the world."
—B. H. Roberts[1]

The Jews have a term, *tikkun olam*, which means "repairing the world." It is both a statement of belief and a commitment to action by individual Jews to heal, repair, and transform the world. Appropriating the concept and inspired by the Jewish passion for repairing the world, I have coined the term *tikkun k'nessiah*—meaning repairing or healing the Church. In this chapter, I hope to explore the dimensions of what *tikkun k'nessiah* may mean to those of us who are members of the restored Church at this critical juncture in its history.

The meaning of *tikkun olam*, as it is used among certain Jews today, can be traced back to the sixteenth-century Kabbalist Isaac Luria. Luria taught that when God created the world, He sought to light it by shaping special lamps or vessels to hold His light. He explains,

> But as God poured the Light into the vessels, they catastrophically shattered, tumbling down toward the realm of matter [that is, the earth]. Thus, our world consists of countless shards of the original vessels entrapping sparks of the Divine Light. Humanity's great task involves helping God by freeing and reuniting the scattered Light, raising the sparks back to Divinity and restoring the broken world."[2]

Many Jews believe it is their duty to participate in the repair and redemption of the world by "freeing and reuniting the scattered Light." In some traditions, this is seen as the shared, sacred work of God and humans.

When I spoke at the Berkeley Institute of Religion several years ago, I asked the students, "Whose church is this?" They responded, "It's the Church of Jesus Christ." I replied, "There are two possessives in the name

---
1. B. H. Roberts, "Two Kinds of Disciples," 713.
2. "Tikkun Olam: The Spiritual Purpose of Life," Inner Frontier.

of the Church: it *is* the Church of Jesus Christ, certainly, but it is also the Church of the Latter-day Saints. It isn't the Church of the First Presidency or the Quorum of the Twelve or the general authorities, it isn't the Church of conservatives or liberals or any particular group, but rather the Church of all those who are or can be called saints. Thus, the Church is our joint stewardship. Ultimately, it will be no better or no worse than we ourselves choose to make it, than we ourselves choose to be."

It is in this sense of joint stewardship that I want to say a few words about repairing and healing the Church. At the outset, I want to make it clear that I don't consider myself a member of the Ark Steadier's Society (whose initials are ASS!) or in any way presume to have an elevated or enlightened position or to have any special calling in relation to the Church. Like other Latter-day Saints, I am simply a member, a disciple, a follower of Christ, one of the workers in his vineyard. But as such, I feel I am called to help the Church more perfectly reflect the truths, glories, and beauties of Christ's gospel: first, by setting right those things that I need to repair and heal within myself, and then, along with others who feel so called, to do the same in the Church. What I am suggesting is that we could learn something important from our Jewish brothers and sisters in relation to the ethic of repairing. Perhaps like Jews, Latter-day Saints could have as part of our devotion "the 'repairing imperative' that things must be mended, a sense livened by the constant perception of God's presence and concern behind all things."[3]

Repairing the world or the Church presumes that it is in some ways and to some degree broken. As Rabbi David Wolpe asserts, "Tikkun olam presupposes that the world is 'broken' and needs to be fixed by the care and application of people working with the guidance of God."[4] The same could be said of the Church. Reading church history, that brokenness is apparent, but it is also apparent in our own time as the Church has grown into a worldwide faith and now faces the challenge of adapting to an increasingly secular society and an increasingly complex and diverse membership. While some might consider it disloyal to speak of the brokenness of the contemporary Church, anyone who has an authentic engagement with the Church knows that, invariably, it is in some ways less than its promise. Saying so is to state a reality, not voice a criticism.

From the beginning, God has known that any earthly manifestation of His Son's kingdom on earth would be imperfect because we who constitute

---

3. David Wolpe, *The Healer of Shattered Hearts*, 93.
4. Wolpe, 65.

the body of Christ as well as those He calls to lead it are imperfect. Both Jesus's parables and Paul's sermons (as well as those of Nephi, Moroni, Joseph Smith, Brigham Young, and a host of other latter-day prophets) are directed at repairing the brokenness of the Church. Throughout scriptural history, we read of God pleading, persuading, cajoling, at times even bribing His children to take ownership of the Church (however it was defined in different dispensations), to build and magnify it, to expand its borders of thought, imagination, and action. I think it is safe to say that at times we have broken God's heart over our reluctance to better shape ourselves, and therefore the Church, to the ideal and standard to which He has called us.

Instead, we have insisted on building golden calves, on wandering in the desert, on, as the scriptures say, "going a-whoring after strange gods" (Deut. 31:16), on being drunk on the nectar of the world and in love with our own narcissism. At times, the Israelites, Jaredites, Nephites, early Christians, and modern Latter-day Saints have all, to one degree or another, allowed the Church to fall into disrepair. At times we have come to our senses (assisted by famine, persecution, or temporary withdrawal of the heavens) and repaired or renewed the Church—whether in the wilderness, in small enclaves of righteousness, in the Great Basin Kingdom, or in great communities like the city of Enoch and the land of Bountiful following Christ's visit to the New World.

In practical terms, how does one go about repairing the Church? As I said at the outset, it should begin by each of us doing (and maintaining) a thorough inventory of our intentions, motives, and integrity. Next, we should carefully consider how and under what conditions to participate in the work of repairing. Most Latter-day Saints I know would immediately shift their attention to the leaders of the Church, but before focusing on them, we should consider reform and repair in our individual lives and among the membership. Where to begin? For me, the following suggests potential brokenness among the body of the Saints and represents opportunities and challenges for grassroots repair. It is my observation that as a body of believers, we are more:

- interested in answers than in questions
- comfortable with certainty than doubt
- inclined to surrender responsibility to those in authority than to trust the integrity of our own thoughts and inspiration
- interested in being right than in being good

- focused on obedience than on love
- interested in the next world than in this one[5]
- inclined to trust our feelings over our thoughts
- committed to the values of our political parties than to those of the gospel
- focused on ourselves than on others and, thus, have a tendency toward cultural egoism

Many of these might be considered virtues, but in their extreme expressions they all constitute brokenness. I believe that repairing the Church means that individually and collectively we need to address these cultural characteristics that essentially prevent change and impede progress.

This means that some of the most important work of repair begins at the local level. That is, the work of *tikkun k'nessiah* begins with oneself and in one's family, ward, and stake. It begins by being willing to accept callings and then magnifying them, by volunteering to do something that needs doing—small things that might make a small difference.

Sometimes the work of repairing requires us to stand up for principle, as a number of California Latter-day Saints did during Proposition 8. I heard of one bishop who refused to follow instructions asking members of his congregation to contribute financially to the effort to enact the proposition. He said to the stake president, "This is not something I feel I can do. If you need to release me, then I will understand." The stake president excused him from the assignment. Others were not treated so charitably but were nevertheless willing to suffer censure and ecclesiastical discipline out of what they considered love of the Church.

There is significant pain in the Church today. Addressing that pain depends on our individual acts of courage, of sacrifice, and especially of love. It is in that realm where much of the most important work of repairing is to be done. But there is also the larger realm, the Church beyond the individual broken heart, beyond the sin and insensitivity with which each of us must contend, and beyond the madness and mystery of trying to make the gospel and the Church work in our lives, families, and congregations. It is in that realm, the macrocosm of the institutional Church, where the work of repair also is required, even though it is more daunting and more

---

5. The Jews have a saying, "Just one world at a time please. God has presently placed me upon planet earth, and I want to be here 100% so I can accomplish the reason for my being."

difficult because it is largely beyond any one person's control. And yet it is also part of our individual and collective stewardship.

Based on my nearly eighty years as a member of the Church, the following is my personal list of things that might be considered in need of repair. It is because I believe the ultimate mission of the Church would be enhanced by intelligently and compassionately addressing such matters that I risk listing them here (and, based on my experience, doing so is indeed a risk):

1. As a large bureaucracy, the Church is less flexible, less open, less efficient, and less effective than one would wish. As a general authority friend said to me a couple of years ago, "We can't get anything done in the Church! I'm not complaining, but I am lamenting." In many ways, the Church has adjusted well to its rapid growth and increasing complexity, but there are problems, one of which is related to what my friend Truman Madsen used to call the "Church Social Service,"[6] Church employees who are more afraid of making mistakes than decisions. This is true of any bureaucracy, of course, but likely more true of a church whose leaders and employees are aware that those who give them direction are sustained as "prophets, seers, and revelators."[7] That is, such an administrative culture, one in which taking independent initiative or engaging in imaginative problem-solving might be seen as disrespectful or in which questioning the judgment of leaders might be seen as "evil speaking against the Lord's anointed," could inhibit the very kinds of actions that might constitute the work of repairing or healing.

2. The Church's method of choosing its president/prophet might be improved by instituting a method of succession based on a different principle than longevity of service. While the present system produces a certain stability and continuity, it also produces significant periods in which the Church is in a sort of limbo because the prophet is cognitively diminished or incapacitated. While that has not

---

6. Personal conversation with the author.

7. A friend who worked for the Church (Bonneville International) told me of several examples of mission presidents not reporting truthfully on conditions in the mission field for fear of being blamed. Everyone is familiar with leaders who seem hesitant to take problems to a higher level as well as those who have an unrealistic idea as to the potential inerrancy of general authorities, something I imagine is not pleasing to those very authorities.

happened under the administration of President Russell M. Nelson, it has happened with previous Church presidents.[8] Having a more flexible process for prophetic succession might open the way for the kind of change one currently sees in the Catholic Church under Pope Francis. At the least, given the miracles of modern medicine in keeping people alive into their eighties and nineties, expanding the status of "emeritus" to the Quorum of the Twelve might be a step in the right direction.

3. The Church is, at least to some in its liberal/progressive wing, too imbalanced toward conservatism and, in some geographic areas, perhaps even toward fundamentalism. While a certain degree of conformity in terms of politics and culture is desirable, some observers contend that the degree of conformity in the center stakes of Zion constitutes a barrier to reform and renewal. Many have the perception that, for example, Saints in the Latter-day Saint heartland (Utah, Idaho, Arizona, and Wyoming) have more in common politically and ideologically with nonmembers in the US South than with their fellow members on the coasts. I'm not sure what, if anything, can be done about this, but I think it is an example of a less diverse, less coherent, and therefore less dynamic, productive, and effective culture. Although some would argue that the Church's conservatism is its strength, I contend that a church that is too conservative can be as problematic as one that is too liberal (although, to work toward some kind of balance, I wouldn't mind seeing the latter experimented with for a period!).

4. Related to and reflective of this imbalance is the perception that the dominant culture influencing the Church on matters of war and peace, the environment, social justice, immigration, politics, and Church polity is the Intermountain West (especially Utah) culture. For an international church, this can be a significant liability. One of the challenges for the future of the Church is the degree to which it can shed its more provincial, US-centric image. As John Sorenson observed many years ago, "When the time comes that Mormons in the central homeland come to the realization that they too are constrained by cultural ways which have nothing directly to do with the gospel they espouse, the result could be a kind of Copernican revolution with attendant new

---

8. See Gregory A. Prince, Lester E. Bush Jr., and Brent N. Rushforth, "Gerontocracy and the Future of Mormonism."

insights into the Church and the scriptures and the meaning of life."[9] The dynamism of twenty-first-century Mormonism depends on the Church's success in truly becoming intercultural and international.

5. Although the Church has made some positive steps toward finding a more favorable balance in terms of gender equality, the situation is currently less than ideal. The Church has not yet figured out what to do with women, especially young, faithful, and progressive women who have less patience with a male-dominant, patriarchy-centered Church culture. Since women once played a more prominent role in the Church, there is precedent for reviving some past practices that might help repair the estrangement that many women, especially Millennials and Zoomers, are experiencing.[10]

6. The same could be said of other kinds of inequity and injustice, especially those relating to sexual orientation and gender identity and choice.

7. Lack of financial transparency. Because the Church does not disclose its finances, there is inevitable speculation about how much money the Church takes in tithes and offerings (an estimated $7 billion annually[11]) and how much it has in assets (estimated at $200 billion in 2023 and a projected $1 trillion by 2044[12]) and therefore how and where and on what it spends members' tithing and other contributions. While disclosing financial data might be considered risky by some, many feel that a more transparent system would diminish suspicion, criticism, and speculation. As contributors and shareholders, many individual Latter-day Saints feel they have a right to an accounting of Church finances.

8. Adjusting to social change. While some argue that the reluctance and slowness of the Church's willingness and ability to change is what creates stability, there is also the sense that the Church is often significantly late in adjusting to social issues that could have a positive impact on its mission. The issue of Black members and the priesthood is a dramatic example. It took 125 years for the Church to change its policy on the denial of priesthood and temple blessings to Black

---

9. John Sorenson, "Mormon World View and American Culture," 17–29.

10. See Jana Riess, *The Next Mormons: How Millennials Are Changing the LDS Church*.

11. Esther Zuckerman, "The Mormon Church Takes In $7 Billion a Year."

12. Tony Semerad, "LDS Church on its way to becoming a trillion-dollar faith." Zuckerman, "The Mormon Church Takes In $7 Billion a Year."

members and another forty years to admit that the scriptural and other justifications for the policy were wrong.[13]

9. Dealing with questions, challenges, and dissent. In other words, the heart of what some call the Latter-day Saint faith crisis. One of the more complicated problems for the Church is how, in the age of the internet, to deal with dissent and criticism as well as open hostility. These kinds of issues are difficult for any organization but especially so for one that makes an ultimate claim to authority, truth, and legitimacy. The modern Church has a history of responding to criticism by not responding, by being defensive, and sometimes by retaliating against those who criticize. The steps the Church has taken over the past several years in publishing the Joseph Smith Papers, underwriting white papers on various controversial subjects, and openly admitting past errors have all helped repair the Church, but additional work is needed.

If these are indeed some of the areas where the work of repairing could be done, the question for individual Latter-day Saints—especially the vast majority without any significant power or position—is when, by whom, and by what means it should be undertaken. This is a critical question, if for no other reason than that many would consider it presumptuous for any individual to feel that he or she could help repair the Church when the consensus is that such work is "best left to the brethren." But, as I have tried to argue, this is the work of all who have covenanted to build and expand Christ's kingdom. It is also the charge the Lord gives us in the Doctrine and Covenants, where, speaking to all members (tenderly calling us his "little flock"), he says, "The kingdom is *yours* until I come" (D&C 35:27). In other words, he is entrusting the Church to the collective care of the Saints and, I believe, will hold us accountable for whatever condition the Church is in, not only when he comes but at each stage along the way.

I have immense respect for those in authority. I have always gladly sustained the general authorities. I do not envy anyone who has the onerous responsibility of governing such a large and diverse church during such a complex period in world history. Being a general authority, from all I can gather, requires both broad administrative skills and deep spiritual sensitivity. It requires those who hold high positions to handle, on

---

13. See "Race and the Priesthood," *Gospel Topics Essays*. Also see my *Dialogue* article, "Truth and Reconciliation: Reflections on the Fortieth Anniversary of the LDS Church's Lifting the Priesthood and Temple Restrictions for Black Mormons of African Descent."

a daily basis, the complexities of a large and growing organization while also being ready to respond to a Saint somewhere in the world who wants a miracle performed on the spot. Judging from what I have been told by the few general authorities I have known personally, I also sense that it is difficult at times for church leadership to distinguish between those who have a genuine desire to affect change and those who may have a frivolous intention, personal grievance, or sinister agenda. Obviously, the general authorities can't have a completely open-door policy as far as such issues are concerned, otherwise they wouldn't have time for anything else. It is extremely challenging for people in such positions to constantly be in the public eye, to always be spiritually in tune, and to be called upon to make Solomonic decisions on the spur of the moment. Probably the last thing a general authority wants to hear is how he might do his job better!

At the same time, if one has made a covenant to consecrate all that one has to the Church for the building up of the kingdom of God on earth and the establishment, strengthening, enhancement, and enlargement of Zion, then repairing the Church is a sacred obligation—albeit one that must be discharged with all the virtues of the priesthood (which apply equally to men and women): "by persuasion, by long-suffering, by gentleness and meekness, and by love unfeigned; By kindness, and pure knowledge, which shall greatly enlarge the soul without hypocrisy, and without guile" (D&C 121:41–42). Especially by "love unfeigned." Whatever we do, however we do it, the important thing is to believe we can make a difference.

I'm aware that to want, out of love, to repair the Church and to hope for change is not easy. Nevertheless, if we don't do this work, who will? As Annie Dillard writes,

> There is no one but us. There is no one . . . on the face of the earth, or in the earth, but only us, a generation comforting ourselves with the notion that we have come at an awkward time . . . and our children busy and troubled, and we ourselves unfit, not yet ready, having each of us chosen wrongly, made a false start, failed, yielded to impulse, and the tangled comfort of pleasure and grown exhausted. . . . But there is no one but us. There never has been."[14]

And, one might add, there never will be.

To illustrate the concept of repairing the Church, I would like to use the metaphor of repairing or renovating a house. Having owned several houses in my lifetime, all of which needed continuous repair and sometimes major renovation, I know something of what it takes to make a

---

14. Annie Dillard, *Holy the Firm*, 56–57.

house work for those who live in it. I'm not very skilled as a carpenter, electrician, or plumber, although I have done such repairs on my homes. Mainly I am a handyman, one who is continually solving small problems and calling on more skilled craftspeople for major, more complicated tasks. I have always felt a sense of satisfaction when I have been able to fix a leaky toilet, a broken window, a jammed garbage disposal, or a faulty electrical junction. I also work outside, when necessary, but I do so with a familiarity and knowledge of what's on the inside.

What I have learned is that almost all repairs have to be made from inside the house. Most of the time, one has to climb into the attic or crawl under the sink, raise floorboards or replace light switches. The same is true for the house of my faith: to have any chance of repairing this house, I have to live in it. I can stand outside and criticize or complain about it, but that's not very useful or very rewarding—and the house doesn't get fixed. Abandoning the Church because of something broken in it is like leaving a house because the plumbing isn't working well.

Some critics of the Church remind me of those who come into a house and see only what's wrong with it but don't volunteer to fix it. They run their fingers over the mantel to see if it is dusty, they complain about the color of the carpet, they make disparaging comments about the smallness of the rooms, and they comment about how poor it is in comparison with their or someone else's house. Others remind me of renters. I have had a couple of rental properties, and my experience is that renters tend not to have the same sense of obligation or care that a homeowner does. The worst renters seldom take pains to fix things and often complain that the owner hasn't created a perfect house for them to live in. Some "renters" in the Church are those who come but don't really participate, who don't really feel the house of the Lord is their house, who don't show up on Saturday mornings to clean it for Sunday services or on Tuesday evenings to work with the youth.[15] Some of these Saints are like those Elder Dieter F. Uchtdorf characterized as "sleeping through the Restoration."[16]

I don't want to sleep through the Restoration or even stroll through it. Its blessings are too great and its promises too grand for me to consider doing so. The Restoration is not an event or series of events that happened in the nineteenth century; it is a process, a continual unfolding. There

---

15. To be fair, one might also argue that the Church can at times seem like a landlord who doesn't fix things that are broken or in need of repair, or who raises the rent without making any improvements!

16. Dieter F. Uchtdorf, "Are You Sleeping through the Restoration?"

are many great and important truths yet to be revealed, some of them to ordinary saints, and I don't want to miss any of them. My guess is that not many of these "great and important things pertaining to the kingdom of God" (A of F 1:9) will be revealed to those who leave the Church.

Latter-day Saints speak of the Church being true, but I would like to consider how a deeper, wider understanding of that word might be instructive in considering how one might repair the Church. Generally, we use "true" as an adjective, as when we speak of "*the* true Church" (especially if we add the qualifiers "one and only"), by which we mean the one that most conforms to or accords with the primitive Church. But "true" can also be a noun, a verb, and an adverb. It is as a verb that I think it has the most relevance to the concept of repairing the Church because in this sense it means to bring something into adjustment, as with a carpenter using a tool to "true" a piece of lumber so as to make it fit. Thus, as individual members, we can help "true" the Church by aligning our own devotion and behavior with what we understand the Lord would like.

As I said at the outset, I have no authority beyond the authority of my own conscience or power beyond that of my own mind, voice, and spirit; I have no knowledge beyond that of an ordinary person who has lived long enough to have learned a few lessons, including, especially, from his own mistakes and misdeeds; I have no calling beyond that which Christ calls all of his followers to fulfill—to love him and the Father with all our heart, might, mind, and strength, and to love others as we love ourselves. Embedded in those two "great" commandments, I believe, is another commandment that involves both deity and humanity—to love the Church enough to try and change it, even if that means risking the displeasure of the Church.

This is Christ's church, and it is also our church. It is part of the Kingdom of God to which we all belong. In repairing the Church with God's help, we can also be, as Isaiah says, healers of shattered hearts. That's the place I want the Church to be for everyone, including you and me—and all of those currently outside the house of the Church, those who have left or are undecided if they want to be inside this house, and those who do not yet know this house. I see our great united charge, our sacred and holy calling as "helping God by freeing and reuniting the scattered Light, raising the sparks back to Divinity and restoring the broken [church and the broken] world."[17]

---

17. "Tikkun Olam: The Spiritual Purpose of Life."

CHAPTER SIX

Imagining "All Are Alike unto God": Lester Bush's Gift of Revelation to the Restoration[1]

Typical of far too many youths of my generation, I grew up in a racist home, in a racist community, and in racist Latter-day Saint congregations. As a young man, I harbored deep racist sentiments and attitudes toward Black people (as well as other racial minorities). I thought of that childhood recently when a friend sent me a copy of a letter from the First Presidency dated November 4, 1949, written in response to a letter from a convert to the Church asking, "What is the Church's attitude (both in theory and in practice) toward Negroes in social life?" The following response was signed by both J. Reuben Clark Jr. and David O. McKay of the Church's First Presidency:

> The church's attitude today is as it always has been, namely, that intermarriage between our members and negroes is forbidden because negroes cannot have the priesthood, and the progeny of marriages between our people and negroes could not hold the priesthood. Since the church's membership is charged by the Lord with carrying on his work, which is done through his priesthood, it is the obligation of every Latter-day Saint to see to it that his progeny, so far as blood and race are concerned, is of a character that can carry on the priesthood. Anything therefore that tends to encourage marriage between negroes and whites is not sanctioned by the Church. Social intercourse with the negroes has this tendency, and for equivalent reasons, it is not sanctioned by the Church. This does not mean that the Church would deny the negro any civil rights nor that it would deny to him any progress which he himself, as to individuals or groups, might be able to achieve in whatever line or endeavor they are able to excel.[2]

---

1. Originally published as "Black Mormons and the Priesthood: A Retrospective Perspective," in a special Fall 2024 issue of *Dialogue: A Journal of Mormon Thought* celebrating the fiftieth anniversary of the publication of Bush's article. Readers are encouraged to read the entire issue, which also includes perspectives by Darius Gray, Gregory Prince, Yvonne Bush, Ross Peterson, and Newell Bringhurst.

2. First Presidency Letter to Waldo H. Anderson, president of the Northern States Mission, November 4, 1949.

Note the exclusionary language: "our members," "our people," and "every Latter-day Saint [apparently, excluding Black church members]." Though starker in its expression, the following statement by apostle Joseph Fielding Smith in 1963 reflects both the tone and the substance the First Presidency's letter: "I would not want you to believe that we bear any animosity toward the Negro. 'Darkies' are wonderful people, and they have a place in our church."[3]

That was the Church in which I came of age. When I went to Brigham Young University in the early 1950s, there was not a single Black student or faculty member on campus. While little at BYU challenged orthodoxy on this subject, serving a mission in Chicago (where we were advised not to return to the homes of any Black families we had inadvertently contacted) and, shortly afterward, serving in the army in Georgia (where I saw firsthand the realities of Jim Crow laws and blatant racism) led me to begin questioning the Church's teaching on this matter. In graduate school at the University of Wisconsin—a dramatically more progressive and inclusive environment than I had experienced at BYU—I grew increasingly uncomfortable with the doctrine and the official justifications for it. Nevertheless, like many Latter-day Saints at the time, I continued to defend the Church's position. As time went by, however, I began to feel a tension between the words I was saying and the misgivings of my heart.

Although I parroted what I had been taught about Black people being less valiant in the premortal existence and the curse of Cain, eventually I developed my own more rational, if still uncomfortable, explanation: "Given the liberating doctrines of the Restoration and the political realities of mid-nineteenth-century racial culture, had the Church given the priesthood and temple blessings to Black members, they likely would have been attracted to the Church in such great numbers that Mormonism would have become essentially a Black-dominated church and therefore lost its ability to proselytize the predominate white (if racist) nations."

It wasn't until the height of the civil rights movement when I began teaching at UCLA, including teaching Black American authors in my English classes, that I became increasingly aware that my attitudes and beliefs were disharmonious with those of the Church. It was during this time when, as editor of *Dialogue*, I opened an envelope and found Lester Bush Jr.'s "Mormonism's Negro Doctrine: An Historical Overview" with its arresting opening sentence: "There once was a time, albeit brief, when

---

3. Jeff Nye, "Memo from a Mormon: In Which a Troubled Young Man Raises the Question of His Church's Attitude toward Negroes," 77.

a 'Negro problem' did not exist for The Church of Jesus Christ of Latter-day Saints."[4] Immediately, the significance of what I was reading became apparent. My feeling was similar to what Herman Melville expressed upon first reading Nathaniel Hawthorne's collection of short stories—"a shock of recognition," which I have described elsewhere as "an immediate and indelible communication of truth to my soul."[5] Bush's article put me in a moral quandary, especially when I learned that he had sent his article and all the documentation for it to church leadership—to Elder Boyd K. Packer, to be precise, who expressed his wish that the article not be published, although, according to Bush, he did not actually forbid it. Other general authorities also voiced objections. According to Bush, Mormon scholar Edward Ashment was present when Elder Bruce R. McConkie, upon studying Bush's article, "slammed the [issue of] *Dialogue* with my essay down on his desk and pronounced it 'CRAP!'"[6]

Although I was warned by Robert K. Thomas, vice president of BYU and a friend and mentor, that there could be grave consequences for me personally if we did publish the article, after much prayer and consultation with my wife and editorial staff, as well as with Gene England and other trusted advisors, we concluded that what Bush had written was so important that morally we had no choice but to publish it. As I wrote to Lester, "It is, of course, a potentially explosive issue, and undoubtedly there will be many people displeased at our efforts, but the time is long overdue, it seems to me, for us to publish some significant work on this subject."[7] If publishing Bush's article was the right decision, publishing it with responses from three trusted Latter-day Saint scholars was an even better one. Together, Gordon Thomasson, Hugh Nibley, and Eugene England created an expanded context in which Bush's words could be more fully understood. I was especially impressed by what England, who called the teaching "The Mormon Cross," said:

> We can get ready for living the higher law, first by working to root out racism in ourselves through getting to know blacks and something of black aspirations and culture. And we can help get Americans ready, black and

---

4. Lester E. Bush Jr., "Mormonism's Negro Doctrine: An Historical Overview," 11.
5. Bob Rees, "A Perfect Brightness of Hope."
6. Lester Bush, "Writing 'Mormonism's Negro Doctrine: An Historical Overview' (1973): Context and Reflections, 1998," 266–67.
7. Devery S. Anderson, "A History of Dialogue, Part Two: Struggle toward Maturity, 1971–1982," 23.

white, by working honestly and vigorously to overcome the burden of our racist past."[8]

Unfortunately, it took a long time following the publication of Bush's article for us to do either.

What none of us could have anticipated was that, according to members of Spencer W. Kimball's own family, Bush's article was not only read by President Kimball, but underlined in red throughout. As Greg Prince informs us, people close to the prophet speculate that Bush's article had a strong influence on his 1978 announcement of the change in policy. In fact, Prince quotes general authority Marion D. Hanks as confirming this: "[Lester's] article had had far more influence than the Brethren would ever acknowledge. . . . It 'started to foment the pot.'"[9]

It is sobering to contemplate where the Church would be today had Brigham Young never authorized nor insisted on his erroneous teaching. Or where we would be if the Church had taken Bush's research to its ultimate conclusion in 1978 and altogether abandoned the historical rationale for the doctrine rather than continuing it for more than three more decades. Imagine the Church over that extended period, unburdened by its heavy racial history!

There is no way to calculate the personal harm suffered by Black people over the more than a century and a half between Brigham Young's teaching and the 2013 "Race and Priesthood" essay.[10] How many more Black people would have joined the Church had they been taught today's liberating policy? How many Black Mormons would have served missions and how many converts might they have brought into the Church had they been allowed to serve during the century between Brigham Young's ban and the lifting of the ban in 1978? How many more Church members would there currently be in Brazil, throughout Africa, and in the United States and Europe? How many Black brothers and sisters would have enjoyed the blessings of temple marriage and eternally sealed families? How many ancestors of Black members would have received saving ordinances through their descendants' temple work? And how many individual Black members would have been spared the pain and humiliation of prejudicial discrimination, rejection, and violence?

---

8. Eugene England, "The Mormon Cross," 85.

9. Gregory A. Prince, "A Tribute to Lester Bush on the Fiftieth Anniversary of the Article that Changed the Church," 71.

10. "Race and the Priesthood," Gospel Topics Essays.

It is also sobering to acknowledge that over a period of 129 years (from 1849 to 1978), ten prophets and hundreds of apostles were wrong in teaching and defending a doctrine and practice regarding priesthood ordination that was counter to what the prophet Joseph Smith taught and counter to the very clear language of the Book of Mormon. It is equally sobering that it took another thirty-four years for the Church to acknowledge the wrongness of earlier justifications when it published "Race and Priesthood" in 2013.

My wife, Gloria, and I were privileged to attend the impressive "Be One" celebration of the fortieth anniversary of the 1978 lifting of the priesthood ban held in the Conference Center in June 2018. We saw and talked with Lester immediately afterward, along with our mutual friend, Greg Prince. We all lamented the fact that those responsible for planning and speaking at the celebration failed to use it to permanently dispel the mythology that had persisted and done so much damage both within and without the Church for nearly two centuries (unfortunately, the remnants of that mythology remain with us).

Those leaving the conference center that night, their hearts filled with the evening's celebratory spirit, were left with the impression that Brigham Young, Spencer W. Kimball, and Russell M. Nelson were all part of a revelatory process and history. Few had any idea that anonymously sitting in the Conference Center that night was a courageous, humble, and devoted Latter-day Saint scholar whose brilliant and respectful service to the kingdom may be of greater import than that of any lay member in the brief history of the Church. The "Be One" celebration would also have been an appropriate occasion to recognize and honor Lester Bush, an extraordinary, ordinary member of the Church who had the faith, courage and, yes, the imagination to see that, indeed, we are all "alike unto God." I say, "Praise to the man!"

CHAPTER SEVEN

Toward a Feminine Mormon Midrash: Mormon Women and the Imaginative Reading of Scripture

"In the Jewish mind, . . . reverence for God's word requires more creative attention. It requires an active, imaginative engagement with language."[1]

"This is what imaginative reading ultimately requires: a willingness to step completely out of the boat and dive into the waters with a God who has declared from the beginning that we will not drown."[2]

—Judith M. Kunst

For millennia, scripture and religious history have been told almost completely from a masculine point of view. Even stories of or about women have been filtered through prophets, patriarchs, and priests. As Jewish scholar Naomi M. Hyman states,

> Traditional Jewish sources see the world through male eyes. Men have determined what is important because they have defined our culture—and they have given us only part of the picture. Women experience the world differently: not inaccurately, not less clearly, but simply differently. A Judaism that includes women's experience will be a more complete Judaism. When we learn to see the world through the eyes of tradition and when tradition takes into itself women's view of the world, both will grow."[3]

For this reason, women have sometimes had difficulty seeing themselves in sacred texts and religious traditions. As Hyman notes, "No matter how I studied those texts, . . . I would never find my own voice, my own experience in them except perhaps vicariously. I felt betrayed."[4] Rabbi Sandy Eisenberg Sasso puts it this way: "Women in the Bible often have neither a name nor a voice. They somehow fit into someone else's story, but rarely is the story about them."[5]

---

1. Judith M. Kunst, *The Burning Word: A Christian Encounter with Jewish Midrash*, 114.
2. Kunst, 86.
3. Naomi M. Hyman, *Biblical Women in the Midrash: A Sourcebook*, xv.
4. Hyman, xv.
5. Sandy Eisenberg Sasso, *God's Echo: Exploring Scripture with Midrash*, 117.

What is true of Jewish women is certainly true of Latter-day Saint women. Since Mormonism as a restored religion includes a continuation of patriarchy and a male-dominated, authoritarian ecclesiastical structure, there has been a paucity of feminine perspectives on our sacred texts and our cultural history. Although, this has changed somewhat for the better over the past several decades as Latter-day Saint women scholars and feminist thinkers and writers have attempted to bring some balance to our understanding. Some Latter-day Saint women have expressed a wish for a more inclusive Church polity or at least the inclusion of more women's voices, and yet there is considerable resistance to this impulse. Without authoritative change in either policy or principle, what options are open to women? Let me suggest one—that in addition to using their scholarly and expressive skills, Latter-day Saint women begin inserting their imaginations, their personal experience, their presence, and their points of view into our scriptural and cultural literature.

A model for such expression can be found both in traditional Jewish midrashic literature as well as in the bold and imaginative writings on scripture by contemporary Jewish women, who are enriching the tradition of midrashic writing by creating new elaborations, extensions, and imaginings of scriptural narratives. While some might object to this as "playing hob with holy things," of presuming to improve on scripture, it is important to remember that much of scripture is an admixture of fact and fancy, a deliberate arrangement of history to make it more persuasive, and an artful telling, even an invention of human events to make them more dramatic. That sixty percent of the Old Testament is poetry suggests that we are to give ourselves to the poetic (that is, the imaginative) *fabrications* of sacred literature (one has only to think of the contrast between the two accounts of Deborah in Judges 4 and 5 to see how much more powerful a conscious arrangement (dare one say *manipulation*?) of facts can be and how powerful one woman acting with boldness and determination can be shown.

The Jewish midrash is a rich repository of such imaginings. Created by the rabbis between 400 and 1200 CE, these stories constitute a rich and engaging collection of rabbinical exegeses, extrapolations, interpretations, and expansions on the Torah. The word "midrash" comes from the Hebrew root *daled-resh-shin* which means to "to examine," "to investigate," to interpret, and to explicate.[6] The traditional midrashim, based on

---

6. Hyman, *Biblical Women*, xxvii. Midrash has been defined variously as "creative interpretation," "a means of extracting meaning" from as well as "a way of reading meaning *into* the text," and "a passionate and active grappling with God's living

both oral and written tradition, constitute an extensive library of Jewish insights into the *possible* interpretations of scripture.

The writers of midrashic literature did not simply look backward to a world already created, but felt that the scriptures were to be reinterpreted for each generation. As Rabbi Sasso writes,

> They believed that the Word spoke to every generation anew. They allowed the biblical stories into their lives, and they let their lives enter the stories. They created midrash, interpretations of Scripture, an imaginative body of literature which enriched the biblical narrative and kept it fresh and vital.[7]

Concern not only about what the text says but also what it does not say, what it suggests, and what is or may be missing was also the objective of the midrashic writers.

The rabbis believed that God himself intended that the scriptural texts be open. As Rabbi Sasso says, "What Moses delivered amidst the thunder and lightning of Sinai was not a final product but rather the beginning of a conversation between God and the people of Israel." She concludes with a statement that reflects Mormon doctrine: "Revelation did not end with Moses but began with him . . . the rabbis highlight Torah as a continuing revelation."[8]

In the midrashic tradition, difference of opinion as to the meaning of a text is not seen as something negative, but rather inevitable: "No one person can claim to hold the key to unlock what God intended, because what God intended was for each generation to read its story into

---

word" (Hyman, xxiii, xxix, xxxiv); "a continuing revelation" of Torah, a way of "deriving a homelitic meaning from [a] passage of scripture," a process that gives "the narrative new life and make[s] it meaningful for another generation" (Sasso, *God's Echo*, 30, 69–70); "reconsideration and reinterpretation," "narrative retellings," (Leila Leah Bronner, *From Eve to Esther: Rabbinic Reconstruction of Biblical Women*, xxi, 185); a process by which the "human imagination" illuminates "the hidden, holy meanings of scripture," "a call to stare straight into the dark holes of scripture, and to use curiosity and questions to dig even deeper into those holes," an "imaginative grappling with scripture," a "uniquely playful, imaginative response to scripture," a process that involves "imagination, intuition, innovation," a way of "connecting literal and non-literal images," a way "to find, in the liquid, living language of Torah, a new way to meet God," a form that "celebrates *conversation* more than information" (Kunst, *The Burning Word*, 5, 30, 35, 57, 61, 67, 76, 128). In short, creating midrash, to use Emerson's term, requires creative reading as well as creative writing.

7. Sasso, *God's Echo*, 5.
8. Sasso, 11.

the text."⁹ This impulse counters fundamentalist, literal, and privileged approaches to the scriptures.

The writers of the midrash saw the Word of God as being like the manna which God provided the Israelites: to the infants, the manna tasted like their mother's milk; to the young, it tasted like sweet bread; and to the elderly, it tasted like honeyed wafers. Thus, "each and every person heard it [the divine Word] according to his own particular capacity." As Rabbi Sasso says, "Just as God had provided manna for the people in the wilderness and yet it tasted different to each person, so did God reveal the divine Word to all who stood at Sinai; yet each person heard something different." And this is according to God's plan, for the Rabbis quote God as saying, "Do not be misled because you hear many voices. Know that I am one and the same: *I am the Lord your God.*"¹⁰

While rabbinic midrashim generally reflect the dominant androcentric world view of ancient cultures, at times they are surprisingly enlightened. As Leila Leah Bronner summarizes, "There is no question that the society in which the sages lived was male dominated. Still, the aggadic discourse of the rabbis gave women greater rights and protections within their limited domestic realm. Moreover, biblical models were treated with respect and comparative open-mindedness by the sages relative to their time."¹¹

The midrash contains a significant body of interesting, provocative, and inspirational literature about women. Female-centered midrashim include not only rabbinic expansions of scriptural narratives but at times fictive inventions that greatly enlarge and expand stories and characters. At times, the sages constructed entirely new narratives based on the smallest of hints or only a sliver of information. For example, the figure Serah is referred to three times in the Bible, yet the only biographical detail given about her is that she was the daughter of Asher (Gen. 46:17, Num. 26:46, and 1 Chr. 7:30). Not content to let her remain a cipher, the rabbis felt emboldened to create a distinct personality for this woman out of whole cloth, "to embroider marvelous, even mythic stories about her."¹² This included the invention that she was the only woman in the Old Testament to be given "the secret knowledge of how to identify the Redeemer."¹³

---

9. Sasso, 14.
10. Sasso, 40, 43, 41.
11. Bronner, *From Eve to Esther*, 185.
12. Bronner, 43.
13. Bronner 46.

Another midrash gives her a prominent role in influencing the Exodus itself. As Leila Leah Bronner explains,

> She is one of the few female characters in the Talmud and Midrash who ventured beyond the limited spheres to which women were relegated in order to participate in activities ordinarily restricted to men, such as learning and political leadership. Moreover, and equally unusual, she achieved this through her own merit, not as the wife or mother of a great man.[14]

Many of the women in the Bible are anonymous, shadowy figures. As Rabbi Sasso says, "It is not uncommon in the Bible to find that women have no names and no stories." For example, she states, "We know nothing of Noah's wife. She has neither a name nor a story. Midrash often fills in those blanks and provides a name and a story."[15] Thus, in the midrash, we find new narratives about Sarah, Noah's wife, Lot's wife and daughters, Pharaoh's daughter, Leah, Rachael, Tamar, Deborah, Hannah, and Esther, among others. In such midrashic narratives, women come alive, perform interesting and sometimes heroic deeds, manifest great faith, and at times even challenge their husbands and the prophets, turning the original text on its head.

Added to this rich lore are the midrashic writings of contemporary Jewish women. In her *Biblical Women in the Midrash*, Naomi M. Hyman cites a number of biblical narratives involving women, recounts traditional midrashim focused on these women, and then presents midrashim newly composed by contemporary Jewish women. One such example is the story of the rape of Jacob's daughter Dinah as recounted in Genesis 34:1–31. In the Genesis account, Dinah is forcibly assaulted by Shechem, the son of Hamor the Hivite. To get revenge, Jacob's sons trick Shechem and all the men of his tribe into agreeing to be circumcised and then, when the men are disabled by this deception, slaying all of them, much to the consternation of Jacob.

The rabbis, in what is a typical (and traditional) male chauvinist interpretation, blame Dinah for being raped: "She brought upon herself her violation by Shechem . . . [because] she went out to see the daughters of the land." That is, by going to the marketplace instead of staying home, Dinah "comes to a state of corruption, to a state of harlotry."[16]

---

14. Bronner, 42.

15. Sasso, *God's Echo*, 123.

16. *Ecclesiastes Rabbah* 10:8, in *The Midrash*, ed. and trans. H. Freedman and Maurice Simon et al., as cited by Hyman, *Biblical Women*, 67–68. Other rabbis give similar interpretations. See citations in Hyman, 68.

To counter this sexist interpretation, Naomi Graetz creates a new midrash, "A Daughter in Israel is Raped." This modern midrash is told in the first person, having Dinah recount the horror and terror of her violation and how inexorably and tragically it altered her life. Her father blames her for what happened, her mother tries to persuade her to forget what happened and marry Schechem, and her brothers, against her will, plot to avenge her violation, not out of concern for her but for "the honor of [her] family." In this telling, she says, "After being raped, my body no longer belonged to me. . . . My privacy was invaded. I had no place to escape." Years later she recalls her brothers' vengeful acts as leading to her "death sentence," condemning her to a life in which her family "go about their business as if I am invisible." She hears them whisper, "Poor Dinah, what will become of her?"[17]

Clearly, this retelling through modern feminist eyes enlarges the narrative and pulls us into the drama of Dinah's life as neither the original nor the classical midrashic interpretations do. The centuries of seeing women blamed for their sexual violations is still with us, not only in fundamentalist cultures, but in modern, progressive ones as well. This imaginative extrapolation on the text speaks truth about women that we still need to hear.

As this example illustrates, both the original writers of midrashim and the contemporary writers of the genre consider the scriptures as alive and inviting to their imaginations. Latter-day Saint women could create their own Mormon midrash, a collection of poems, dramas, stories, and other imaginative elaborations; retellings and transformations of scriptural narratives from the New Testament, the Book of Mormon, the Pearl of Great Price, and the Doctrine and Covenants; and Restoration history. Consider for example the story of "a woman" (she is identified only as such in Mark's gospel but as "Mary" in John's) anointing Jesus's feet with a precious ointment of spikenard. The disciples and others are critical of her for what they see as "waste," murmuring, "It might have been sold for more than three hundred pence, and have been given to the poor" (Mark 14:3–5). Jesus famously rebukes her critics: "She hath done what she could: she is come aforehand to anoint my body to the burying." And then he makes this amazing prophesy: "Verily I say unto you, wheresoever this gospel shall be preached throughout the whole world, this also that she hath done shall be spoken of for a memorial of her" (Mark 14:8–9).

---

17. Hyman, *Biblical Women*, 68–71.

Can anyone imagine this story told from her point of view? Can anyone tell us how her life might have unfolded with Jesus's promise held close in her heart? What kinds of memorials might she have experienced in her lifetime? How was she regarded and treated afterwards by Jesus's male disciples, by her family, by other women? This is a tale worth imagining, worth telling.

Let me cite some other examples of women who need to be clothed, not just in flesh and blood but in silks and linen, adorned with pearls and rubies, and given songs to sing, prophesies to speak, and wisdom to share. Consider:

- I've often wondered how Martha felt when she is rebuked by the Lord for her concern over her sister Mary not helping with domestic duties. What did she experience doing the dishes and mopping the floor while Mary was locked in intimate conversation with Jesus? What happened after she was reprimanded? Did she, like her sister, choose "that good part" and leave the household duties to others? As someone who often got stuck with the dishes, I have always had a tender spot for Martha!

- What did Mary experience when "the Holy Ghost came upon her"? What did she mean by "He that is Mighty hath done unto me great things"? In "Leda and the Swan," Yeats imagines what Leda experienced when she was ravaged by a divine being and asks, "Did she / put on his knowledge with his power?" Could one imagine this young Jewish girl, recalling this powerful, mystical experience, revisiting it in hours of grief and visiting it in her dreams? Did she recall it at the foot of the cross when doubts were crowding her mind and her heart was breaking?

- How would the story of the prodigal son be different if it were the story of the prodigal daughter, with a mother and two daughters as the main characters? Would a wastrel and destitute daughter behave differently from the prodigal son? And how would the mother and older sister behave different from the way the father and older son behave in the biblical story?[18]

- What if the story of the Good Samaritan were reconstructed with the characters as women? In this story (as I imagine it), a Jewish woman

---

18. For an example of a midrash on his parable, see "The Prodigal Daughter" in Imaginative Interlude 4A that follows this chapter.

who has been physically and sexually assaulted is lying by the roadside. Priests and other men and women pass her by without coming to her aid. Then a good Samaritan woman comes by, binds up her wounds and takes her, not to an inn, but to her own home where she nurses her back to health, in spite of the criticism of neighbors and the disapproval of priests. The two women set aside their cultural differences, live together, and nurture one another—bearing living testimony to the fact that Samaritans and Jews, both descended from Abraham, could live peaceably together, not simply as neighbors, but as friends.

- In the Book of Mormon, women's voices are fewer and more muted than in the Bible. As Camille Williams states, "Latter-day scripture contains far fewer stories of individual women than those in either the Old or the New Testament."[19] In fact, we know the names of only three women from Nephite/Lamanite culture: Sariah, Nephi's mother; Abish, the Lamanite convert; and Isabel, the harlot who consorted with Alma's son Corianton. The other three named women in the Book of Mormon—Eve, Sarah, and Mary—are biblical figures. The rest of the women in the record are identified either by their association with men or by their societal roles. Thus, we have Morianton's Maid (Alma 50:30–31), Jared's Daughter (Ether 8:8–17), Lamoni's Wife (Alma 19:2–11), et al.[20] In *Charting the Book of Mormon*, anonymous women are referred to by their generic identities: wife/wives (80 times), daughter/daughters (76), woman/women (55), mother/mothers (17), concubine/harlot/harlots (15), widow/widows (7), female (5), and maidservant/maid/mistress (3).[21]

In another article, Williams cites Carol Lynn Pearson as concluding that this is evidence of a "'strong anti-female statement made by Nephite society,' in whose record we see a few 'spiritually dependent [women]'

---

19. Camille Williams, "Women in the Book of Mormon: Inclusion, Exclusion, and Interpretation."

20. "KC," "Ten Women in the Book of Mormon." In a blog response, "Juliette" comments, "I love Morianton's Maid, and I wish we knew her name. She illustrates strength and independence—she left an abusive relationship, did some good on her own, and was instrumental in averting the hostile occupation of the entire northern territory. An empowering story for women if there ever was one."

21. "Charting the Book of Mormon," BYU Studies; See also J. Gregory Welch and John W. Welch, *Charting the Book of Mormon*.

and a plethora of faceless, nameless women listed as part of their husband's possessions."[22]

Although Williams states, "All interpretations of scripture are, in some sense, a dialogue with the text, or, as Old Testament scholar Phyllis Bird notes, 'an exercise in cross-cultural understanding,'" she reveals a very different approach to scriptural interpretation by citing Bird's contention that readers should avoid "interpretations that 'distort the ancient writer's understanding or intention, whether to a "negative" or "positive" effect.'"[23] But such distortion is precisely the aim and the advantage of midrashic narratives. I contend that such intentional counter imaginative, even boldly inventive readings, could make the Book of Mormon, as well as other Restoration scriptures, richer and more relevant to modern readers.[24] Here are some possible examples for modern Mormons to consider:

- Not long after Nephi and his brothers return from Jerusalem, Laman and Lemuel seek to do violence to Nephi, but as Nephi reports, "One of the daughters of Ishmael, yea, and also her mother, and one of the sons of Ishmael did plead with my brethren, insomuch that they did soften their hearts" (1 Ne. 7:19). Who is this woman with such persuasive powers? Did she become Nephi's wife and play a role in the journey to the New World?[25]
- In 1 Nephi we learn of Lehi's and Nephi's dreams. Did any of the women in this culture have dreams? And if so, of what might they have dreamed? What were their lives like in bearing children in the

---

22. "Charting the Book of Mormon"; Williams's reference to Pearson can be found in Carol Lynn Pearson, "Could Feminism Have Saved the Nephites?" 35–36.

23. Williams, "Women in the Book of Mormon"; the reference is to Phyllis Bird's *Missing Persons and Mistaken Identities: Women and Gender in Ancient Israel*, 6–7.

24. See my "The Midrashic Imagination and the Book of Mormon," 44–66.

25. Orson Scott Card speculates that this woman became Laman's wife: "A lot of people leap to the conclusion that this must have been the woman who ended up marrying Nephi. My own feeling is that Laman would hardly have listened to the pleading of Nephi's wife-to-be. It seems far more likely to me that the woman who pleaded for him was Laman's intended. The very fact that Nephi didn't name her supports this, I think, because, while he had to include this woman in his story, he couldn't very well point out that it was the woman who ended up marrying Laman." Orson Scott Card, "The Book of Mormon - Artifact or Artifice?" Of course, Card's speculation is exactly the kind that the rabbis engaged in when considering elements that are not clear in the Torah.

wilderness, in helping to build the ship, and in trying to keep their children from being terrorized during the long ocean voyage to the Promised Land? What did they do while the male-dominated internecine conflicts raged on for generations?

- Abish, the Lamanite woman who converted through a vision of her father, kept her beliefs secret in the hostile Lamanite society. When the king and the queen fall into a trance, she runs "from house to house" explaining to her Lamanite neighbors what has transpired. When they refuse to believe her, she boldly takes the hand of the queen and raises her up (Alma 19:16–31). One of the few women given a name in the Book of Mormon, what can we imagine happens to her following this episode? Did she become celebrated among the Lamanites? Had she kept her secret even from her husband? What was the vision her father had that so transformed her life? What was her relationship like with the queen afterward?[26]

- And what of the queen herself who has faith in Alma's words, is overcome by the spirit, and praises Jesus when she revives (Alma 19:2–30)? This extraordinary woman loves her husband and knows his unique bodily odors so well that she can exclaim to those who are convinced he is dead, "To me he doth not stink." She then speaks in tongues and raises the king from his own spiritual trance. Who is willing to bring this royal personage to life, to give her a story both before and after these dramatic events? In spite of the fact that she is anonymous in the text, she must have been legendary among her own people, for, according to Ammon, her faith exceeded that of all the Nephites: "Blessed art thou because of thy exceeding faith; I say unto thee, woman, there has not been such great faith among all the people of the Nephites" (v. 10).

As far as women in Mormon history are concerned, here, too, is a need for contemporary Mormon women (and men) to use their imaginations to fill in some of the gaps, to enlarge our understanding of the role of women in our cultural history, and to balance our account of the past with feminine elaboration and invention. Let me cite just one example.

In her article, "Joseph Smith's Sisters: Shadowy Women of the Restoration," Lavina Fielding Anderson reminds us of how little we know of Sophronia, Katherine, and Lucy Smith:

---

26. See "Abish" in Imaginative Interlude 4B.

From adolescence on, Lucy's daughters faithfully followed their prophet-brother, supporting and sacrificing to advance the family mission of restoring the gospel, arguably subordinating even their own marriages and the needs of their children to advancing the cause of the Kingdom, and always remaining overshadowed by their dazzling brother. Once more they were faithfully present, their grief as great, their loss as rending, but their presence unremarked and apparently unvalued. Not one account in all that I have read of the martyrdom and funeral mentions them by name, nor were their husbands, Joseph's and Hyrum's brothers-in-law, given any responsibilities or roles in the services. Even at a time and in a place—not just in Mormondom—where women had virtually no public role, I still see Joseph's sisters as among the most obscure women in the Church.[27]

Could contemporary Latter-day Saint women speak for these sisters, give them voice, as if from the dust, to provide some insights that would help us better understand the Restoration? What, for example, was Sophronia's reaction to Joseph's account of his encounter with Moroni? Anderson states:

Sophronia was twenty-four when Joseph returned from his midnight excursion to the Hill Cumorah bringing the plates. What had Sophronia's participation been in the family circle as he had told them Nephite stories for the previous three years? Was she allowed to view the plates, bundled in their wrappings, as other family members were? Was she allowed to touch the Urim and Thummim, as Lucy was? The historical record is silent on the matter.[28]

Silent, yes, but the imaginative record by contemporary Latter-day Saint women, I contend, need not continue the silence. And if these sisters could be given voice, what about Emma (there are volumes to be written!) and other women who helped establish Joseph's New World religion? And what of the possible midrashim out of Mormonism's storied polygamous past?

Perhaps one of the most fertile areas for midrashic exploration is the enlightened Mormon teaching that we have a Mother as well as a Father in Heaven. A number of years ago in an article titled "Our Mother in Heaven," I asked,

Why do we not know [more of] this mother of all creation, this mistress of light and space? . . . I believe that hers is also a powerful voice, rolling at times like thunder and cutting through the darkness like lightning. What explains the fact that many Mormon women, and an increasing number of

---

27. Lavina Fielding Anderson, "Joseph Smith's Sisters: Shadowy Women of the Restoration," 230–31.
28. Anderson, 232.

Mormon men, are beginning to feel her presence in their lives, other than that our consciousness of her identity has been awakened? The freeing of the social and emotional bondage of women has also liberated our Heavenly Mother from the silence in which men have held her. An increasing number of Mormon women testify to hearing her voice and are finding lyric modes in which to tell us about her. Like Procne in Greek Mythology, her liberation from the bondage of silence has been a transformation into song."[29]

In the fifteen years since this paper was presented at the Sunstone Symposium, those songs and the singing of them by Latter-day Saint/Mormon women and men constitute a rich flowering of revelation, of restoration in such works as *Dove Song: Heavenly Mother in Mormon Poetry*[30] and *The Mother Tree: Discovering the Love and Wisdom of Our Divine*.[31]

I believe singing that song of Heavenly Mother, placing her in the middle of the divine drama that constitutes the Latter-day Saint understanding of the Plan of Salvation, would inspire Mormon women to explore deeper dimensions of their own mothering, to open scriptural narratives about mothers and mothering that would bless Mormon culture. One might even consider what Jesus learned from his Heavenly Mother as well as his Heavenly Father. Perhaps it is also true that Jesus did nothing that he had not seen his Heavenly Mother do! The fact that he identifies so closely at times with the feminine (consider his metaphor of himself as a mother hen), suggests this possibility.

Eliza R. Snow, our pioneer poetess, pointed the way to such midrashic invention with her great hymn, "Oh My Father." If we are indeed eventually to greet them, "Mother, Father" in their "royal courts on high," perhaps Mormon women could help us all begin preparing for that grand reunion by bringing her and the other scriptural mothers—Eve, Sarah, Rebecca, Hannah, Mary, and Sariah—into our twenty-first-century imaginations.

Like all good writing, scripture is a mirror in which we see reflections of ourselves. When I was traveling in China with a group of American writers, one of our Chinese hosts asked Toni Morrison how she became a novelist. Her reply was that she couldn't find herself in any of the books written by white people or Black men, and so she started writing fiction

---

29. Robert A. Rees, "Monologues and Dialogues: Our Mother In Heaven," 49–50.

30. Tyler Chadwick, Dayna Patterson, Martin Pulido, ed., *Dove Song: Heavenly Mother in Mormon Poetry*.

31. Kathryn Knight Sonntag, *The Mother Tree: Discovering the Love and Wisdom of Our Divine*.

that included her experience. I think that is a good justification for Mormon women to begin writing their own midrashic literature.

Just as "every word [of the Torah has been] mediated through rabbinic sources," so could every word of the Book of Mormon, Pearl of Great Price, and Doctrine and Covenants be mediated through the minds and imaginations of contemporary Mormon women. As Bronner argues, "If in the mundane role women appear inferior to men, in the realm of the spirit they are on a level equal to, if not higher than, that of men." As such "through the hermeneutic process of feminist reinterpretation [they can] breathe an air of both authenticity and fairness" into scriptural narratives.[32]

Jane Sprague Zones summarizes the importance of such work:

> One way for women to relieve the tension created in a relationship between the static written Torah and the modern changing world is for each generation to read the text with fresh and open eyes. Women's roles in the Torah were circumscribed and limited while women's roles in the modern world are expanding. Therefore, it is incumbent upon contemporary women to study the text and to write modern stories that maintain a relationship with the text, incorporating their own experiences and consciousness into Judaism. This midrashic process allows Judaism to grow and develop a healthy relationship with all of its people.[33]

Consider how different this is from most traditional Christian and Mormon attitudes toward scriptural texts. Most Catholic, Protestant, and Mormon readers see the text as fixed, its meaning clear and certain. God and the prophets have spoken and we are to listen and act. Biblical literalists are uncomfortable with any openness, ambiguity, or uncertainty in the Bible. Consider how most gospel doctrine classes approach scripture: the lesson materials are delivered as if from Sinai (or certainly Salt Lake City), and the teacher and most of the students start to squirm with any unorthodox, speculative, or imaginative discourse about meaning. For this reason, our lessons tend to be mechanical and confirming. As soon as a scripture is read, class members know the interpretation by heart—but, I would argue, not always *in* their hearts.

Rabbinic reading is dramatically different. As Judith Kunst observes,

> Midrash reads the Hebrew Bible not for what is familiar but for what is unfamiliar, not for what's clear but for what's unclear, and then wrestles with the text, passionately, playfully, reverently. Midrash views the Bible as one side of

---

32. Bronner, *From Eve to Esther*, x–xi.
33. "Introduction: Begetting a Midrash," in *Taking Fruit: Modern Women's Tales and the Bible*, 6, as cited in Hyman, *Biblical Women*, xxxii.

a conversation, started by God containing an explicit invitation, even command, to keep the conversation—argument, story, poem, prayer—going.[34]

According to Naomi Hyman, Jewish tradition contends that the Torah was written in black fire on white fire "and that the white spaces around the black letters hold meanings that we have yet to uncover." Further, as Hyman states,

> It has also been said, more recently, that we have received only half of the Torah, because the Torah as we know it was written by men and the women's Torah has yet to be revealed. I like to think that the women's Torah can be found in the white fire, in the white spaces whose meanings we have yet to uncover, and that a part of each of our souls is still standing at Sinai, ready to receive it.[35]

It may also be that the white fire of the Book of Mormon and other Restoration scriptures is yet to be discovered and that part of our souls is still waiting to receive it—from Zarahemla and Bountiful, from Cumorah and Far West, from Nauvoo and beyond. It is delightful to imagine that future inspired and imaginative expansions and explorations of Latter-day scripture will come from Latter-day Saint women living in Mongolia, Indonesia, Uganda, Guatemala, Ghana, the islands of the Pacific, and elsewhere who employ both their feminine sensibilities as well as their unique cultural perspectives in creating imaginative readings.

B. H. Roberts argued that "not half—not one-hundredth part—not a thousandth part of that which Joseph Smith revealed to the Church has yet been unfolded, either to the Church or to the world." He adds, "The work of the expounder has scarcely begun."[36] Perhaps part of that unfolding lies in opening ourselves to the imaginative possibilities in our scriptures. Judith Kunst argues that God's invitation for us to bring our imaginations as well as our minds into dialogue with him may be seen as an invitation to greater intimacy with him: "Another lesson [from the Midrash] is that God is not so much hiding *from* us as he is hiding *for* us. He is purposefully creating the places where, with curiosity and perseverance, we can find him"[37]—in the burning bush, in the black and white fires of the Torah, in the fire he has placed in our own hearts and minds.

---

34. Kunst, *The Burning Word*, 4.
35. Hyman, *Biblical Women*, xvii.
36. B. H. Roberts, *The Seventy's Course in Theology*, iv–ix.
37. Kunst, *The Burning Word*, 37.

INTERLUDE 4A

The Prodigal Daughter

Once there lived in a far country a woman who had two daughters. In her youth she had married a young nobleman, but he was often gone to war in the king's service. Each time he sallied forth to battle, she waited patiently but nevertheless made good use of her time. From her mother and grandmothers she had learned the ancient arts of weaving, of making beautiful yet useful pottery, of singing and telling stories, and of dancing the dances that only women did in that country. She also learned the names of all the herbs and spices and how to cook with them so that both taste and aroma delighted all who sat at her table. She was devout without being pious and graceful without being obvious. She made daily devotions to God and gave generously to the poor.

Not content to learn only womanly skills and crafts while her husband was at war, she learned how to bargain in the marketplace, how to manage those who tended the flocks and harvested the crops on their estate, how to negotiate with the men who came to take advantage of what they perceived as her inexperience. And she in turn taught these skills to her daughters.

One morning after prayers while waiting for the sun to rise on her fields and orchards, she saw a lone horseman riding out of the forest beyond her home. She knew what news the messenger carried, but nevertheless allowed him to sorrowfully tell her of the death of her husband. She had known it in her bones from the moment he had fallen on the battlefield. She immediately went to her daughters and told them the news, comforting and weeping with them all through that long day and into a longer night. The next morning, they all put on blackness and waited for ten days until the body was brought for burial.

After a year of mourning, the mother and the younger daughter resumed their lives of learning the arts, of supervising workers and entertaining guests, of worshiping God and serving others. But the elder daughter, who had been her father's favorite and had something of his temperament, continued to mourn and cast angry words at her mother and sister for taking off their black garments. She went for long walks in the woods and often returned home late at night. They tried to understand, but, as they knew, the world continues spinning and affairs need tending to. Without her elder daughter's help, the mother relied more heavily on her younger daughter, assigning her duties that once belonged to her older sister—going to market and bargaining with the men who sold sheep and goats and fruits and vegetables and managing some of the household duties.

In time, seeing her sister taking over her duties, going to market in her stead and counseling with her mother, the elder sister became resentful. Jealousy and pride cankered her so that she spoke indifferently to her mother, was silent to her sister, and was rude to servants and workers. Her mother, who understood how grief had darkened her daughter's soul, tried to console and comfort her, but such tenderness only crowded the daughter's heart the more.

One morning when the mother awoke to begin her day, she felt a giant absence in the house. Going immediately to her elder daughter's room, she found a note saying that the daughter had gone away. The mother immediately called her chief servant and commanded him to ride after the girl and bring her back, no matter how long it took. Every day the mother and the younger daughter looked to the distance, hoping to see the servant returning with their daughter and sister, and every night the sun went down on their disappointment.

After a week, the rider returned alone, reporting that he had been to every hamlet and village within a hundred miles. In some he had heard that the young woman had been there a day or two before, but though he rode after her, he could never find her. The mother and younger daughter embraced and wept. They fasted and prayed many days for the return of their daughter and sister. After a year, with her mother's permission, the younger daughter also went to look for her sister but returned after many days without success. Once again, the mother and younger daughter put on black clothing and the blackness seeped into every corner of their lives.

The elder daughter had taken the fastest horse she could find and ridden into the night. Within days, she was at the seashore and took passage on a ship bound for the country where her father had fallen. When she arrived, all she could find were dead animals, broken swords, and fresh mounds of earth. She went to the nearest village and after a few days caught a ship to a faraway port. In time, her money ran out and she had to sell her jewelry and her fine silk clothing for food. She took jobs much beneath her status, working first at an inn and then in a place where she milked goats and made cheese.

Inexperienced in the ways of the world, she sought the help of strangers, only to be taken advantage of. Captivated by her beauty, men sought her company and promised her many things. At first, she resisted their entreaties, but one night, hungry, cold, and desperate, she allowed a friendly stranger to take her to his home. In the middle of the night, he forced himself upon her and she fled in shame. Not many days following, she knew that something inside her had changed, knew even before the first swelling of her belly that the long road home had become even longer and overgrown with brambles. That shame led to further shame and a descent into a world she had never imagined existed. Thereafter, she avoided men all together and her life grew more lonely and more desperate. Wandering from village to village, from port to port, begging for morsels of food, she lost track of days and weeks and months. At times she thought of her mother and her home, but she felt too ashamed to return to them. At last, she felt she could live no longer and sought out an old woman who dealt in special potions. She told the woman of her long descent into darkness and surrendered her last coins for a small vial that would allow her to forget all she had done. She took the vial to an old manger where swine slept and, crawling to a corner, drank it fully and lay down.

The potion did not kill her but instead put her in a deep sleep. She dreamed of her home and saw her mother yearning toward her with outstretched arms. Through a dark forest of troubled dreams, she saw a light shining through the trees. As she reached out to take the light, monstrous beasts began devouring it and an army of men with red eyes came toward her. Struggling to run, her mind racing but her muscles frozen, she awoke with a scream. She heard a grunting sound and, looking around, saw a giant sow suckling its piglets.

She arose and, dusting straw and dirt from her tattered dress, said, "I will go to my mother and beg her to let me be a serving woman at her table." She walked many days and then caught a boat to the land where she was born, arriving late at night. Seeing there was a full moon, she determined to go at once to her mother's home, even though it would take her the entire night. Walking laboriously with the extra weight upon her, she went with anxious heart. As dawn approached, she was still a long way off, but she could see the sun beginning to shine in the windows of her mother's home, which sat high on a hill. Seeing the house in which she was born and from which months before she had left in anger, she slowed her pace, suddenly doubtful of her journey and fearful of its end. As she was about to turn back, she saw a figure walk out onto the porch of her home.

The mother, as was her morning and evening custom as well as intermittently throughout the day, looked toward the path that disappeared into the forest at the end of her fields. Since the sun had not yet cast its light on the place where the path wove out of the forest, she simply looked, as she had for endless days, although she had long given up looking with hopeful eyes. As she was about to turn back into the house to begin her daily duties, she saw a figure moving slowly along the path. She squinted and then her heart leapt within her.

She ran forward a few steps and then shouted back toward the house, calling for her younger daughter. The daughter, sensing alarm in her mother's voice, came running, still in her sleeping gown. The mother pointed to the small figure wending its way upward through the fields of ripe wheat and mother and daughter ran with all haste, forgetful of their garments and their uncombed hair.

And the daughter, returning from her long self-imposed exile, saw the two figures running toward her and ran as fast as her feet could carry her, cutting through the tall wheat to shorten the distance. And the mother and younger daughter turned through the wheat as well, the daughter outrunning the mother the last furlong. The younger daughter fell upon her sister and embraced her so fully that for a moment they seemed as sisters bound together from their mother's womb. A few long moments later the mother, breathless and staggering with the years upon her body, opened her arms wide and took them both in, embracing them with such fullness, such intensity that they seemed lost in one another. They wept. They laughed. They danced. And they sang as if their whole lives were compressed into this very moment.

Exhausted at last, they walked slowly up the hill to the house where they had last been together, the mother in the middle with a daughter on each side. The servants and the hired men, hearing the tumult, the shouting, the joyous laughter, stood looking in amazement at the three women coming toward them. As they began ascending the hill to their home, a warm, gentle rain began to fall so that by the time they arrived, their garments were soaked through and their hair was as wet as if they had just stepped from the sea. Still, they continued laughing and weeping and embracing one another.

When they arrived at the house, the elder daughter turned toward her mother and said, "Mother. I have lived a dissolute life. I have sinned against heaven, and I have sinned against you and against the memory of my father. I felt so unworthy that I tried to take my life so you would never have to see me as I now am. But God is merciful and showed me his light in a dream, and so even though I was dead, now I am alive, and all I ask is to be a servant in your house for the remainder of my days." She turned to walk to where the servants were standing as if to take her place among them, but her mother grabbed her by her ragged sleeve and pulled her into a hug, and her sister embraced her as well. Her mother had no words to speak and so placed her hand on her lost daughter's heart and held it there for a long moment.

That night as the younger daughter lovingly washed her sister's weary feet, their mother bathed her prodigal daughter's bruised body with warm water, anointed her head with aromatic oil, and embraced her swollen belly with tenderness. And when they had clothed her in new garments, her mother took both daughters into her bed, and they slept in one another's arms through the night.

In the morning, the mother told the servants to begin preparations for a feast to honor her daughter. She sent servants into the fields to gather fruits and grains and flowers. She instructed the workmen to build a long table and benches out of newly cut cedarwood. She called the kitchen maids to bring fresh yogurt and aged cheeses from the cellar and raisins, dates, olives, and pomegranates from the pantry. The cooks baked dozens of fresh loaves. When her groom said he had selected the fattest calf for the feast, she said, "No. We will not have meat. I don't want any living creature to die on a day we celebrate my daughter's new birth."

When the preparations had all been completed, the mother called all the neighbors and all the servants and gave them a place at the table. She dressed her daughters in new robes. Then she and her daughters poured the wine she had saved from the day her daughter had left. Next, they brought in all the specially prepared dishes and served all who were seated at the table. Then the mother invited her younger daughter to sit at her side and, before sitting herself, seated her elder daughter at the far end of the table where she herself had sat when her husband was alive. When all were seated, the mother bowed her head and thanked God for their bounty and blessings. Then she raised her wineglass and, looking toward her elder daughter, said simply, "Welcome home my dear, dear daughter." Her daughter bowed her head and wept.

Not many months following the feast, the daughter who had been prodigal but now was restored, gave birth to a son who bore the image of his grandfather. In time, the daughters married, and in time, there were more children and then many grandchildren, and every year on the anniversary of her daughter's return, the mother invited everyone for a great feast to honor the day they all began to live again.

INTERLUDE 4B

Abish

Abish had held a secret in her heart since she was a young girl. Helping her father tend his flock one day, she noticed that her favorite lamb was gone, a black orphan whose mother had died giving birth and which Abish had nurtured to life. As she wept, her father told her to tend the other sheep while he went to look for the stray. After hours of anxious waiting and watching, Abish finally saw her father returning with the lamb in his arms.

Quickly she ran to where they came over the hill and then stopped. There was something in her father's face she had never seen before, something that made her eyes open wide and the hair on her arms and neck rise and coldness wash all over her. She stopped, looked again, and stepped back. Something had changed him. There was so much light in his face, it was as if he was walking in the sun. At first, she was frightened, but when he set the lamb down and reached toward her, she ran to him.

The story was hard to hear and harder to believe, and yet she did believe. He told her of finding the lamb caught in briars and seeing wild animals moving toward it. He heard the lamb cry out. Frightened, not knowing what to do, he remembered the story of David and the bear and lion and ran to save her lamb. After he had done so, an angel appeared to him and said, "As in faith and courage you have saved this lost lamb, so shall your lamb, your daughter, save your people. Following the traditions of your fathers, you have lost knowledge of the Holy One, but you and your people have been in his heart from the days they left Jerusalem and crossed the great waters to this Promised Land. One day, he will send the son of a Nephite king to rescue your people from darkness. As you sought and saved this lamb, so has the God of your fathers sought you and blessed you with such a daughter as Abish. Teach her to hold this promise in her heart and to await the day when she will be guided to bring great light to your people." So, from that day forward, Abish watched and waited, wondering when and where the light in her father's face would light her way. Even after he passed, she looked for that light.

For years Abish had been a servant of the queen, attending to her every wish throughout the day and bathing her at night, always with kindness, and always waiting.

One day, her heart leaped within her when she heard rumors of a Nephite named Ammon who had come among them. There was much talk in the palace as other servants told stories about this stranger who had been bound and brought before the king. Some believed the king might slay him or put him in prison. Others said that, like his fathers, Ammon had come among them to steal their gold and silver and precious things and to make them servants of the Nephites. Still others said that he was powerful with the sword and could not be slain. Still others were greatly disturbed when one of the king's chief retainers reported that King Lamoni had invited this son of their enemies to dwell in their land and even offered one of his daughters to be his wife. Imagine! And Abish did imagine.

The next day, a servant ran into the room saying that the king had just called this Nephite "the Great Spirit of whom our fathers have spoken." Some of the men immediately withdrew their swords, saying the king was surely deceived and that Ammon was the son of the Devil.

Wanting to see and hear for herself, Abish went to the royal chambers of the king and queen and quietly crept in as Ammon was answering the king's questions. Her heart rejoiced to hear words like those she had heard from her father so many years before. She was astonished when she heard her king say, "Oh Lord, have mercy, according to your abundant mercy, which you have had upon the people of Nephi, have upon me and my people." Immediately, the king fell to the earth as if he were dead. Confused, Abish and other servants carried him to the queen's chambers. For two days and nights, Abish, still waiting for direction as to what she should do, heard the loud lamentations of the king's family, believing him dead.

But the queen, who loved the king, saw light in her husband's face and did not believe he was dead, and having heard that Ammon was a prophet sent from God, she sent Abish to bring him to her. Seeing Abish and immediately recognizing her as a daughter of God, Ammon told her that the light she had seen so many years before in her father's face was the same light which lighted Lamoni's face, even though he appeared to some as if he were dead. He said, "My dear sister, this light I see in you and which you saw in your father is the light of the glory of God, which is a marvelous light of goodness. It is the light that has filled your king's heart with great joy and will bless your people as they embrace it."

When Abish brought Ammon before the queen, knowing the queen's wish, he said, "Your husband, O Queen, is not dead but is asleep in God and tomorrow he shall rise. Do you believe this?" The queen replied, "I believe it shall be according to what you have said." And Ammon said, "You are blessed with great faith, O Queen, even greater than I have seen among my own people."

The next day as the king's family and servants stood over his body, he arose, filling the room with light and exclaiming, "I have seen my Redeemer; and he shall come forth, and be born of a woman, and he shall redeem all his children who believe in his name." Having said these words, the king, overcome with joy, collapsed once more. And the queen, also overcome with joy, fell to the ground, as did Ammon. And then the servants, calling on God with all the energy of their souls, also fell to the earth. Seeing all this, Abish, remembering the vision of her father, stood alone among the company, her heart and mind on fire.

And that fire, shut up in her heart and bones for so many years, burst forth as she ran from house to house telling everyone to come and see what had happened. But when they came, running breathlessly into the palace and seeing the king and queen and Ammon and all the servants lying prone and still, they were frightened and confused and began to murmur among themselves. Some said Ammon was the Great Spirit; others said he was a monster who had been sent by the Nephites to torment and enslave them. Still others said he was sent to afflict them because of their wickedness.

Abish, observing the contention among the people growing and becoming more intense, began to weep. This was not how she imagined it unfolding. In the midst of the tumult, she quietly went over and, taking the queen's hand, tried to raise her from the ground. As soon as she touched the queen's hand, the queen stood and exclaimed, "O blessed Jesus, who has saved me from an awful hell! O blessed God, have mercy on this people!" Filled with boundless joy, she spoke many words which could not be interpreted.

And then the queen took the king's hand, and he, too, arose and began to teach his people what he had leaned about the love and joy of God. Together they bore witness that their hearts had been changed and that they no longer had a desire to sin and do evil things. As they spoke, angels came and ministered unto them, filling the palace with joyful singing.

A few days passed as they rejoiced together in the outpouring of light and joy that now filled their hearts. One evening as Abish came to bathe the queen, the queen reached out and took her hand, the hand that had raised her up. She kissed Abish's hand and, embracing her, said, "My dear sister. You have brought so much love and light to our royal house that you will no longer be my servant but my princess. Come, let us rejoice in our Redeemer."

For all the years after, when people spoke of the great turning of Lamanite history, Abish's name was spoken with reverence and thanksgiving.

CHAPTER EIGHT

All In the Family: Opening Our Hearts, Homes, and Chapels to Our LGBTQ Members

For reasons I can't explain, over the past nearly fifty years I have felt called to minister to gay, lesbian, bisexual, and transgender Latter-day Saints. Doing so has brought me both great joy as I have walked with them but also great sadness and sorrow as I have seen them treated as pariahs, as outcasts, as foreigners, and as strangers in their own homes and congregations. In championing their cause, I have risked and have experienced the opprobrium of some leaders and fellow members. In looking for a solution to what I consider one of the great failings of the modern and contemporary Church, the following words of the old Shaker hymn "More Love, More Love" keep coming to me:

> If ye love not each other
> in daily communion,
> How can ye love God
> whom ye have not seen?
> More love, more love;
> The heavens are blessing,
> The angels are calling,
> O Zion! More love.

Families

"Call it a clan, call it a network, call it a tribe, call it a family: Whatever you call it, whoever you are, you need one. You need one because you are human."
—Jane Howard[1]

What is a family? The word "family" comes from the Latin *familia*, which means "household" or, more broadly and generously (from 1620), "any group of things classed as kindred based on common distinguishing characteristics." In its broadest sense, we all belong to groups that might be considered families (clubs, classes, neighborhoods, parties, etc.). Latter-day Saints speak of their "ward family," see themselves as belonging to the broader family of Latter-day Saints or their Church family, and, with

---

1. Jane Howard, "All Happy Clans Are Alike: In Search of the Good Family," 37.

everyone else in the world, consider themselves part of the universal human family. In addition, Latter-day Saints identify themselves as part of an eternal family, including generations of those to whom they are related who have passed onto the next world or are yet to be born.

There is some question in Latter-day Saint theology as to whether we choose our families, as some believe; have them chosen by our heavenly parents before we are born into them, as others believe; or simply don't know the process by which we have the families we do. But once we are born into a family biologically or become part of one through marriage, adoption, or simply acceptance, it is the family with which we identify most personally and intimately—the setting where we have the opportunity to learn some of life's most fundamental lessons and, at times and in most families, experience some of life's most fundamental challenges. If we are fortunate enough to be born into a stable, loving family, it is where we learn about ourselves, cultivate relationships with those closest to us, prepare to go out into the world, and, hopefully, discover our divine destiny as spirit children of loving heavenly parents. As President Russell M. Nelson has observed, "Our family is the focus of our greatest work and joy in this life; so will it be throughout all eternity."[2] These sentiments are expressed in the following Latter-day Saint children's song:

> I have a fam'ly here on earth
> They are so good to me.
> I want to share my life with them through all eternity.
> Fam'lies can be together forever
> Through Heav'nly Father's plan.
> I always want to be with my own family,
> And the Lord has shown me how I can.
> The Lord has shown me how I can.[3]

Sometimes, however, contrary to expectations and gospel principles, our families are not good to us—or good for us—as when they are unloving, abusive, hurtful, and rejecting. This unfortunately often happens in families with LGBTQ members. As one lesbian said, "But what do you do when you have made all the 'right' choices and that sadness, that yearning, that soul-deep aching never lets up? What do you do when all the efforts to keep you from knowing about queerness succeed and all you're left with is the inexplicable sorrow? The sense that the very divinity inside you is a sin?"[4]

---

2. Russell M. Nelson, "Set In Order Thy House."
3. *Children's Songbook*, The Church of Jesus Christ of Latter-day Saints, 188.
4. Kerry Pray, "To Dance in the Dim Light: Meditation on Joy pt. 1."

In such families, the idea of being "together forever" may not be inviting or reassuring. When parents of LGBTQ children lament that their children will not be part of their eternal family, these children often feel lost to both their earthly and heavenly families and may in fact feel homeless in both spheres.

Ward leaders and ward families also often judge, reject, cast out, and exclude from fellowship LGBTQ congregants. In the last century especially, LGBTQ members were often spoken about and spoken to in extremely condemning language and rhetoric. Sometimes such language came from top leaders, which made it even more difficult to hear. As one gay man reported, "One Sunday I heard Elder Joseph Fielding Smith say that homosexuality was so filthy and abhorrent that he would rather see his sons dead than unchaste or homosexual."[5]

Rather than endure such rhetoric and rejection, some gay and lesbian Saints sought refuge in other churches, although for some their indelible ties to the restored gospel caused them to long for (and continue to seek) fellowship within their own faith community. This was brought home to me dramatically a number of years ago when I was invited by a gay Latter-day Saint friend to attend services at a church where he and other gay Latter-day Saints had found a welcoming home—St. Thomas the Apostle Episcopal Church in West Hollywood. The church's motto read, "Called by God to be in a holy place where love is found, where all are named and where hearts are freed to change the world." When we went to lunch after the service, these Latter-day Saints, all of whom had served LDS missions, spoke with sadness that they did not feel welcome to worship in a Latter-day Saint congregation. As I wrote in an article about my visit that Sunday:

> I believe many homosexuals feel not only like motherless but also like churchless children, and many hope for both earthly and heavenly homes where they will be welcomed with unconditional love. It is reassuring that the keeper of the gate for the final home we all will enter is the Savior of the world himself. In the meantime, we are all keepers of our own hearts and homes (and churches), and we are responsible for nurturing all who seek fellowship and refuge there.[6]

I was grateful to the clergy and parishioners of St. Thomas for opening their church and hearts to my gay brothers and for giving them opportunities to serve, as many of them had learned to do so faithfully as missionaries in Germany, Japan, Mexico, and elsewhere.

---

5. "Anonymous," "Solus," 94–99.
6. Robert A. Rees, "Finding Christ at St. Paul the Apostle Church." (The name of the church is actually St. Thomas the Apostle Church.)

As far as I know, there are no empirical studies showing the percentage of LGBTQ Latter-day Saint individuals and families with LGBTQ members who have, either formally or informally, separated from the Church, but those of us working with this demographic over the past decades would likely estimate it as at least a majority and likely a high percentage. This is bolstered by a recent study reported by Jana Riess in the *Salt Lake Tribune*: "Who is leaving the LDS Church? Eight key survey findings." One such finding is that "in the survey, only 4% of current members identified as LGBTQ, compared with 18% of former members."[7] That significant difference is likely attributable to various factors, including the number of LGBTQ people who have left the Church, the reluctance of attending LGBTQ members to identify as such due to a culture generally inhospitable to non-heterosexual and non-binary members, and the fact that certain characteristics of those who have left and don't intend on returning (higher divorce rate and smaller family size) fit the profile of LGBTQ members who attempted to adapt to the Church's requirements (marrying heterosexually and beginning families) but ultimately were unable to do so.

Mythologies of Sexual Orientation and Gender Identity

Until recently, in regard to sexual orientation and gender identity, Latter-day Saint parents and leaders, as with nearly all societies and faith communities, have labored within what might be termed the shadow world of misinformation and mythology. That is, LDS doctrine, policy, and practice have been heavily influenced by traditional social and cultural beliefs that have little grounding in sound science or true religion.

In the twentieth century, this led to beliefs that homosexuality and other non-heterosexual diversities are chosen and therefore changeable, that homosexuality is a curable disease that can be infectious to others, that non-heterosexual desires are temporary and will disappear once people marry heterosexually, and that even having non-heterosexual, non-binary romantic and erotic desires constitutes a grievous sin.

One of the most damaging of these myths, and one that dominated Mormon culture at least until the twenty-first century, was that any deviation or variation from the heterosexual and cisgender norm was a disorder stemming from family or early childhood pathologies. Since the "disorder" was thought to be learned or chosen, it was believed that it could be

---

7. Jana Riess, "Jana Riess: Who is leaving the LDS Church? Eight key survey findings."

unlearned or unchosen. It was thought curable through various folk and psychological therapies or through heterosexual marriage. Those identified as having such "attractions," "inclinations," and "desires" were told to just stop them and honor their natural, God-given heterosexual orientations and gender identities (male and female as assigned at birth).

In a statement shared with me, Jim Carlston, a contributing author in Kerry Pray's anthology, *The Book of Queer Mormon Joy*, speaks about his eight years of experience with reparative therapy:

> I started therapy for my same-sex attraction during my sophomore year at BYU, both because I wanted to be "healed" and because my mother, who had a doctorate in Child Psychology, assured me I would be happier. It wasn't until nearly a decade later that I met Carol Lynn Pearson. She was the very first person, including half a dozen BYU and LDS Social Services therapists and multiple bishops, to inform me of the extensive research confirming that sexual orientation is neither chosen nor changeable. In reading such research I saw how pained and tortured those trying to change had been. Becoming more comfortable with being myself is the crowning achievement in my life, and it has brought years of happiness despite life's pains.

Readers wishing to read courageous, touching, and at times heart breaking personal voices are directed to two collections of personal essays by present or former LGBTQ Latter-day Saints: *The Book of Queer Mormon Joy* and *I Spoke to You In Silence*.[8]

When I served as bishop of a Latter-day Saint singles' congregation in Los Angeles during the 1980s, I came to see that such mythologies were ungrounded and harmful. I wondered why anyone would deliberately choose a "lifestyle" within a community so hostile, rejecting, and punitive toward it. I also concluded that if sexual orientation and gender identity were so amenable to change, as many asserted, why did change not happen for those Latter-day Saints who faithfully worked, prayed, and sacrificed, sometimes for years, in a desperate attempt to rid themselves of something so abhorrent to their ecclesiastical leaders, fellow members, friends, family, and apparently to God Himself?

I think of those with whom I counseled as a bishop who had fasted and prayed, served missions, paid extra tithing, gone to the temple often, and been furiously active, hoping God would change them. When change didn't come, some separated from the Church. Others blamed themselves,

---

8. Kerry Spencer Pray, ed., *The Book of Queer Mormon Joy* (Signature, 2024); Kerry Spencer Pray and Jenn Lee Smith, ed., *I Spoke to You in Silence: Essays from Queer Mormons of Marginalized Genders* (University of Utah, 2022).

feeling they were unworthy of such a blessing. Still others, discouraged and depressed that no change resulted from their extraordinary devotion and sacrifice, sought to escape their pain through drugs and alcohol. Far too many took or attempted to take their own lives. Many no longer sit in our pews, and few, in my experience, have sought fellowship in other churches.

About myths, Latter-day Saint author Irene Bates observes, "Myths may have a purpose. They can be comforting, familiar frameworks for our faith, but that is all they can be—they can never serve as pillars of our faith. They are too vulnerable . . . and they cannot be allowed to stand guard over truth itself."[9]

The Science of Sexuality and Its Implication for Families

For millennia, science was not advanced enough to offer any empirical understanding of sex, sexual orientation, or gender identity. More recently, as individuals have felt freer and safer to identify as LGBTQ, science has responded with evidence about the origin and nature of these identities. The evidence counters and contradicts traditional mythologies and some deeply established societal norms that have influenced Latter-day Saint theology and cultural beliefs.

An emerging body of research has led scientists to a broad consensus that sexual orientation and identity are neither chosen nor changeable, but rather are explained by biology. In his "The Biological Origin of Sexual Orientation," Latter-day Saint scientist William S. Bradshaw cites a large body of evidence showing that steroid hormones acting on the brain during embryonic development program sexual orientation after birth. In his words: "Non-heterosexuality is an inborn, inherent state for a minority segment of the human race. It is very important to emphasize that this is a *normal* variant." He adds, "There is considerable evidence that sexual orientation is an unchangeable feature of human personality, and not subject to reversal as might be predicted if social events were the responsible factors. No one chooses his or her sexual orientation."[10]

Also relevant are Bradshaw's observations about gender dysphoria: "Gender identity also has a biological basis. For example, transgender people differ from cisgender individuals in a number of physical traits (neuroanatomy of the brain, steroid hormone exposure, and genetics). The biological mechanisms responsible for gender identity, like those

---

9. Irene Bates, "Another Kind of Faith," 22.
10. William S. Bradshaw, "The Biological Origin of Sexual Orientation," 10, 28.

responsible for sexual orientation, can ultimately be traced to the function of genes."[11] In other words, contrary to what many have adamantly and dogmatically asserted, LGBTQ individuals are born that way. (Given the complexity and range of sexual orientations and gender identities and the evolving scientific research in these fields, this does not mean that some individuals may not be tentative, uncertain, or even confused about their own particular experience, but it does call for kindness, compassion, and patience—none of which has been in abundance, especially among religious communities.)

There also seems to be a possible genetic influence in relation to these sexual orientation and gender identity variations. In relation to same-sex orientation, rather than finding a "gay gene" as some have speculated, a recent (2019) genome-wide association study of twins and families titled "The Genetics of Sexual Orientation" reveals "insights into the genetic architecture of same-sex sexual behavior."[12] According to Jocelyn Kaiser, the study presents "the most solid evidence to date linking specific genetic markers to same-sex sexual behavior." Another study, "Genetic Link Between Gender Dysphoria and Sex Hormone Signaling," tentatively concludes, "Gender dysphoria may have an oligogenic [i.e., a trait that is influenced by a few genes] component, with several genes involved in sex hormone-signaling contributing."[13] While such studies may not be definitive, they at least suggest greater complexity regarding sexual orientation and gender identity than has heretofore been assumed.

Although there have been no such studies of strictly Latter-day Saint gay, queer, or transgender populations, anecdotal observation and reports seem to point to the same conclusion of these scientific studies. That is, it is not unusual to find multiple LGBTQ individuals in intergenerational Latter-day Saint families. I know of one family where two lesbian sisters each had several gay sons, and in another large Latter-day Saint family of seven children, their spouses and numerous grandchildren, a surprising number are gay, lesbian, bisexual, or transgender.

Given the prominence of genetics in sexual orientation and gender identity, and the evidence of genetically influenced diseases found in Latter-day Saint families (including cancer, cardiac arrhythmia, and a

---

11. Bradshaw, 26–27.
12. Jocelyn Kaiser, "Genetics May Explain Up to 25% of Same-sex Behavior, Giant Analysis Reveals."
13. Madeline Foreman et al., "Genetic Link Between Gender Dysphoria and Sex Hormone Signaling."

rare genetic disorder called fumarase deficiency), one could speculate that because of the practice of polygamy among Latter-day Saints in the nineteenth century—which led to a greater degree of intermarriage in the following generations—there may be a higher incidence of non-heterosexual and non-binary individuals in families descended from polygamous ancestors. The cooperative alliance between the Church and the University of Utah's Human Genetics program, which has led to the establishment of the Utah Population Database (UPDB), may open the way for further research on the genetic factors influencing sexual orientation and gender dysphoria. Such studies, coupled with basic gospel principles, should cause us to revisit our attitudes toward and treatment of our LGBTQ members.

"What's Love Got to Do with It?": Forming and Nurturing Families

As argued earlier, nearly all human beings, whatever their sexual orientation or gender identity, are born with a deep desire, even a primal need to emotionally, socially, and physically connect to and bond with others. In addition, beginning in puberty, we develop a powerful, intrinsic desire to bond romantically and intimately with a few individuals with whom we experience an extraordinary attraction that is a combination of what we call romantic love and sexual and erotic desire, which the restored gospel suggests is also fundamentally spiritual in nature.

Such connection is described by Lewis Thomas and his coauthors of *A General Theory of Love* as "a full-throated duet, a reciprocal interchange between two fluid, sensing, shifting brains . . . we call *limbic resonance*— a symphony of mutual exchange and internal adaptation whereby two [individuals] become attuned to each other's inner states." They explain:

> When we look into the ocular portals to a limbic brain our vision goes deep; the sensations multiply, just as two mirrors placed in opposition create a shimmering ricochet of reflections whose depths recede into infinity. Eye contact, although it occurs over a gap of yards, is not a metaphor. When we meet the gaze of another, two nervous systems achieve a palpable and intimate apposition [i.e. sameness].[14]

This is beautifully expressed in the last stanzas of Pablo Neruda's Sonnet XVII:

> I love you without knowing how, or when, or from where.
> I love you straightforwardly, without complexities or pride;
> so I love you because I know no other way than this:

---

14. Thomas Lewis et al., *A General Theory of Love*, 63.

where I does not exist, nor you,
so close that your hand on my chest is my hand,
so close that your eyes close as I fall asleep.[15]

Whether such intimate, electric connections happen between people of opposite or similar sexual orientations or gender identities, they are, as Bill Bradshaw argues, hardwired from birth. As the authors of *A General Theory of Love* assert, "The brain's Byzantine conformation determines everything about human nature, including the nature of love."[16] In other words, they argue that something deep and yet amazingly powerful leads nearly all of us to become attracted to, infatuated with, and "fall in love" with another person. They explain: "*In love* twists together three high-tensile strands: 1) a feeling that the other fits in a way that no one else has before or will again, 2) an irresistible desire for skin-on-skin proximately [as they call it], and 3) a delirious urge to disregard all else. In the service of that prismatic blindness, *in love* rewrites reality as no other mental event can."[17]

Forming Earthly and Eternal Families

In many if not most cases, the result of falling in love and bonding intimately with another person, regardless of sexual orientation or gender identity, leads to the desire to create a family with whom such love can be shared. This may be especially true for Latter-day Saints, who from their earliest years are taught the importance and eternal nature of families. While some argue that an ideal parent combination is a man and a woman, a comprehensive research study conducted by the American Sociological Association concludes that "there is a clear consensus in the social science literature indicating that American children living within same-sex parent households fare just as well as those children residing within different-sex parent households over a wide array of well-being measures."[18] Given these findings and the fact that the United States has the world's highest percentage of children under eighteen living in single-parent households

---

15. Pablo Neruda, *One Hundred Love Sonnets: XVII (I don't love you as if you were a rose).*
16. Thomas Lewis, et al, *A General Theory of Love*, 20.
17. Thomas Lewis, et al., 206.
18. Wendy D. Manning, Marshal Neal Fettro, and Esther Lamidi, "Child Well-Being in Same-Sex Parent Families: Review of Research Prepared for American Sociological Association Amicus Brief."

(23%, compared with 7% worldwide),[19] one can conclude that having two emotionally healthy parents of any sexual orientation or gender diversity leads to healthier children and more stable homes.

The implication of such findings for Latter-day Saint culture and society is that a number of LGBTQ individuals have formed, and trends suggest they increasingly will form, family units. While no studies reveal the extent to which LGBTQ Latter-day Saints marry, the fact that in 2022 the Church announced that it was accepting the legality of gay marriage (while still disapproving of it doctrinally) likely supports the possibility that such marriages are increasing among transgender, gay, lesbian, and bisexual Latter-day Saints and likely will continue to do so.

How the church culture responds to such families constitutes a significant religious, spiritual, and social challenge. At present, few Latter-day Saint congregations welcome non-heterosexual, non-binary individuals, couples, or families into fellowship. What might provide hope, however, is that traditionally, at least over the last five decades, the Church has welcomed unmarried, cohabiting *heterosexual* couples and, when they have children, also welcomed their families, often without any limitations, conditions, or disciplinary measures. At present, no such flexibility or accommodation exists for married or non-married gay, lesbian, bisexual, or transgender Latter-day Saint couples and their families, which I believe means, sadly, that most such couples and families who wish to be part of a religious or spiritual community must seek fellowship outside of Latter-day Saint congregations—or, as is the case with many Latter-day Saints who are deeply embedded in and bonded to the restored gospel, do not seek it in any faith community. This means, in addition to other losses, that the children of such relationships are growing up with little knowledge of, let alone grounding in, the faith of their fathers and mothers.

This would seem to present both a challenge and an opportunity for Latter-day Saint leaders and members. While at present The Church of Jesus Christ of Latter-day Saints recognizes only one form of marriage for its faithful adherents—between a straight, biological male and a straight, biological female—since a number of people who do not fit that category have a spiritual identity with and a deep commitment to the restored gospel and the Church, as well as an apparent God-given desire to bond intimately with another person and create a family (as they have been

---

19. Stephanie Kramer, "U.S. Has World's Highest Rate of Children Living in Single-Parent Households."

taught from their early youth is their heavenly parents' wish), what are they to do—and what is the Church to do?

Expanding the Definition of Marriage

When I was released as bishop of the Los Angeles First (Singles') ward more than thirty years ago, having had the calling and privilege of befriending and ministering to a number of LGBTQ Latter-day Saints, I remember saying to my wife: "As I look into the future, it seems to me that the greatest challenge the Church faces is what to do with its single members, including those who are gay, lesbian, or bisexual. I see only one path forward: the Church should not compromise its fundamental principles of premarital chastity and post-marital fidelity, but that means that it must be flexible with regard to its definition of marriage." My experiences and observations over the past decades affirm that conclusion.

The history of the Church would seem to suggest the possibility of such flexibility. At the end of the nineteenth century, in its best interest, the Church made a dramatic and enlightened—if difficult and painful—change in its teaching and practice by abandoning a form of marriage that was generally seen not only as illegal but even barbaric by most citizens of the United States. That was a painful but necessary choice for the future flourishing of the Church. While some leaders and members felt (and some offshoots of Mormonism still feel) that decision was wrong and even counter to God's will, and while it caused tension among leaders and significant suffering for some families, it is likely that the Church would not have survived without it.

Since its establishment, the Church has made various changes, accommodations, and adaptations with regard to marriage: as noted above, it established polygyny (polygamy) as an acceptable (even divinely revealed) mode of marriage and then ceased the practice and forbade it (at least for mortals); for a period of time the Church honored common law marriages; in countries where divorce is (or was) illegal, the Church made some accommodation for converts who were in non-legal relationships; until 1978 the Church not only discouraged and strongly disapproved of interracial marriages but also "social intercourse" between whites and Blacks of African descent;[20] in 2019, the Church eliminated the one-year

---

20. A letter from Presidents McKay and J. Ruben Clark, dated November 4, 1949, stated, "The church's attitude today is as it always has been, namely, that intermarriage between our members and negroes is forbidden because negroes

waiting period for temple marriage for people first civilly married;[21] and in 2022, the Church began recognizing the legality of same-sex marriages (although not its legitimacy for members).

Expanding its definition of marriage to include some alternate modes may be the wisest and most practical choice the contemporary Church could make, especially if it wishes to improve its record of retaining LGBTQ individuals, couples, and families. While, as with the abandoning of polygamy, there will be resistance to accepting some alternate forms of marriage and accepting a more flexible definition of families, the advantages to doing so could well prove a blessing to the Church.

Several recent studies suggest that there may be signs of changing demographics and attitudes among Latter-day Saints regarding sexual orientation and marriage. The most surprising (and possibly most alarming to church leaders) is the report by Jana Riess of a 2023 study, conducted by the Foundation for Individual Rights and Expression, which claims that 22% of LDS students between the ages of eighteen and twenty-five identify as "lesbian, gay, bisexual or something else."[22] According to Riess, the study's finding that 78% of LDS students identified as heterosexual is nearly identical (77%) to a 2021 Nationscape Survey of LDS Gen Zers (those born between 1997 and 2012) conducted by Benjamin Knoll.[23]

Also promising are data that show a dramatic increase in the percentage of Utahns who approve of same-sex marriage (from 40% to 75% over

---

cannot have the priesthood, and the progeny of marriages between our people and negroes could not hold the priesthood. Since the church's membership is charged by the Lord with carrying on his work, which is done through his priesthood, it is the obligation of every Latter-day Saint to see to it that his progeny, so far as blood and race are concerned, is of a character that can carry on the priesthood. Anything therefore that tends to encourage marriage between negroes and whites is not sanctioned by the Church. Social intercourse with the negroes has this tendency, and for equivalent reasons, it is not sanctioned by the Church." See First Presidency Letter to Waldo H. Anderson, President of the Northern States Mission, November 4, 1949. Permission to publish granted by Waldo Anderson's grandsons, James and Neil Anderson.

21. Sarah Jane Weaver, "First Presidency Discontinues One-Year Waiting Period for Temple Sealings after Civil Marriage."

22. Jana Riess, "A fifth of LDS college students in the U.S. don't identify as heterosexual."

23. Riess argues for some caution in considering the data. Jana Riess, "Update—Jana Riess: There are more young lesbian, gay or bisexual Latter-day Saints than previously believed."

the past decade). Although not as high, another study shows a percentage of Latter-day Saints "in favor of allowing same-sex couples to marry" nearly doubled between 2015 and 2022, "from 27% to 50%" (the figure diminished by three points by 2023).[24] In addition, Utah has one of the highest rates of marriage in the US among its LGBTQ population (61% as compared to the national rate of 58%).[25]

Adding to this is a dramatic change in rhetoric from top church leaders, especially over the past decade. For example, in 2017, Apostle Russell M. Ballard expressed:

> I want anyone who is a member of the Church who is gay or lesbian to know I believe you have a place in the kingdom and I recognize that sometimes it may be difficult for you to see where you fit in the Lord's Church, but you do. We need to listen to and understand what our LGBT brothers and sisters are feeling and experiencing. *Certainly we must do better than we have done in the past* so that all members feel they have a spiritual home where their brothers and sisters love them and where they have a place to worship and serve the Lord.[26]

Newly called Apostle Patrick Kearon's words are even more helpful and hopeful:

> We need to treat them [LGBTQ people] like everybody else, treat them as the Savior treated those he ran into. . . . He blessed them. That's our model. The invitation to all of us is to get better at being like him. When we treat people the way he would have us treat them, we feel more peace, we feel more joy. And that's what we want for them.[27]

Welcoming LGBTQ parents and their families into full fellowship could be a healthy counter to slowing growth and to divisive sentiments over LGBTQ issues in the Church. Beyond that, its LGBTQ members and their families who deeply desire fellowship could play a vital role in the great unfolding of the Restoration, including in its missionary and temple work. Is it possible to even allow ourselves to entertain such a more diverse, inclusive, and possibly more dynamic church?

---

24. Tamarra Kemsley, "Study shows shifting Latter-day Saint views on LGBTQ rights."

25. Megan Banta, "Utahns' opinions on same-sex marriage have shifted dramatically over the past decade."

26. Marianne Holman Prescott, "Elder M. Russell Ballard tackles tough topics, shares timely advice with BYU students" (emphasis added).

27. Peggy Fletcher Stack, "LDS Church's newest apostle talks singles, women and LGBTQ members in sit-down interview."

If, as shown above, contemporary science attests and human experience affirms at least some varieties of sexual orientation and gender identity are determined *in utero* and therefore fixed at birth, and if the indelible desire for intimate bonding is implanted by God into the human psyche and body, then one might conclude that such intimate connection and fulfillment are part of our heavenly parents' design for Their mortal children. And if, as the Church teaches, sexual expression within marriage is not only for the purpose of procreation but "also to strengthen the emotional, spiritual, and physical connection between spouses,"[28] then it raises the fundamental moral question of what God intends for and expects of those who have such desires and wish to express them with integrity but have no present Church-sanctioned means of doing so.

If one argues that any sexual orientation or gender identity outside of or beyond those accepted by the Church are not eternal but rather only mortal conditions, then one might posit that those who experience these variations deserve some means by which they, too, can fulfill the measure of their mortal creation as it relates to bonding with another person. Following such an argument would seem to lead to a justification for a *mortal* moral system in which such individuals could enter into marriage relationships with someone of their own orientation or gender *for time* and be held to the ethical requirements of a faithful marriage for this life and then trust God for whatever might obtain in the next world. That is, if, as the Church argues, celestial exaltation is a prelude to heterosexual godhood, wouldn't our heavenly parents want their children who have been born with non-heterosexual capabilities and desires to have the mortal experience of learning to love and be loved by another, in order to better prepare them for exaltation in the unique way marriage and families make possible? Surely, one could conclude that the initial decree immediately following Adam's creation that "It is not good for man to be alone" would apply not to just heterosexual men and, once Eve was created, just to heterosexual women, but to all God's children. I realize what I am proposing is bold and even shocking to some, but I fear that without some accommodation, we will continue to lose the majority of our LGBTQ members whose unique gifts enrich the Church. I sincerely believe that losing them will hamper the growth and mission of the Church.

---

28. Chelom E. Leavitt, "Conversations about Intimacy and Sex That Can Prepare You for Marriage."

An Exercise in Empathy

A number of years ago I was invited by a group of members to speak about my experience in ministering to LGBTQ Latter-day Saints. The group, who lived east of Oakland, California, consisted of six or seven older couples who, as friends and fellow believers, had been holding discussion groups for years. My first question to them that night was, "When did you make the decision to be heterosexual?" Their initial response to the question was puzzlement: "What do you mean? We have always been this way?" I then said, "I want to ask you a second, more challenging question, which I don't expect you to answer tonight, but would like you to ponder. You are all sitting next to someone with whom you fell in love many years ago. Since then, you have married, had children and grandchildren, and have helped one another grow and evolve socially, intellectually, and spiritually. I would guess that under the influence of the gospel you would consider your personal and family lives rich and rewarding because of your marriage."

After letting this sink in, I said, "Now I want to ask you a more challenging question. I want you to go back to the time when you first fell in love with the person sitting next to you and decided to get married. What would you have done had you been told that you couldn't marry one another but rather had only two choices: you could remain celibate for the remainder of your lives, or you could marry someone of your own gender. Those were the only acceptable choices. What would you have done? The question becomes even more challenging if you were told that remaining celibate would deprive you of the growth, rewards, and joys that marriage affords and that marrying heterosexually would put you in great disfavor with the Church. As you think about the question, consider that this is similar to the choice our gay brothers and sisters face. Now imagine how you would feel if the Church changed its policy and made heterosexual marriage legal and accepted by the Church."

More Love, More Love

I fully acknowledge that I do not have the calling or the authority to change church doctrine, policy, or practice. My only motive in suggesting accommodation for our faithful non-heterosexual and non-binary LGBTQ brothers and sisters is that I wish for them the same opportunities for and blessings of emotional, intellectual, and spiritual growth that I and other married heterosexual Latter-day Saints are privileged to enjoy, so that they, like us, can work out their salvation, not only with fear and trembling, but with the unique hope and joy that marriage makes possible.

Clearly it is not up to me or other lay members of the Church to establish doctrine, policy, or practice. That daunting calling and challenge is reserved for the First Presidency and the Quorum of the Twelve Apostles. What is given to us as individuals, families, and congregations is the challenge of aligning and living our lives in harmony with the basic principles and teachings of the Savior.

Part of the function of churches, including any church founded on the mission and teachings of Jesus Christ, is to create a home for all of us who have taken upon ourselves his name, including any we consider the least among us (which, for some, includes LGBTQ people) and to welcome them into the family of Christ. The central calling of churches and all those who belong to them, therefore, is to show more love, to allow the gracious love and sweet grace of Christ to work its miracle in our lives and all those with whom we live and serve.

I return to the words of the Shaker hymn with which I began:

> If ye love not each other
> in daily communion,
> How can ye love God
> whom you have not seen?
> The heavens are blessing,
> The angels are calling,
> O Zion! More love.

I bear grateful witness of that love and the way it has changed my life—and I testify that Christ and his angels are calling us to have and show more love for our LGBTQ brothers and sisters. I truly believe that doing so is among our most urgent and holy callings.

By fully welcoming our LGBTQ brothers and sisters, we would be following Jesus and in doing so, realizing the vision Rumi has of the Lord's disciples: "Where Jesus lives, the great-hearted gather. We are a door that's never locked. If you are suffering any kind of pain, stay near this door. Open it." I believe Jesus would add, "That door leads to your heart, your home, and your chapel."

CHAPTER NINE

Imagining a Holier Holy Week

Because our own Latter-day Saint faith tradition does not celebrate the events of Holy Week—with the exception of Easter—our family has often found ways of marking these holy days. Before she passed, I often attended Good Friday services with my wife Ruth at other churches. When our children were young, we sang hymns and read from the gospels on Good Friday. One year we continued this tradition with the next generation when two of our young grandsons and their parents visited us on Good Friday. When they asked us why the day Jesus died was called "Good Friday," we told them that in Middle English the word "good" actually meant "holy" and also that what Jesus did for us on that day results in enormous good for all who believe in and follow him, including giving us hope that we can make our lives better by following his teachings. I have since remarried, and now my wife Gloria and I and some of our adult children continue this and other Holy Week traditions.

Early in our marriage, Ruth's and my friends David and Susan Egli first introduced us to the tradition of celebrating a Passover meal or seder on Maundy or Passover Thursday—a tradition we continued with other Latter-day Saint friends. In the seder, each part of the meal has meaning for both Jews and Christians. As we celebrated that meal and what it symbolizes, I couldn't help but think of what it might mean for the Church if Latter-day Saints regularly had such an opportunity.

Our Holy Week celebrations have always included generous time for listening to great sacred music. While our musical fare during this season is drawn from such works as Handel's *Messiah*, Beethoven's *Missa Solemnis*, Mozart's *Mass in C Minor*, and a number of other sacred choral works, we are particularly drawn to Bach's exquisite music, to his Passions (derived from *passio*, the Latin word for suffering) according to St. Matthew and St. John, his Holy Week cantatas, his *Easter Oratorio*, and his magnificent *Mass in B Minor*. No Christian, I believe, can listen to Bach's Passions dispassionately or without being immediately and deeply enveloped in the drama of Christ's last mortal week. The ariosos, arias, recitatives, choruses, and chorales tell the story of Christ's suffering with such dramatic and lyrical power that we are imaginatively and emotionally present at the sorrowful events of his last week. This is particularly true with the chorales, which were traditionally sung by the congregation. Bach wrote these

Passions for Holy Week services in the German Lutheran church, and no composer before or since has so completely captured the intense devotion and deep spiritual immersion it is possible to experience in the felt presence of Christ's passion. As Professor Robert Greenberg of the San Francisco Conservatory of Music says, "Bach's Passions demand engagement."[1] At the same time, no composer has helped us feel the power of the resurrection more powerfully than Bach does in the B minor Mass. The chorus of "Et resurrexit," which follows the quiet, almost indiscernible last notes of the "Crucifixus," explodes with such musical force that there is a powerful kinesthetic sensation that seems to symbolize Christ rising boldly from his tomb. As one of our Jewish friends (who considers himself an atheist) said, after listening to the B minor Mass, "I don't believe in God, but if I did, that's what He would sound like!"

To my mind, these works also constitute the music of Zion—certainly so in the original meaning of that word—"the pure in heart." I imagine that when heavenly beings attend services, this is among the music they hear!

During the time I served as bishop and for periods when Ruth served as ward choir director, we were able to create special worship services on Palm Sunday and Easter Sunday and, on one occasion, Good Friday. Ruth prepared wonderful musical offerings for these occasions, including performances of cantatas, motets, and selections from Bach's "Christ lag in todesbanden" ("Christ Lay in Death's Prison"), his Passions, and on several occasions his *Easter Oratorio*. These were glorious occasions for all present.

Some of my most memorable Holy Week devotions have taken place in other churches. Let me name just two. A number of years ago, Ruth and I had the privilege of attending the National Cathedral in Washington, DC, on Palm Sunday. It was a beautiful spring day. The landscapes were resplendent with the cherry blossoms that gossamer our nation's capital during this season. Tulips, daffodils, and crocuses were all in bloom. As we entered the cathedral along with other worshipers, we were given a strand of a palm frond. Palm branches have been used for centuries as symbols of joy and victory.

As the service began, the celebrant said, "Blessed is the King who comes in the name of the Lord," and the congregation answered, "Peace in heaven and glory in the highest." There followed a reading of Christ's entry into Jerusalem from Luke. The celebrant said, "On this day Jesus Christ entered the holy city of Jerusalem in triumph and was proclaimed

---

1. Robert Greenberg, "Bach and the High Baroque."

as King of Kings by those who spread their garments and branches of palm along his way. Let these branches be for us signs of his victory, and grant that we who bear them in his name may ever hail him as our King, and follow him in the way that leads to eternal life." The celebrant again said, "Blessed is he who comes in the name of the Lord," and the congregation, each holding our strand of palm on high, responded, "Hosanna in the highest."

The music that day, which focused on Palm Sunday, included the following hymns: "Procession of the Palms," "All Glory, Laud, and Honor" (the only hymn in the LDS hymnal specifically related to Palm Sunday), and the joyous spiritual "Ride On!":

> Ride on, king Jesus. No man can a-hinder me.
> He died for you and he died for me
> He died to set poor sinners free.
> He died for the rich and He died for the poor.
> He ain't come here to die no more.

After the hymn, the tone of the service shifted from joyful praise to somber contemplation as the darkening clouds of Holy Week began to gather. Now the words and music focused on Christ's betrayal, trial, and crucifixion. The Passion from Luke's gospel was read by Charles Robb, former governor and US senator from Virginia, with various other voices representing Jesus, Peter, the chief priest, Pilate, and witnesses. The congregation represented the crowd. Thus, those of us who earlier had shouted "Hosanna! Blessed is he who comes in the name of the Lord," were now shouting, "Away with this fellow! Release Barabbas for us!" and "Crucify, crucify him!"

I must confess that these last words were difficult for me to say, but say them I did, and as I did so, I instantly assayed the measure of my devotion to the Lord. I wondered if I would have been among those who shouted him welcome the previous Sunday and then cried his death these few days later. It was a sobering moment.

The service continued with Reverend Nathan Baxter, the dean of National Cathedral, delivering a sermon on the conflicting emotions between Palm Sunday and Good Friday, between the shouts of "Hosanna!" and "Crucify him!" Speaking of those ambivalent first disciples, he said, "We, too, are caught between the poles of devotion and disobedience, between praise and peccata, between wanting to welcome him into our lives and wanting also to crucify him." I looked up at the carved wooden statue of Christ hanging high at the crossing of the cathedral and was filled with remorse for those things I had done to add to his sorrow. I joined my prayer with that of Reverend Baxter: "Almighty God, we pray you graciously to behold this your family, for whom our Lord Jesus Christ was willing to be betrayed, and given into the hands of sinners, and to suffer death upon the cross."

The service ended with the choir and congregation singing "O Sacred Head, Sore Wounded" ("O Savior, Thou Who Wearest a Crown" in the LDS hymnal). I was particularly moved by the third verse, which is different from the one in the LDS hymnal:

> What language shall I borrow to thank thee, dearest friend,
> for this thy dying sorrow, thy pity without end?
> Oh, make me thine forever! And should I fainting be,
> Lord, let me never, never, outlive my love for thee.

Needless to say, this was a fitting way to begin the celebration of Holy Week. The spirit of that service echoed throughout that week, and still echoes during times of reflection about my bond with Christ.

The second experience took place on Easter Sunday when my daughter Julianna and I attended services at Grace Cathedral in San Francisco. It was a stunningly beautiful day, the sky a cerulean blue and the city sparkling like a giant dew-lit field lying below and beyond the cathedral itself, which sits on a hill. As we approached the cathedral, we were struck by how the stained-glass windows bejeweled its massive gray walls. Upon entering, we passed a labyrinth floor tapestry (patterned after the labyrinth at Chartres Cathedral) representing, according to a pamphlet we picked up in the church, "a symbolic diagram of the pilgrim journey" that signifies the winding path to the center of the world, which is Christ. We took our seats and listened to the prelude music, organ renditions of "Offertoire pour le Jour de Paques" ("Offertory for Easter Day") by Jean-Francoise Dandrieu and "Christ lag in todesbanden" ("Christ lay in Death's Dark Prison") by Bach.

A few moments of silence were followed by three raps at the giant bronze Doors of Paradise at the front of the cathedral. The three raps startled me for a moment since I had heard three similar raps not long before at the veil in the Oakland Temple. I turned around to see the heavy doors, which are patterned after the famed doors by Lorenzo Ghiberti that hang on the Florence Babtistery, swing open. Sunlight flooded the nave as the dean, chapter, and choir entered, singing the introit by Christopher Tye, accompanied by brass ensemble and timpani:

> "O who shall roll away the stone,"
> the faithful women said;
> "the heavy stone that seals the tomb,
> and shuts us from our dead?"
> But looking up, at dawn, they saw
> the great stone rolled away,
> And from the empty tomb a light
> more dazzling than the day

The choir and congregation together sang "Jesus Christ Is Risen Today," with its repeated alleluias. Following scripture readings from the Old and New Testaments, William E. Swing, the Episcopal Bishop of California, delivered the sermon. He spoke of a recent murder in Johannesburg and of the murderer's refusal to see his victims and their families as real people because he saw them as through a telescope. He said, "It is hard to see humanity through a telescopic lens." He then spoke of Paul's inability to see Christ until he was "blinded by the resurrection" on the road to Damascus. He concluded his sermon by saying, "Easter has everything to do with a new way of seeing. The angel at the tomb said to the women, 'Look!' The last word was no word at all, but an empty tomb."

In the Episcopal Church, Easter Sunday is a day of renewal of baptismal vows, so following the bishop's sermon, all who wished to do so reaffirmed their denunciation of sin and recommitted themselves to Christ. This reaffirmation of our discipleship took the form of answers to a series of questions, including the following:

> Will you proclaim by word and example the Good News of God in Christ?
> I will, with God's help.
> Will you seek and serve Christ in all persons, loving your neighbor as yourself?
> I will, with God's help.
> Will you strive for justice and peace among all people, and respect the dignity of every human being?
> I will, with God's help.
> May Almighty God, the Father of our Lord Jesus Christ, who has given us a new birth by water and the Holy Spirit, and bestowed upon us the forgiveness of sins, keep us in eternal life by his grace, in Christ Jesus our Lord. Amen.

As I listened to these questions and tried to answer them honestly, I felt a renewal of my bond with Christ in an expanded way; I felt the purifying waters of baptism wash over my soul anew.

The service continued with the Eucharist or sacrament, additional musical numbers by the choir and congregation, the bishop's blessing of the congregation, and, as we walked out into the spring sunshine, the organist playing Widor's majestic *Toccata*.

Needless to say, I was filled with the Spirit during and after this service. My heart was full of praise. I felt like Joseph Smith, who described his feeling after the First Vision: "My soul was filled with love and for many days I could rejoice with great Joy."[2]

I am aware of the fact that these were unusual Palm Sunday and Easter services and that they took place in churches with a professional clergy and many of the trappings of large, wealthy, urban churches. While the sublime drama of such services can be appealing, it isn't necessary to celebrate Holy Week in such grand style. Some of my most memorable Holy Week experiences have taken place in simple, humble church services, including Latter-day Saint services, where we gathered as Christians to center our lives on Christ and renew our devotion to him. What is important for Latter-day Saints, I believe, is that we elevate the significance of Holy Week and expand and deepen our ways of expressing praise and devotion to our Lord during the season that marks his triumph over sin and death. The seeds of such worship exist both in the primitive Church and in the first years of the Restoration. Perhaps it is time that we allow them to flower among us.

I hope for the day when The Church of Jesus Christ of Latter-day Saints recognizes and celebrates the full significance of Holy Week, when honoring Christ's suffering and death as well as his resurrection becomes more important than a stake or general conference scheduled on Palm or Easter Sunday, a celebration of the restoration of the priesthood, or a remembrance of the coming of the pioneers into the Salt Lake Valley. I don't want to be misunderstood—I value these important events of the Restoration, just as I value being instructed and inspired by modern prophets in conference, but my ultimate commitment is to Jesus Christ, whose sacrifice and resurrection have imparadised my heart and whose amazing grace has set me free.

I have always seen the Restoration as an ongoing process, an enlightened unfolding which continues to this day and will continue until the glorious return of Jesus makes it complete. Anyone with eyes open knows that we need continuing restoration as well as continuing revelation. I respectfully submit that observance of Holy Week is one of the things that awaits our preparation.

---

2. "History, circa Summer 1832," The Joseph Smith Papers.

INTERLUDE 5A

Calvary

She dared not look
at his feet
for fear she would feel
the hammer blows
on her heart
as she had heard them
from afar,
spikes driven
into flesh,
into feet
she had washed
and anointed with spikenard,
feet she had bathed in tears
and kissed,
knew each contour and callus.
Reaching up,
she touched them tenderly,
felt the iron,
hard as the hearts that had
nailed him.
Slowly, she unraveled her hair
and wound it round his wounds,
his blood deepening her crimson
tresses.
She rose and, embracing both feet,
kissed them,
remembering that
first time she had seen
his sandals
walking toward her,
each step coming nearer
until he reached down and touched her.
And now those hands were also nailed,
but still she could not look up.

> She stood there until darkness
> slowly enveloped her,
> and walked away
> not knowing where she would go.

INTERLUDE 5B

The Empty Tomb

The cross fading
in the darkness,
the women followed the procession
to the empty tomb where,
enshrined in white linen,
his body was laid to rest.
Not knowing what to do or where to go,
they wept their way into the night.
Reaching their abode,
they lay down together,
cradling one another,
weeping and mourning
as Israel's women had before them.

. . . .

That night, the Magdalene
slept fitfully,
hearing hammering
through flesh,
the agonized cries,
seeing the blood
dropping
as if into eternity,
her own tears
incarnadine.
She dreamed
that she, too,
was wrapped in linen
lying beside him,
spice and perfume
flowering the air.
She heard thunder,
which startled her awake.
Not knowing where she was,
she touched her hands and feet
and her side at the place

where the spear had entered him,
covered her face
and wept bitterly.

. . . .

Obediently, they kept the sabbath,
the hours seeming days
and the night eternal,
then arose early,
taking myrrh and aloe,
cassia and cinnamon,
aromatic oils and ointments.
They were astonished to find
the great stone rolled away
and the tomb empty.
And then there were angels,
luminous as the sun,
"He is risen!"—
She remembered the story
of Jesus weeping
over unbelief at Bethany,
and imagined Lazarus
his winding cloths
lying at his feet,
and felt a sweet coldness wash over her.

. . . .

The unbelieving and then believing disciples
gone,
she sat in the tomb holding
the empty linen to her face,
then went into the garden,
her heart daring not to hope.
She heard but did not recognize the voice,
"Why are you weeping?
Whom are you seeking?"
Supposing the gardener, she said,
"If you have taken him, tell me where
and I will take him away."
"Mary!"

She turned, reaching toward him, "Rabboni!"
Stepping back,
"I know you want to touch me
but we must wait
until I return
from our Father."
And then he was gone. . . .
She turned toward Jerusalem
and ran.

CHAPTER TEN

Imagining a Whole and Healthy Planet: Earth Stewardship in Light of Matthew 25

"It is only a little planet, but how beautiful it is."
—Robinson Jeffers

"The earth is the Lord's and the fullness thereof."
—Psalm 24:1

I

According to Latter-day Saint theology, this earth was created by the Gods expressly for the grand purpose of giving Their most precious creation—*us*—a place where we could become like Them and thus have the potential to create other worlds like this one, inhabited by other beings like us and by the rich diversity of flora and fauna with which we share this planet. Our theology argues that there are innumerable other planets like ours swimming in space, also inhabited by the offspring of deity; yet, with all our scientific knowledge, this is the only planet within the scope of our discovery with the conditions exactly right to sustain life. Its complexity and beauty are astonishing—and, as we have discovered in the past century, astonishingly vulnerable to our indifference, selfishness, and greed.

I was fortunate to have Hugh Nibley as a teacher, mentor, and friend. My attitudes toward earth stewardship are influenced by Nibley's inspired and enlightened teachings about our divine mandate to be lords *of* (rather than lords *over*) the earth. It is an important distinction—one we seem to have lost. According to Terryl B. Ball, Nibley's attitude toward the earth can be summarized by the following four principles: "(1) humankind has a divine mandate to properly care for creation; (2) humankind's spiritual health and environmental heath are linked; (3) creation obeys, reverences, and provides for humankind, as humankind righteously cares for creation; and (4) humankind should not sacrifice environmental health for temporal wealth."[1]

In a 1972 article in the *New Era*, Nibley argued that with our stewardship in regard to the environment and the earth and all its living plants

---

1. Terry B. Ball, "Nibley and the Environment."

and animals—as with all things—God allows us to choose the way of light and love or the way of darkness and destruction. Unfortunately, evidence shows that for at least the last half century, both as a religious community and as a world community, we have been choosing the latter. Consider the following:

- According to a recent UN report, "around 1 million animal and plant species are now threatened with extinction."[2] A separate report from Penn State University titled "Species Extinction," expands on this threat:

    > Our planet is now in the midst of its sixth mass extinction of plants and animals—the sixth wave of extinctions in the past half-billion years. We're currently experiencing the worst spate of species die-offs since the loss of the dinosaurs 65 million years ago. Although extinction is a natural phenomenon, it occurs at a natural 'background' rate of about one to five species per year. Scientists estimate we're now losing species at 1,000 to 10,000 times the background rate, with literally dozens going extinct every day. It could be a scary future with as many as 30 to 50 percent of all species possibly heading toward extinction by mid-century.[3]

- Recent news from climate scientists reveals an acceleration of the glacial melt in Antarctica. According to the *Washington Post*, "We may have irreversibly destabilized the great ice sheet[s] of West [and East] Antarctica," which together would cause a rise in sea levels of more than twenty feet.[4] Imagine New York, Los Angeles, Miami, Bangkok, Calcutta, Amsterdam, and many other of the world's great cities and rural areas under water! What we may have already unleashed portends a slow-motion flood of biblical proportions.

- The earth seems to be warming at an accelerated rate, leading to dramatic increases in violent storms, floods, droughts, and fires, which lead to massive losses of jungles, forests, plains, and food and water sources, ultimately leading to starvation, disease, and death.

---

2. Sustainable Development Goals, "UN Report: Nature's Dangerous Decline 'Unprecedented'; Species Extinction Rates 'Accelerating.'"

3. Environmental Issues, "Species Extinction"; see also, Elizabeth Kolbert, *The Sixth Extinction: An Unnatural History*.

4. Chris Mooney, "The melting of Antarctica was already really bad. It just got worse."

- According to the World Health Organization, within a decade "climate change is expected to cause approximately 250,000 additional deaths per year, from malnutrition, malaria, diarrhea and heat stress."[5]

In his powerful essay "The Passing Wisdom of Birds," Barry Lopez writes about Hernando Cortez's destruction of Tenochtitlan, the "Aztec Byzantium" known today as Mexico City. Having been driven out of the city a year earlier by Montezuma, Cortez returned with a larger army and, with vindictive violence, "laid siege to the city. Canal by canal, garden by garden, home by home, he destroyed what had been described by Charles V as 'the most beautiful city in the world.'"[6] In an ultimate act of cruelty, Cortez set fire to the great aviaries and to the nests of wild birds that were found throughout the city. The deliberate destruction of all that beauty and civilization reminds me of what we are doing to the earth today. Lopez writes, "The image I carry of Cortez setting fire to the aviaries in Mexico City that June day in 1521 is an image I cannot rid myself of. It stands, in my mind, for a fundamental lapse of wisdom . . . an underlying trouble in which political conquest, personal greed, revenge, and national pride outweigh what is innocent, beautiful, serene and defenseless—the birds. . . . Indeed, one could argue, the same oblivious irreverence is still with us, among those who would ravage and poison the earth to sustain the economic growth of Western societies."[7]

II

In his parable of the sheep and the goats in Matthew 25, Jesus gives the ultimate challenge to his followers—they are always to consider those whom they see as "the least" as if they were Jesus himself. Here, Jesus speaks of this challenge of discipleship in the past tense, but he clearly intends for his followers to apply it to the present and, in terms of earth stewardship, to the future—to those who *will be* adversely affected by our indifference and inaction. In other words, he is saying that we should consider those who *will suffer* disease, destruction, and death because we failed to act in the interest of future generations as far as the earth is concerned—just as if they were Jesus himself. Paraphrasing Francisco Goldman, "The great metaphor at the heart of the Gospel According to Saint Matthew is that those who suffer and those who show love for those who will suffer are

---

5. "Climate change," World Health Organization.
6. Barry Lopez, *Crossing Open Ground*, 196.
7. Lopez, 207.

joined through suffering and grace to Jesus Christ."[8] Likewise, in the Book of Mormon, the Nephite King Benjamin articulates an ethic that enjoins us to "love one another and serve one another" without judgment and with special emphasis on those who suffer because of want, which increasingly will include those affected by our inaction on climate change.

The Book of Mormon prophet Alma (the elder) suggests that redemption is directly related to our imaginatively identifying with those who suffer—or who will suffer. He asks candidates for baptism if they are "willing to mourn with those that mourn; yea, and comfort those that stand in need of comfort, and to stand as witnesses of God at all times and in all things, and in all places that ye may be in, even until death, that ye may be redeemed of God" (Mosiah 18:9). One assumes such mourning and comforting of others (at "all times," in all things," and in "all places") includes those who will suffer as a result of our degrading and destroying the earth. Further, scripture suggests that *the earth itself mourns* because of the desolation caused by such wickedness (Jer. 4:28; Isa. 24:4–5; Moses 7:48–49).

Latter-day Saint theology also teaches that our heavenly parents mourn with the suffering and extinction of other creatures due to our violence and indifference (see D&C 77:2). Global warming is not a figment of anyone's imagination; its effects were all too visible to a group of us from the Bountiful Children's Foundation who visited the island nation of Kiribati in 2015. Kiribati, located in the middle of the Pacific, is one of the poorest nations of the world; it also happens to be among the highest in terms of LDS population density—some 17%. It is predicted to be the first nation to lose all its land mass to rising seas. Everyone there will have to relocate to other nations in the next several decades. In the meantime, there are high levels of poverty, malnutrition, disease, and social dysfunction on the island.

In 2018 my wife Gloria and I visited Madagascar, also on behalf of the Bountiful Children's Foundation. Madagascar is one of the most beautiful yet most environmentally devastated and endangered countries in the world. Although it has abundant plant and animal life found nowhere else on the planet, Madagascar has lost 90 percent of its forests and is rapidly losing more. While there, I read that 45,000 illegal miners were devastating forests and rivers in pursuit of sapphires. In visiting a lemur reserve, I was delighted to have a lemur leap onto my shoulders in an affectionate manner. I wondered how many years remain before all the lemurs are gone.

---

8. Francisco Goldman, "Introduction," xv.

I believe that Latter-day Saints have a special stewardship in relation to the earth. In the near future, in my imagination, the president-prophet of the Church will receive a revelation calling the Church to establish earth stewardship as its fifth mission, realizing that fulfilling the other four major missions—perfecting the saints, preaching the gospel, redeeming the dead, and caring for the poor and needy—all depend on a healed and whole planet. That is, without clean air and water, without sustainable natural resources, without the delicate balance in the atmospheric, oceanic, and biological spheres, the only area of growth for the Church of the future will likely be work for the dead! I realize that that is a somewhat macabre attempt at humor, but climate change is already producing enormous increases in disease and death in many places around the world and obliterating resources that could be used for urgent human needs. Sobering views of a world allowed to continue descending into ecological apocalypse are Naomi Oreskes and Erik M. Conway's imaginative projection, *The Collapse of Western Civilization* (2014), and Kim Stanley Robinson's science fiction novel, *The Ministry for the Future* (2020).

III

A powerful metaphor for the modern Church in relation to earth stewardship might be seen in two of Utah's most prized natural resources—the Great Salt Lake and the Pando aspen grove near Fish Lake.

Great Salt Lake, which has nourished life within the Great Basin for centuries, is presently, like other saline lakes abound the world, in serious danger of being desiccated, thereby endangering human, animal, avian, and other life that has depended on it from the time Lake Bonneville collapsed during the Late Pleistocene period. So serious is the Great Salt Lake's condition that in 2022, the *New York Times* published an article, "As the Great Salt Lake Dries Up, Utah Faces an 'Environmental Nuclear Bomb.'" The subheading elaborates, "Climate change and rapid population growth are shrinking the lake, creating a bowl of toxic dust that could poison the air around Salt Lake City." (Not "could," but presently seriously does!) "The lake bed contains high levels of arsenic and as more of it becomes exposed, wind storms carry that arsenic into the lungs of nearby residents, who make up three-quarters of Utah's population."[9]

---

9. Christopher Flavelle, "As the Great Salt Lake Dries Up, Utah Faces an 'Environmental Nuclear Bomb.'"

A study out of Brigham Young University reports that in addition to the exposed lake's deleterious impact on human health (increased cancer, stroke, and lung and other diseases), pollution from the lake leads to an annual increase of 3,500–8,000 premature births and, most alarmingly, a dramatic diminution of longevity (1.1–3.5 years) for the more than three million people who breathe the air from off the lake.[10]

The average loss of two years for the three million residents who live along the Wasatch Front totals six million years (or sixty-thousand centuries). Imagine that many lost human years. Imagine further what those lost years mean in terms of lost creativity, invention, exploration, and production—of opportunities to advance civilization and to serve and bless others, to say nothing of the enormous loss of compassion, kindness, generosity, forgiveness, and, especially, love that gives hope of humanity not merely existing or enduring but advancing and prevailing.

Also endangered is Pando, a grove of aspen trees near Fish Lake in central Utah. Within this grove, "The Trembling Giant," an eighty-thousand-year-old clonal colony of quaking aspens that has a single root system for thousands of individual trees, with an intertwined root system consisting of nearly 50,000 stems covering over one hundred acres and weighing 6,000 tons. It is both the largest and oldest living organism on earth, and—ironically or, as I imagine, perhaps by divine design—it, along with Great Salt Lake, is located in of what Latter-day Saints sometimes refer to as Zion, a sacred space requiring a sacred stewardship.

Could God have placed these two remarkable natural resources in this specific environment intentionally? Could they represent an opportunity or an invitation to a covenant for Latter-day Saints to set an example on behalf of the planet? As inhabitants of the earth, we could be likened to Pando's intertwined root system. Like individual aspen trees, humans live and die, but like the forest itself, humanity has hope of survival. Therefore, while one stem has a comparatively short life span (50–150 years), "the entire clone can live for tens of thousands of years!"[11]

---

10. Isabella M. Errigo et al, "Human Health and Economic Costs of Air Pollution in Utah." The report states, "This loss of life is distributed across most of the population rather than only affecting 'sensitive groups.' For example, 75% of Utahns lose 1 year of life or more because of air pollution and 23% lose 5 years or more."

11. "Quaking Aspen," The National Wildlife Federation.

Although it has been thought "virtually impossible to kill," Pando may be dying "an ugly death, according to a recent report."[12] When I stood in the forest several years ago, I witnessed what some consider the first indication that this amazing living organism is dying due to climate change.

In Latin, Pando means "I spread." In his yet unpublished book, *The Lens of Love, Eye of Universal Consciousness,* Raymond Bradley argues that there is an interrelatedness of love among all humans—"whether as group bonds of positive attachment or as a positive emotion experienced by the individual, love generates a coherent rhythm . . . which radiates outward as a wave field of bio-emotional energy in all directions."[13] One could speculate that if enough individuals and groups took seriously our collective stewardship of the earth, it would establish coherent bioenergetic fields that could radiate outwards to both the present and the future and therefore influence every living organism on earth. That seems a much more hopeful future than the one we presently seem headed toward. Certainly, more hopeful than what took place in the Valley of Mexico when, in the words of Barry Lopez, "we behaved as though we were insane."[14]

I believe a more hopeful future is embedded in the promises of the Restoration envisioned by Joseph Smith. According to Kathleen Flake (as cited in this volume's introduction), "Smith's narrative history of human and divine interaction was ultimately oriented *to a future time that served as a basis for acting in the present.* It provided a world of meaning by which his believing readers understood themselves existentially, including their future and not merely their past." This is precisely what I am proposing—that we orient ourselves to a reimagined future of the earth and all its living entities by acting in the present. Flake adds, "Most fundamentally, Smith's writings give his believing readers a different sense of what was and what will be."[15]

If we choose, as individual Latter-day Saints and as a church, to act with passionate intent to save the earth by applying the principles embedded in Jesus's parable of the sheep and goats, we could have a powerful impact on others—both present and future. When we are motivated by love—love of our fellow beings, love of other creatures, and love of the earth—we fulfill the charge given to Adam and Eve and all the generations

---

12. Brigit Katz, "Pando, One of the World's Largest Organisms, Is Dying."
13. Copy of manuscript in author's possession.
14. Lopez, *Crossing Open Ground,* 208.
15. Kathleen Flake, "Translating Time: The Nature and Function of Joseph Smith's Narrative Canon," 524–25 (emphasis added).

of God's people since Eden—to act in relation to the earth as God does and as God does with each of us—with love.

As Nibley says,

> The ancients taught that Adam's dominion was nothing less than the priesthood, the power to act for God and in his place. The idea is that God, while retaining his unshakable throne in the heavens, "extended his glory to a new world below in the work of the Creation; then as the culmination of that work he created man to be in charge [*li-mshol*] of all the beings he had created," with the understanding that "from this time forth man must work to improve the earth and preserve and take of all that is in it, exactly as God had done before."[16]

I believe that saving the earth is *the* moral imperative of our own and future generations. Arthur Zajonc says, "Morality concerns the nature and quality of our relationship with other people and, by extension, to the world of which we are a part."[17] In my imagination, I see the Church becoming known worldwide as one of the leaders in a movement to redeem the living, including the living planet for the generations who will inhabit it for the rest of this century and beyond. We could begin by revising our tenth Article of Faith from its present passive voice, "The earth will be renewed . . ." to "*We* will renew the earth so it can receive its paradisiacal glory." That, I believe, is what Jesus calls us to do: to save and preserve the great gift of the world that has been entrusted to us so that we and those who will come after us can truly fulfill the measure of our creation.

---

16. Hugh W. Nibley, "Subduing the Earth," *Nibley on the Timely and the Timeless*, 88.

17. "Transcript for Arthur Zajonc and Michael McCullough—Mind and Morality: A Dialogue," On Being.

CHAPTER ELEVEN

Forgiving the Church and Loving the Saints: Spiritual Evolution and the Kingdom of God[1]

During the five years I served as bishop, I became increasingly aware of the fact that what we speak of as "the Church" has a much more complex, multifaceted, and variable set of meanings than I had ever before realized. Since then, I have also become aware that we tend to act and to govern in the Church as though everyone has a common understanding of the gospel and an equal ability to live its principles. Because of this, at times we may tend to misjudge others, to condemn them for not abiding by our personal view of what the Church should be, and to exclude them from what we may experience—or assume—as our more advanced, enlightened, and elevated devotion. Our spiritual work as both individuals and as a church is impeded by our failure to recognize that the Church has many faces and that we are all at different stages of moral development along a continuum we call the Plan of Salvation.

These realizations have come as I have heard many individuals express their feelings and thoughts about the Church and as I have become increasingly aware of the evolution of my own relationship to the Church and of the complexity of my feelings about and devotion to it.

The Church as Mirror

What is the Church? To different people under different circumstances, the Church may be experienced as the kingdom of God on earth, an entrenched bureaucracy, a rigid hegemony, a safe haven, the political kingdom of God, a monolithic social structure, a place of refuge, a male chauvinist enclave, a rigid religious order, a cult, and the one and only true church.

---

1. Published in *Sunstone* (February, 1992):18–27. An earlier version of this paper was presented at the Sunstone West Symposium in Los Angeles in 1990. At the time I was living in Los Angeles and serving as bishop of the Los Angeles First (Singles') ward.

I once had a conversation in print with my friend and fellow academic Karl Keller, entitled "Letters of Belief," in which we offered divergent views of the Church. Karl said that the Church is a society that "is indeed a clean, safe, pleasant, hope-filled place . . . but it is also mindless, artless, anti-humanistic, simplistically nationalistic, crudely authoritarian, uninteresting." I countered, "The Church . . . is imperfect. [However,] it is the best instrument the Lord has, given our agency, to effect His purposes. If it is at times inefficient, backward, repressive, it is also at times instructive, progressive and liberating. The Church is like *us*. . . . I'll go one step further: the Church *is* us; it is no better or no worse than we are (and that includes *you* and me), for the Church is what we make it."[2]

The Church, which so readily serves as a symbol for either ambivalent feelings about authority or for a nurturing family, tends to call forth strong emotions. Consider the variety of feelings people have expressed to me about the Church: they love the Church, they hate the Church; they respect the Church, they fear the Church; they are devoted to the Church, they are indifferent to the Church; they feel nurtured by the Church, they feel excluded from the Church. Some seem to experience no negative feelings toward the Church; others seem to be in a constant state of conflict with it.

About a year ago, I received a letter from a friend who had this to say about the Church: "I find myself more and more at odds with the institution of the Church. My resentment about how women are treated and the authoritarianism that seems to be growing in this growing institution are making my activity in the Church very uncomfortable to me. What seemed to be a community of which I could feel a part is now a kind of machinery that moves the work along. My activity in my own ward seems empty and meaningless. I feel a part of the huge machine, and I don't believe in the machine anymore."

This woman and I have been friends for a number of years and have had countless discussions about the gospel and the Church. During the time she wrote this letter, she was feeling estranged from the Church. She is a bright woman with a far-reaching intellect, and she is also an artist whose work is original and imaginative. During our many conversations, I have tried to listen to her feelings, to express understanding, and to reaffirm my faith in the enduring goodness of the Church.

---

2. Anonymous, "Letters of Belief: An Exchange of Thoughts and Feelings about the Mormon Faith," 11–13. (The "Anonymous" authors were Karl Keller and Robert Rees.)

Not long after she wrote to me, this woman took a trip to Utah to attend a family reunion and visit friends. The trip was a turning point in her relationship with the Church. This is what she wrote upon returning: "As the plane touched down in Salt Lake, a peaceful feeling came over me, a longing, and memories of all that was Mormon about me. This was my homeland and I was coming home." After a week of remarkable personal spiritual experiences, most of which came as surprises to her, she wrote, "And so I came home from this week-long trip having felt gently led by the spirit on a special journey. This journey was one of healing, of discovery, of reconciliation, of reuniting, of the sweet peace that such openness [from friends and relatives] in such a place can bring. I came back wishing I could live there. But soon I realized that it was meant to renew me, to revive the spirit in me so I can undertake the journey of my life."

Reveling in her newfound peace and reconnection to her Mormon cultural roots, she returned to church with renewed hope. She wrote, "I went to church again for the first time in a long time. . . . I shared my newfound enthusiasm to reconnect and get to know people on a spiritual, personal level. I have stopped asking why the Church doesn't meet my intellectual and social needs and started asking how I can serve people—how I can come to know and love them. And I already feel love flowing back and forth as the barriers come down."

Feelings are rarely so simple nor life trajectories so happily ever after as the story to this point would indicate. Recently this same friend had her name removed from the records of the Church.

To illustrate how individuals may react in vastly different ways in relation to a common experience, I cite an example from Herman Melville's *Moby Dick*. In this novel, Ahab, in his megalomaniacal quest for the white whale, nails a gold doubloon to the mast of the *Pequod* as a reward to the first man who sights the whale. As they seek the elusive leviathan, each of the characters on the ship comes up and looks at the doubloon, and each sees something different. For Ahab it is the prophetic emblem of his quest; for Starbuck it is a Puritan sermon; for Stubb it is an almanac of the zodiac; for Flask, the pragmatist, it is "but a round thing made of gold . . . worth sixteen dollars"; for Queequeg it is merely "an old button off some King's trousers"; for the dark and ghostly Fedallah it is the sign of the Devil; and, finally, for the mad Black boy Pip it is a reflection of the mad world itself: "I look, you look, he looks; we look, ye look, they look. And I, you, and he; and we, ye, and they, are all bats." As Ahab says, "This round gold is but the image of the rounder globe, which, like a magician's glass, to each and every man in turn but mirrors back his own mysterious self."³

Like Ahab's doubloon, the Church is a mirror into which all the Saints look and see a reflection of their unique, individual selves. It reflects back to each of us what we are and where we are in our moral or spiritual development. Obviously, there are a variety of views about the Church, a variety of attitudes toward it, and a variety of possible relationships with it.

Kohlberg's Stages of Moral Development

To develop this idea further, I refer to the research of Lawrence Kohlberg, a Harvard psychologist who in the 1950s developed what is now commonly referred to as "the Kohlberg Perspective." Based on his research, Kohlberg postulated a paradigm consisting of six stages of moral development. He concluded that the different motives people have for doing what is right depend on their stage of moral development.

At Kohlberg's first stage, people are motivated by the avoidance of punishment, loss, or discomfort. Here people see the power of authority as superior and tend to be obedient for the sake of obedience itself. At the second stage, motivation is based on serving one's own needs and interests. At the third stage, people are motivated by the need to be seen as good in their own eyes and in the eyes of others. They have a "desire to maintain rules and authority which support stereotypical good behavior." The motivation at the fourth stage of moral development is related to the interests of and allegiance to institutions. The emphasis here is on obedience to laws, rules, and authority. Those at this stage seek to avoid the breakdown of the system that results when everyone acts out of self-interest. At the fifth stage, there is a "sense of obligation to law, because of one's social contract to make and abide by law for the welfare of all, and for the protection of people's rights." The guiding principle at this stage is "the greatest good for the greatest number." Finally, the sixth stage is characterized by a rational belief in "the validity of universal moral principles, and a sense of personal commitment to them." The emphasis here is on the welfare of individuals rather than on rules or laws.⁴

---

3. Herman Melville, *Moby Dick*, 1253–58.

4. Lawrence Kohlberg, Charles Levine, and Alexandra Hewer, *Moral Stages: A Current Formulation and A Response to Critics*, 489. See also Kohlberg's essays on moral development in the first and second volumes of *The Philosophy of Moral Development*. Kohlberg is only one of many scholars to postulate stages of moral

Because his original research was conducted primarily among white Western males, Kohlberg's ideas have been challenged, and legitimately so, as having both cultural and gender biases.[5] My purpose here is not to delve into the controversy over Kohlberg's research methodology; it is rather to use his paradigm of moral reasoning as a construct for talking about the Church and our respective relationships to it. In fact, the extent to which Kohlberg's ideas can be expanded to include even more complex levels or kinds of moral reasoning based on gender or cultural conditioning only increases their usefulness and strengthens the proposition that there are many ways to experience the Church.

The scriptures suggest that the Lord recognizes a progressive system of moral development. We are told that we must have milk before meat, that we are to be taught "line upon line, precept upon precept," and that light is added as we are able to live by the light we have (Heb. 5:12; Isa. 28:10; D&C 98:10, 50:24). The contrast between the Mosaic and the Christian laws suggest that entire groups of people may be at different stages of moral development. Paul states that the Children of Israel were incapable of living the law of faith and therefore were given a lesser law as a "schoolmaster to bring [them] unto Christ" (Gal. 3:24). It is generally held that it was because the people of Enoch achieved such a high state of spiritual development as a community that they were translated as a body into heaven.

In his teachings, the Savior recognized differences in moral development in his followers. For example, the parables of the sower, of the

---

development. For a summary of some of the most significant research in this area, see James R. Rest, *Moral Development: Advances in Research and Theory*.

5. One of Kohlberg's critics is Carol Gilligan, who argues that because women generally are more sensitive to the needs of others and more naturally oriented to taking care of others than are men, their moral development and moral values are in some ways different from those of men, and, because of this, they have often been judged unfairly by men as being morally inferior. Citing a number of studies, including Kohlberg's, Gilligan notes, "The repeated finding of these studies is that qualities deemed necessary for adulthood—the capacity for autonomous thinking, clear decision-making, and responsible action—are those associated with masculinity and considered undesirable as attributes of the feminine self. The stereotypes suggest a splitting of love and work that relegates expressive capacities to women while placing instrumental abilities in the masculine domain." Carol Gilligan, *In a Different Voice: Psychological Theory and Women's Development*, 17. For Kohlberg's response to Gilligan and other critics, see *Moral Stages: A Current Formulation and a Response to Critics* cited in footnote 3 above.

talents, and of the wheat and tares all recognize various stages of readiness to receive and embrace his gospel. In his behavior toward others, the Savior was always willing to accept people at all levels of spiritual development as long as their hearts were right. Even among his chosen Twelve, he recognized a wide spectrum of spiritual readiness to embrace his teachings and follow him.

Levels of Moral Behavior in the Church

One way to understand how moral reasoning operates in a religion like Mormonism is to look at differing attitudes toward a commandment or principle. For the purposes of illustration, let us consider the law of tithing in relation to Kohlberg's six stages:

At the first stage, people pay tithing out of fear. They don't want to be punished for not paying tithing. At times one hears people refer to tithing as "fire insurance," taking literally the promise, "He that is tithed shall not be burned at his coming" (D&C 64:23).

At stage two, people pay their tithing to be rewarded. We often hear people at this level tell faith-promoting stories about how paying tithing brought them immediate tangible rewards. Often people at this stage say, "I can't afford *not* to pay my tithing."

At stage three, people tend to pay tithing to get approval—of their fellow members, their bishop, or the Lord. They pay tithing because of what people would think of them if they didn't. At this stage, bishops get questions like the following: "My grandfather gave me $5,000 but he tithed on the money before he gave it to me, so do I have to tithe on it as well?"

At stage four, people tend to pay tithing out of practical considerations and for the social good of the Church and its members. They recognize that their tithes contribute to the successful functioning of the Church and see it as their duty to contribute their share.

Saints at stage five pay tithing because they recognize that they have made a covenant to do so, that it is part of their spiritual contract with the Lord. These people generally do not focus on the technical stated requirements of the principle, but are instead motivated by an inward sense of personal obligation and covenant.

At stage six, the highest stage of moral development on Kohlberg's scale, people pay their tithing out of a deep personal commitment to moral principles and the welfare of others. They don't pay their tithing out of fear or to get a reward; they don't pay it out of a sense of duty or obligation; they pay it because they recognize that in giving this offering freely and out of love, the progress of the kingdom is enhanced, their brothers and sisters are blessed, and the world is made better. It is not unusual for people so motivated to give more than the specified ten percent. I know one couple who over their adult lives donated millions of dollars to support the Church's missionary program. They did not keep their wealth for themselves or their family and in fact lived modestly, considering the money they were blessed to have as a stewardship that should be returned to the Lord with interest.

Tithing, like most commandments, opens a wider ethical lens or framework, the kind that Jesus's parables challenge us to consider. How, one might ask, would Jesus respond to the following possible cases or scenarios in which people seek a temple recommend: (A) a sister who pays the equivalent of her tithe to a humanitarian foundation in order to keep peace with her nonmember husband who has requested that she not pay tithes to the Church; (B) a returned missionary who says he doesn't pay tithing but instead pays more than the tithing he owes in fast offering funds to an African country where he served his mission; (C) a brother who said he is in difficult financial straits and is unable to pay a full tithing but has paid more than a full tithing in previous years; (D) a couple who pays tithing on their net rather than their gross income; (E) a divorced sister with small children on government welfare who receives financial assistance from the Church but still does not have enough to pay tithing; and (F) a widowed, faithful, tithe-paying temple worker who confesses she is not financially able to pay a full tithing but hopes for a recommend because she is the only member of her family doing genealogy work on her family line.

Based on my experience as a bishop and as a lifelong tithe payer, I can imagine some bishops and stake presidents approving at least some of these requests for recommends and others who would approve none of them. We can imagine Jesus giving us a parable on this subject. Perhaps he would quote Rumi: "Out beyond wrong doing and right doing, there's a field. I'll meet you there." It is important to recognize that members of the Church live at many different levels of moral development or spiritual awareness. However, as pointed out earlier, most of our Church governance is performed and the majority of our teaching is conducted as if we had not only a common moral ground but a uniform understanding of the policies, practices, and doctrines of the Church. Because of this, we tend to expect more of the Church than it can possibly give and also expect a higher level of Christian behavior from some members and leaders than they can or choose to abide.

The Character of the Church

Some Latter-day Saints tend to regard the Church as if it were a perfect reflection of the mind and voice of God. Often, these members think of the organization of the Church in almost anthropomorphic terms. Thus, one hears such statements as: "The Church is sexist," "The Church is homophobic," "The Church is generous," or "The Church is supportive." Each of these statements contains truth, but none is entirely true. What we may be expressing by such statements is that in our experience in the Church (most probably with individual church leaders), we have encountered people who are sexist, homophobic, generous, or supportive.

This isn't to say that there aren't dominant attitudes and ideas that shape the essential character of the Church; it is to say that when speaking of the Church, one should keep in mind that the Church includes all of us who have taken upon ourselves the name of Jesus Christ and given our allegiance to his restored gospel. The Church includes the limitations, weaknesses, and prejudices as well as the faith, hope, and charity of all of us who call ourselves members, from the apostles and prophets in Salt Lake City to the latest converts in New Guinea, Nigeria, and Ukraine. We are all members of the body of Christ. We all constitute that phenomenon known as his church, and therefore we must be careful in not having unrealistic expectations of the Church by ascribing to it oversimplistic characteristics or by seeing it in terms of our own or someone else's invariably limited point of view.

We may also tend to think of Church leadership as if it consisted of a unanimous, always harmonious entity. It is not uncommon, especially in certain quarters, to hear people make such statements as: "The brethren wouldn't like that," or "The brethren have said . . ." as if all the general authorities were in agreement on all issues. Even a casual reading of church history would suggest that this is not the case, nor should we expect or even want it to be so. Except for doctrinal pronouncements, no one person speaks for the Church, and even in these matters there are sometimes dissenting opinions. The brethren present matters before the Church as a unified body, but this doesn't mean that every one of them personally agrees with what is said, or, as verified by the evolution of doctrine on the question of Blacks and the priesthood, that they are at times inerrant.

Since Kohlberg and the work of other early investigators into the stages of human development, our understanding has expanded significantly with regard to the sophistication and complexity in this area of scientific, humanistic, and spiritual study. Among the leaders in this field is Latter-day Saint evolutionary thinker John Kesler, originator of the Integral Polarity Practice, a systematic understanding of human psychological, social, and spiritual development. Kesler's work consists of a spiritually grounded character and virtue practice consistent with the restored gospel that supports principles of flourishing through the full spectrum of human development.[6]

The spiritual evolution of the Church depends to some extent on the diversity of lifestyles, cultural backgrounds, and social experiences of its members as well as the openness of all members to the possibilities of revelation through the many sources that the Lord has shown he is willing to make his will known. Since we believe that the Lord will "yet reveal many great and important things pertaining to" his kingdom (A of F 1:8), we need to prepare our hearts and our minds for what changes these revelations may portend for the Church.

Forgiving the Church and One Another

While Kohlberg's paradigm of moral development focuses on individuals, I believe it can be usefully applied to organizations as well. If the Church is part of the earthly embodiment of the kingdom of God, then, like God's people and the earth itself, it must also be renewed and receive its celestial glory. Participating in the spiritual evolution of the Church is one of our most sacred callings, as individuals and as the body of Christ.

Because the Church cannot possibly be all things to all people, it will at times be hurtful to some in its policies and practices. The idealist who wishes the Church to be an active agent for change based on the social

---

6. According to Susanne Cook-Greuter, PhD, one of our most prominent researchers and theorists of human development, "John Kesler has created the richest matrix that covers development through the whole spectrum of consciousness from birth through personal individuation into the heart of Big Mind. Kesler provides exquisite detail within an elegant and comprehensive structure. His polarity map illuminates the still points between polar opposites at multiple developmental junctures along the way. By clarifying just what the fundamental tensions are, he has deepened our understanding of human development and experience in a profound way." "About the IPP Institute: Who We Are," Integral Polarity Practice Institute.

and political realities in the United States and Europe will surely be disappointed. The realist, who may be more aware of the implications of social change for an international church, may be grateful for the degree to which the Church responds to social issues at all. Institutions are at best cumbersome and inefficient instruments of human progress. Most of us would probably subscribe to the oft-quoted dictum, "That government is best which governs least,"[7] and some would also likely applaud Thoreau's variation, "That government is best which governs not at all."[8] Nevertheless, in our more sober moments, we likely would agree that in spite of their limitations, organizations and institutions not only do much good but are necessary.

Those of us who belong to the Church should keep in mind that as part of the expansive kingdom of God on earth (which includes believers of all faiths), it is an institution with a special destiny. In giving our allegiance to it, we pledge to commit our lives to making it as true a reflection as possible of the heavenly kingdom it ought to reflect. Our vision of its possibilities must include the whole earth, including Africa, South America, and Asia—those places where the highest priority may be surviving political conflict or getting enough to eat. That means that we all must work to make the Church a more responsive, more effective, and more charitable institution. We also need to forgive it when it fails to meet all our expectations and needs.

It helps to consider Kohlberg's perspective in relation to church leadership. We tend to regard church leaders as if they always lived at the highest stages of morality. Actually, church leaders, like the rest of us, live at varying stages of moral development. While they usually respond from Kohlberg's more advanced stages of moral development, at times bishops, stake presidents, area authorities, and even general authorities respond from lower ones. They will on occasion act out of a moral perspective that seems unenlightened or without charity. Such concerns as practicality and securing the greatest good for the greatest number—Kohlberg's stage four—are likely to figure frequently in their decisions.

Recognizing that church leaders, too, are involved in the process of moral development and act out of a complex moral context should make us more tolerant of their weaknesses, more forgiving of what we might see

---

7. Attributed to John O. Sullivan in his introduction to *The United States Magazine and Democratic Review*.
8. Henry David Thoreau, "Civil Disobedience."

as their faults, and more willing to sustain them in their callings when they fall short of our expectations.

The Church has undergone various spiritual transformations from its beginning. I believe, for example, that the Church is less racist today than it was in previous periods. I also believe that there is a diminishing sexism in the Church. There is clearly less emphasis now on literal and legalistic aspects of church governance, and there seems to be more emphasis on being a good church rather than being the one and only true church. I hope there is more emphasis on being Christian than being merely Mormon.

But there are other ways in which the Church needs to grow and change. Women need to have a yet greater voice, a greater sense of their true equality before God and His priesthood leaders, and an enlarged hope not only that there is a place for the Church in them but a place for them in the Church. Our diverse and underrepresented populations need to be empowered by the Church to play a central role in its divine mission, to have their cultural traditions honored on an equal basis with the dominant Eurocentric tradition that has shaped the Church to the present. Alternative visions need also to be given voice and alternative voices given opportunities to shape the visions of the Church's future. A tendency to silence these voices—feminine, culturally and racially diverse, intellectual, and otherwise—does not serve the Church or its ultimate mission well. While there has been significant progress in some of these areas over the past several decades, being more open to these voices is perhaps one of the ways in which the contemporary Church can evolve to a higher spiritual plane.

Loving the Saints

One of the dangers for those who are at any but the highest levels of spiritual awareness is that they tend to expect everyone to conform to their standards. Those at the highest levels have the charity and magnanimity to accept people where they are and to help them to grow spiritually. The following Zen story about fixed and open rules of morality illustrates the danger of judging others by our standards of morality.

> Tanzan and Ekido were once travelling together down a muddy road. A heavy rain was falling. Coming around a bend, they met a lovely young woman in a silk kimono and sash who was unable to cross the road. "Come on," said Tanzan at once. Lifting her in his arms, he carried her over the mud and set her down on the other side. He and his companion set off down the road again. Ekido did not speak to his companion again until that night

when they reached their lodging temple. Then he could no longer contain himself. "We monks do not go near females," he told Tanzan, "especially young and lovely ones. It's dangerous. Why did you do that?" "I left the girl there by the side of the road," replied Tanzan. "Are you still carrying her?"[9]

Recognizing that people don't fall neatly into Kohlberg's categories should make us more tolerant. We are all on a continuum in our eternal progression, and God is present at every level. In reality, none of us ever acts consistently with moral maturity. With our families, in our business dealings, or even while stuck in traffic, we may regress all the way back to stage one. On the other hand, we may also occasionally stretch ourselves to reach stage six. Thus, we need to be open to what we can learn from others whose spiritual development may be as uneven as our own. As Emerson said, "In my walks, every man I meet is my superior in some way, and in that I learn from him." No one of us is ever in a position to completely know the heart of another. This truth became increasingly evident to me during my service as a bishop. In counseling with hundreds of church members, I came to recognize that there is an entire category of people who have been physically, psychologically, and sexually abused and who therefore often have an impaired sense of moral reasoning or an impaired ability to live certain commandments. Others, through trauma, tragedy, or even rigid upbringing, may be hindered in developing into morally responsible adults.

One story will illustrate my point. An attractive woman moved into our ward. She dressed and carried herself in a provocative manner. She attracted men quickly and was openly flirtatious, even with me, her bishop. Through a series of interviews, her troubled history unfolded. I discovered that she had been born out of wedlock, abandoned by her mother at an early age, and sexually abused by a grandfather and uncle while still a toddler. She was taken into several foster homes in which sexual abuse continued. She was promiscuous in her teens, during which time she was taken in by an LDS family where the father made sexual advances toward her. Yet when she was twenty-one, she served a successful mission. One would have thought that her life had changed completely. Following her mission, she became engaged to a fellow missionary with whom she later became intimate. Her self-esteem crumbled and the engagement was broken. Six months later she was working as an escort in Los Angeles.

---

9. Kees Bolle, "The Buddhist Revolt Against Fixed Ideas," 12.

While a member of my ward, this woman was given a new beginning when she began to work with a psychotherapist. It was clear that it would be very difficult to overcome the burden of such an abusive and troubled past. Through long hours of counseling with me and with her therapist, loving attention from home and visiting teachers, financial assistance, and various other forms of fellowship, we supported her efforts to break the pattern of her desperate and self-destructive need for male attention. After some time, she made a carefully planned move to be near her mother in another state. Unfortunately, I learned recently that she was back in Los Angeles working as an escort for rich businessmen.

While she was in our ward, though some were loving and supportive, this sister was also the subject of criticism by some ward members who only saw the surface of her behavior. Being aware of her history, I knew it was completely unjust to judge her by normal standards of morality, and yet I couldn't betray her confidence by telling others why she should be treated with greater patience and charity.

Every Sunday as I looked out over the congregation during sacrament meeting, I was aware of the pain, the sorrow, the suffering behind some of the faces I saw. While some members of my congregation would have been comfortable citizens of the City of Enoch, others were only steps away from addiction, serious transgression, or, in extreme cases, suicide. While some appeared to have unlimited freedom in determining their destinies, others, whose lives had been seriously damaged, compromised, or squandered, seemed to have little true agency.

For the first six months I was a bishop, I worried a great deal about inconsistency in dealing with transgression. Then I realized that it was impossible to be both consistent and charitable and decided to try to be consistently charitable—to treat each individual not according to strict policies but with understanding and love for his or her unique situation.

For most of us, saintly behavior is not a steady state but one to which we rise on occasion. For most of us, our behavior tends to be inconsistent as we fluctuate among the various levels of moral conduct. At one moment we may respond with Christlike compassion to a stranger in need and the next be irritable and even cruel to a spouse or child. We may be generous in paying tithes and offerings and yet turn away a hungry beggar. The fact that our spirituality is neither constant nor ever increasing in its intensity should leave us humble in regard to our own ability to abide by ideal standards, and it should make us tolerant of others who fail to meet our expectations.

Let me again observe that in the Church we tend to judge one another for failure to understand the gospel as we understand it or to abide by the commandments as we do. In every ward there are those who speak disparagingly of others, who question the spiritual devotion and commitment of some of their brothers and sisters. Sometimes intolerance divides a ward along generational, ideological, or political lines.

I confess that at times I get caught up in such polarization, to see myself on the side of truth, wisdom, and good taste, and to be critical of those whose ideas, opinions, and tastes differ from my own. I can be especially intolerant of those who attack or reject my ideas or lifestyle. What helps me is to remember how accepting, forgiving, and long-suffering the Lord is with me. He doesn't reject me because of my ignorance and sinfulness or condemn me for my limitations and shortcomings. Instead, he stands always ready to forgive me, to urge me to higher standards of ethical and moral behavior, and to be patient with me as I struggle to reach them. Therefore, we should strive to accept others as God accepts us—for whatever we are, wherever we are. His grace on our behalf is always beyond our deserving. As Paul says to the Romans, "God's act of grace is out of all proportion to Adam's wrongdoing. . . . [W]here sin was multiplied [through us], grace immeasurably exceeded it" (Rom. 5:15, 20, REB).

It is in Romans where Paul gives his strongest argument about the importance of the Saints having tolerance and charity for one another. To those who may make judgments about others in regard to living the Word of Wisdom, he says,

> Accept anyone who is weak in faith without debate about his misgivings. For instance, one person may have faith strong enough to eat all kinds of food, while another who is weaker eats only vegetables. Those who eat meat must not look down on those who do not, and those who do not eat meat must not pass judgement on those who do; for God has accepted them. (Rom. 14:1–3 PHILLIPS)

Disputations about the Sabbath day are seen in the same light:

> Again, some make a distinction between this day and that; others regard all days alike. Everyone must act on his own convictions. Those who honour the day honour the Lord, and those who eat meat also honour the Lord, since when they eat they give thanks to God; and those who abstain have the Lord in mind when abstaining, since they too give thanks to God. For none of us lives, and equally none of us dies, for himself alone. . . . Let us therefore cease judging one another. . . . Let us, then, pursue the things that make for peace and build up the common life. (Rom. 14:5–7, 13, 19 REB)

Building that common life is our common stewardship, and when we take it seriously, we progress as individuals, as families, as congregations and communities, and as a church.

Spiritual Evolution

M. Scott Peck defines spiritual growth as the evolution of consciousness. He describes the movement from "undeveloped spirituality" to "spiritual competence" as spiritual evolution. He also says that this evolution is anti-entropic and that the force that drives this spiritual evolution is love:

> It is through love that we elevate ourselves. And it is through our love for others that we assist others to elevate themselves. Love, the extension of the self, is the very act of evolution. It is evolution in progress. The evolutionary force, present in all of life, manifests itself in mankind as human love. Among humanity love is the miraculous force that defies the natural law of entropy.[10]

Peck states that love comes from grace. He says, "To explain the miracle of grace . . . we hypothesize the existence of a God who wants us to grow—a God who loves *us*."[11] Latter-day Saints who have read *The Road Less Travelled* undoubtedly have been astonished to discover what Peck has to say about the ultimate end of spiritual evolution. He is the only believer I am aware of outside of the Church who seems to understand that the purpose of our mortal existence is to evolve toward godhood. He says,

> Why does God want us to grow? What are we growing toward? Where is the end point, the goal of evolution? What is it that God wants of us? . . . No matter how much we may like to pussyfoot around it, all of us who postulate a loving God . . . eventually come to a single terrifying idea: God wants us to become Himself (or Herself or Itself). We are growing toward godhood. God is the goal of evolution. It is God who is the source of the evolutionary force and God who is the destination.[12]

Conclusion

I believe that, like other faith traditions and communities that take seriously God's invitation to increase in light and love and thus grow toward greater holiness, The Church of Jesus Christ of Latter-day Saints

---

10. Scott Peck, *The Road Less Travelled: A New Psychology of Love, Traditional Values and Spiritual Growth*, 268.
11. Peck, 269 (emphasis added).
12. Peck, 269–70.

is evolving through the stages of moral development because we, as its constituent parts, are also evolving. It is the divine design of loving deity that all who wish to do so will arrive at a point where their faithfulness will be rewarded with paradisiacal glory.

I am convinced that the purpose of the Church is to make it possible for us all to have three central experiences, all of which are designed by loving heavenly parents to help us move to higher planes of spiritual evolution.

The primary purpose of the Church is to make it possible for us to experience the love of God. Ideally, all the Church's programs and activities should reflect this purpose. Perhaps locked in our deepest preexistent memories is a remembrance of what it felt like to be held in the loving embrace of our Father and Mother in Heaven. I am convinced it was the purest experience we have ever felt, an experience so profound and so joyful that when we are in touch with it, we are motivated to spend our entire lives trying to get back into Their presence so that we might feel that love, both physically and spiritually, for eternity.

The next purpose of the Church is to help us love ourselves. This is not merely a wish on the Lord's part, but one of His great commandments. He has revealed the gospel and the design of His church and kingdom so that we will truly know that we are unique, eternal creatures begotten out of love and of inestimable worth to those who begot us and to Their Son who gave his life that we might return to their presence.

Being able to love ourselves makes it possible for us to love others and to receive their love, which is the third central purpose of the Church. Notice how much of the gospel is focused on the commandment that we love one another. It is very difficult for people to feel the love of God if they have not first experienced the love of other human beings. Those who doubt the love of God generally are those who doubt the love of their parents and others, who on some deep level are convinced that they are unlovable. In reality, we can't accept the Atonement until we are able to love those who, like ourselves, are undeserving of Christ's love. It is through loving others that we participate with God in the redemption of his children, and it is in being loved by others that we receive the power to seek redemption. For there can be no redemption without love—not just God's love, but the love we give to and receive from others.

When as individuals or as a church we fail to enable these central purposes, as sometimes happens, it frustrates the work of God. We are called of God to help make the Church fulfill its central mission of making love possible in all its heavenly and earthly manifestations.

I used to think that in order to get to the celestial kingdom I had to keep all the commandments. I now believe that I need to live as perfectly as possible one commandment—the commandment to love. Further, I believe that those who enter that kingdom will do so because, having learned to love purely, they alone will be comfortable in the presence of the pure love of God. Others who have loved less completely and less purely will seek lower kingdoms.

I believe that the celestial kingdom is reserved for those who have learned to love themselves, others, and God; the terrestrial kingdom for those who have learned to love themselves and others; and the telestial kingdom for those who chose to love only themselves. The love of the first will be as bright and as warm as the sun, while the love of the second and third will be comparable, respectively, to the light and warmth of the moon and stars. Outer darkness is reserved for those who, in spite of all the opportunities given them in mortality, are unable to give or receive love of any kind. As Father Zosima says in *The Brothers Karamazov*, "Fathers and teachers, I ponder 'What is hell?' I maintain that it is the suffering of being unable to love."[13] Thus outer darkness is merely the reflection of inner darkness, the heart of darkness in which there is no love and therefore no light.

As we learn to love, we move through the stages of our divine lives, from the beginning where our love is focused on ourselves, to loving those who love us, to loving God. And when we learn to love God, our capacity to love is extended to our enemies, to the unlovely, to those we do not know but for whom we feel compassion because they belong to the human family, to the world itself and all its creatures and living things, and ultimately to the vastness of space with all of its stars and galaxies and other worlds—because all are part of the handiwork and the habitation of those who begot us in love, who now nurture us in love, and who will welcome us home and crown us as exalted beings through that same love.

---

13. Fyodor Dostoyevsky, *The Brothers Karamazov*, quote at subsection letter "I."

CHAPTER TWELVE

Why the Imagination is Essential for the Ultimate Flowering of Mormonism

> *Not "Revelation" 'tis that waits,*
> *But our unfurnished eyes.*
> —Emily Dickinson[1]

My hope is that the previous chapters demonstrate not only the importance of the imagination but its essential role in the unfolding of the Latter-day Saint Restoration. What seems clear from the other revelations and scriptures that unfolded after that astonishing theophany is that it was the beginning of a new liberal religious revolution—*liberal* in the original meaning of that word: "generous, selfless, noble, gracious, munificent." During the English enlightenment, "liberal" also came to mean tolerant and free from prejudice. Unfortunately, for many in today's Church the word "liberal" has retained none of these positive connotations. My intention in using it here is in keeping with the meanings Joseph Smith had in mind when he taught that "our heavenly Father is more liberal in His views, and boundless in His mercies and blessings, than we are ready to believe or receive."[2]

That the Prophet intended the positive qualities of the word "liberal" I listed above seems confirmed by what he taught a couple months earlier: "The nearer we get to our heavenly Father, the more we are disposed to look with compassion on perishing souls; we feel that we want to take them upon our shoulders, and cast their sins behind our backs"[3]—in other words, the kind of compassionate care and generous forgiveness at the center of Christ's gospel. This usage is in keeping with Joseph's contemporary dictionary, *Webster's 1828*, which defines "liberal" as "of a free heart; free to give or bestow; not closed or contracted; munificent;

---

1. Letter to Thomas Wentworth Higginson, 1862–63, in Mabel Loomis Todd, ed., *Letters of Emily Dickinson*, 260.

2. Alonzo L. Gaskill and Richard G. Moore, comp., *The Revised and Expanded Teachings of the Prophet Joseph Smith: Compared with the Earliest Known Manuscripts*, 332.

3. Gaskill and Moore, 310.

bountiful; generous; giving largely."[4] It is those qualities I have in mind when I speak of the role of imagination in our quest for the ultimate flowering of Mormonism.

Since Jesus stated, "Truly, truly, I tell you, the Son can do nothing by Himself, unless He sees the Father doing it. For whatever the Father does, the Son also does" (John 5:19), we know that Jesus's liberality is identical with that of the Father, who again, according to Joseph Smith "is more liberal in his views, and boundless in his mercies and blessings, than we are ready to believe or receive." Examples of the Savior's liberal imagination are found on every page of the Gospels, throughout the Book of Mormon, in his words to modern prophets, and in the lives and witnesses of his most devoted disciples in all religions. One example of many from a modern prophet is the following from President Stephen L. Richards:

> When the gospel was restored in this age all the goodness and mercy of Christ was restored.... The essence of the ... whole restored gospel was and is election without coercion, persuasion not compulsion, no unrighteous dominion, only patience, long-suffering, meekness, kindness and love unfeigned."[5]

I want to be clear that I believe there is harmony between the definition of liberalism mentioned above and the conservatism that is reflected in many of the Church's doctrines, principles, and practices. In a world of often capricious change, the Church's stability is to be admired; in a world of increasing moral relativism, the Church's doctrinal consistency can be seen as a virtue; in a world of wanton disregard for standards of modesty, sexual morality, and decency, the Church's clear and certain standards offer safety and refuge; and in a world in which the family is under siege from many quarters and by many forces, the Church's teachings on this core institution are a great blessing to members as well as to society in general. My own life has been immensely blessed by these conservative virtues as well as by the Church's liberal ones. In the future I imagine, these would be more equally balanced, thereby making the Church more reflective of the fullness of the gospel and more appealing to a wider humanity.

Such a social-political balance was sought by the Church's First Presidency when Utah was vying for statehood at the end of the nineteenth century. They argued that "the more evenly balanced the parties become

---

4. Webster's Dictionary 1828, Online Edition, s.v. "liberal."

5. Stephen L. Richards, "Bringing Humanity to the Gospel," 43–44. President Richards is reiterating counsel from D&C 121:39–42. Although the address was delivered in the April 1932 general conference, it did not appear in the printed version of the proceedings.

the safer it will be for us [Latter-day Saints] in the security of our liberties . . . and the more evenly balanced the parties, our influence for good will be far greater than it possibly could be were either party overwhelmingly in the majority"[6] (as is the case in Utah and the Intermountain Region at present).

The Quest for a More "Progressive" Mormonism

Just as the word "liberal" has undergone a dramatic change in terms of its original meaning, so has "progressive." The definition I prefer, in relation to expanding our religious imaginations, follows denotations common during the time when Joseph Smith made his declaration to the world: "using one's efforts toward advancement or improvement" and "striving for change and innovation";[7] in other words, the subject of this concluding chapter.

Let me shift my attention to some specifics. I am a scholar and poet, not a prophet, and so what I suggest in the following pages is a result of my imaginative projections, the longings of my heart, and the deep yearnings of my soul for a more expansive and enlightened Mormonism—"enlightened" in the sense of the Lord's words in Doctrine and Covenants 50:24–25: "That which is of God is light; and he that receiveth light, and continueth in God, receiveth more light; and that light groweth brighter and brighter until the perfect day." One of the functions of that light is "that you may know the truth, that you may chase darkness from among you." In my view, our imagining the future of the Church is a reflection of our hope for diminishing darkness and moving toward the light of that promised brighter day.

In addition to subjects covered in the preceding chapters (e.g., Heavenly Mother, earth stewardship, racial inclusion, and so on), I would like to focus on several additional ones I feel have particular importance in imagining and reimagining the Restoration—ways in which our imaginative discipleship might have particular focus and fulfillment. These include the status of women, the state of the poor and those whom Jesus classifies as "the least of these," our call to be peacemakers, a quest for a more unified and harmonious political and social community, a more liberal education, and becoming a more Christ-centered church. To make

---

6. First Presidency to Joseph W. Young, May 29, 1891, as quoted in Eugene England, *Making Peace*, 86.
7. Online Etymology Dictionary, s.v. "progressive."

any or all of this possible, love must be the essential force driving it. In other words, an imagined future inspired and motivated by love will not only be more realizable, but also more in harmony with heaven.

O Daughters of Zion: Imagining the Whole Latter-day Saint Woman

I believe one of our most important tasks in reimagining the Restoration is to visualize a church and a world in which all women, the daughters of Zion and all their sisters throughout the world, truly feel equally valued—not solely for their roles as wives and mothers nor as only joint heirs in some far otherworldly kingdom, but for all they are and have to offer here in this world in which we live and move and have our being. For all our rhetoric to the contrary, the reality is that many women do not feel equally important, valued, or loved, either in the Church or in the world, essentially because they most often are not. Consider the following grave statistics:

> Currently, an estimated 160 million females are "missing" worldwide due to infanticide and femicide. "This is the equivalent of an entire generation of girls being wiped from the face of the earth."[8]
>
> Rape continues to be widespread and is a particularly egregious form of violence against girls and women. In many countries rape is endemic. According to the World Health Organization (2013), "more than a third of all women are victims of physical or sexual violence." That's over one billion women—or more than three times the entire population of the United States.[9]

Add to this list honor killings, genital mutilation, child marriages, dowry deaths, and other forms of abuse and violence, and one can only conclude that as far as women and girls are concerned, we live in a brutal, barbarous, uncivilized world.

In the United States, including in the Latter-day Saint heartland, women suffer inordinate sexual and other kinds of abuse. According to a recent report from the Utah Women & Leadership Project, "one in three Utah women has been sexually assaulted, and one in six women report having been raped."[10]

---

8. Jimmy Carter, *A Call to Action: Women, Religion, Violence, and Power*, 116.
9. Roni Caryn Rabin, "Nearly 1 in 5 Women in U.S. Survey Say They Have Been Sexually Assaulted."
10. Susan R. Madsen, Tiffany Turley, and Robbyn T. Scribner, "Sexual Assault Among Utah Women," 1.

Neither the Church nor individual Latter-day Saint can hope to solve such gross and serious problems, but we could all imagine and work toward a world in which the girls and women within our families, congregations, and communities are accorded full respect, dignity, and equality. This is what Neylan McBaine calls for in her book, *Women at Church: Magnifying LDS Women's Local Impact*. She writes,

> I have written this book as an inducement toward greater empathy for those who feel unseen, unheard and unused, and a strategic guide for improving our gender cooperation in local Church governance. . . . I believe we have the opportunity and the responsibility to adapt our local practices to include our women more comprehensibly.[11]

I would argue not just locally but also generally and globally, perhaps especially in cultures where women's rights are severely limited or under attack.

In my lifetime I have seen progress in the Church regarding women. In just one generation women have been given more recognition, responsibility, and rewards. Recently, in speaking to women, President Russell M. Nelson said that the Church needs "your strength, your conversion, your conviction, your ability to lead, your wisdom, and your voices. The kingdom of God is not and cannot be complete without women who make sacred covenants and then keep them, women who can speak with the power and authority of God!"[12] *Speak and act with such power and authority!* Referring to women having "power and authority" seems a new and more enlightened way to speak of the unique gifts and promises of Latter-day Saint women.

Can we imagine even more? I know for some it is considered impolitic if not impolite to speak of women's being ordained to the priesthood but given the references in scripture to women prophets and apostles and the promise of the restoration of all things, it seems to open that possibility. Paul speaks of Junia as being "preeminent among the apostles" (Rom. 16:7). In reference to other female apostles, New Testament scholar Bart Ehrman asks,

> Were there other women apostles? Other women, who understood themselves, and were understood by others, to be commissioned by Christ in order to spread the word of his death and resurrection? We know of at least

---

11. Neylan McBaine, *Women at Church: Magnifying LDS Women's Local Impact*, xiii.
12. Russell M. Nelson, "A Plea to My Sisters."

one other, one who could be thought of, in fact, as the original apostle: Mary Magdalene. Mary is called an apostle by some early Christian writers.[13]

Having been involved in interfaith work for the past fifty years and having spent a dozen years teaching at Graduate Theological Union in Berkeley, I have had the privilege of working with many women ministers, priests, rabbis, and other ecclesiastical leaders. I have seen firsthand how these women bring their unique gifts to various altars in ways that bless and serve others and glorify God in ways that differ from but also complement those of men. Whether our heavenly parents intend for such gifts to bless the Latter-day Saints is not something I can predict, but I can envision it, and that envisioning is indeed joyful to contemplate.

Who knows what other amazing advances await Latter-day Saint women in the future! Our imaginations will fail us if we don't consider the possibility that many of "the great and important things pertaining to the kingdom of God" (D&C 97:14), we are encouraged to seek and work for will come through women. That is, I believe, what our Mother in Heaven wants. It is what I imagine her imagining Latter-day Saint women doing!

The Least of These: Poor Wayfaring Men and Women

Women's status is not all that needs to be reimagined. We must also reimagine the place of racial, ethnic, and religious minorities, as well as those considered inferior because of their sexual orientation, gender identity, disability, economic or social status, or any other kind of "otherness" that prevents us from seeing them as fully human and equal citizens of society and of Christ's kingdom. I believe Jesus's statement "The poor you have always with you" (Matt. 26:11) is a condemnation rather than an observation of inevitability—especially knowing that the City of Zion had no poor among them (Moses 7:18). As a religious community, we Latter-day Saints are known for our generosity. In fact, because we are tithe payers, our per capita charitable giving is larger than that of any other religious group in the United States, and yet many of us live far beyond our needs while many of our brothers and sisters live in extreme, even grinding poverty—poverty that could be significantly ameliorated by even modest additional giving on our part. In an article in *Meridian Magazine* titled "Feed My Lambs," I argued that Jesus's question to Peter, "Lovest thou me more than these [meaning materials things]?" (John 21:15), is also directed at us. I wrote:

---

13. Bart Ehrman, "Women Apostles in Early Christianity."

> To those of us living in the modern, developed-world church, I think Jesus is saying . . . , "I have blessed you with enormous wealth. You live in large houses more spacious than you need and often some of your bedrooms lie empty; you drive expensive cars and pass by the poor on roads and byways. You eat three meals (or more) a day and your larders and pantries are fully stocked. . . . You have more of everything than you actually need and have more luxuries than any previous generation in history. What do you intend to do with all of these things? Do you love me enough to follow me and give generously to the poor?"[14]

During the Great Depression, President Heber J. Grant said that he would go so far as to "close the seminaries, shut down missionary work for a period of time, or even close the temples" rather than "let the people go hungry."[15] More recently, Presiding Bishop H. David Burton underscored this by telling the Saints,

> No matter how many temples we build, no matter how large our membership grows, no matter how positively we are perceived in the eyes of the world—should we fail in this great core commandment [and] . . . turn our hearts from those who suffer and mourn, we are under condemnation and cannot please the Lord.[16]

Jesus was the Lord of everyone, especially—given the emphasis of the New Testament—the poor. He cannot be pleased with the enormous gap between the rich and the poor in this generation where, according to the BBC, the "richest 1% now has as much wealth as the rest of the world combined."[17] In the United States, the top 1 percent earn 25 percent of the nation's annual income and possess 75 percent of the nation's wealth.[18] Just as startling, the top 1 percent own nearly four times as much as the bottom 80 percent—all shocking statistics. The consequence of such inequality is that even in this, the richest nation in history, there is grinding poverty, hunger, despair, sickness, and unnecessary death related to poverty. For example, according to researchers at the Harvard Medical School, "45,000 people die in the United States annually because they lack health insurance."[19]

---

14. Robert A. Rees, "'Feed My Lambs': Jesus' Last Great Teaching."
15. As quoted by H. David Burton, "The Sanctifying Work of Welfare."
16. Burton.
17. "Oxfam says wealth of richest 1% equal to other 99%," BBC.
18. Jill Lepore, "Richer and Poorer: Accounting for Inequality."
19. Susan Heavey, "Study links 45,000 U.S. Deaths to Lack of Insurance."

I don't wish to preach a jeremiad, but I cannot see anything but disaster coming from an economic system so severely imbalanced in favor of the rich. As Hugh Nibley warned, "The calamitous effect of wealth, according to the Book of Mormon, is the inequality it begets."[20] Such inequality could have a negative impact on the Church. As we read in Third Nephi, because of "a great inequality in all the land . . . the church began to be broken up" (3 Ne. 6:14). Some economists predict that unless it becomes less severe, this level of inequality could lead to significant political and social unrest.

In the conclusion to his *And There Was No Poor Among Them: Liberation, Salvation, and the Meaning of the Restoration*, Ryan Ward reminds us that there are two salvations, spiritual and temporal, and that both are related to the cross: "This is the covenant he revealed to his followers that was solemnized on Calvary's cross, and this is the new and everlasting covenant that is revealed and calls us from the crosses of the world today. *This is the meaning of the Restoration.*"[21]

"Study War No More": Blessed are the Peacemakers

In 1976 President Spencer W. Kimball critically observed, "We are a warlike people." That he was referring to the Latter-day Saints is evident by what he says next: "[We are] easily distracted from our assignment of preparing for the coming of the Lord. When enemies rise up, we commit vast resources to the fabrication of gods of stone and steel—ships, planes, missiles, fortifications. . . . When threatened, we become anti-enemy instead of pro-kingdom of God."[22] President Kimball's words echo First Presidency statements at the beginning of both the First and Second World Wars.[23]

Our consistent, even enthusiastic support of war is in direct opposition to the Lord's commandment in the Doctrine and Covenants that we "renounce war and proclaim peace, and seek diligently to turn the hearts of the children to their fathers [and mothers], and the hearts of the fathers [and mothers] to the children" (98:16). As Hugh Nibley elaborates, "'renounce' is a strong word: we are not to try to win peace

---

20. Hugh Nibley, *Since Cumorah: The Book of Mormon in the Modern World*, 394.

21. Ryan Ward, *And There Was No Poor Among Them: Liberation, Salvation and the Meaning of the Restoration*, 224 (emphasis in original).

22. Spencer W. Kimball, "The False Gods We Worship," 4.

23. See Joseph F. Smith, "Our Duty to Humanity, to God, and to Country," 645–56 and Joseph F. Smith, "Message of the First Presidency," 88–97.

by war, or merely call a truce, but to renounce war itself, to disdain it as a policy while proclaiming . . . peace without reservation."²⁴ Significantly, this commandment links renouncing war and establishing peace with intergenerational healing: turning the hearts of parents and children to one another.

In modern revelation, the Lord speaks of the saints being gathered to Zion, which will "be called the New Jerusalem, a land of peace, a city of refuge, a place of safety for the saints of the Most High God" (D&C 45:66). This is a pre-millennial city, where, we are told, the wicked will not come (v. 67) and where those who will not take up their swords (or their guns!) against their neighbors will "flee . . . for safety" (v. 68). Further, we are told that "there shall be gathered unto it out of every nation under heaven; and it shall be the only people that shall not be at war one with another" (v. 69). Consider the implications of Zion being the *only* place in the entire world where there will be no war or contention among the saints. That seems unlikely to happen in the Latter-day Saint heartland today!

We can begin to reimagine our attitude about war with the following statement from the First Presidency's 1981 Christmas message:

> To all who seek a resolution to conflict, be it a misunderstanding between individuals or an international difficulty among nations, we commend the counsel of the Prince of Peace, "Love your enemies, bless them that curse you, do good to them that hate you, and pray for them which despitefully use you, and persecute you; That you may be the children of your Father which is in heaven." . . . This principle of loving one another as Jesus Christ loves us will bring peace to the individual, to the home and beyond, even to the nations and the world.²⁵

This indeed is radical theology, but it is also Christ's theology!

In his article titled "Can Nations Love Their Enemies? An LDS Theology of Peace," my friend and Latter-day Saint scholar Eugene England writes,

> LDS theology offers a guide to better conduct. I believe its fundamental message is that "effective pacifism"—even unilateral disarmament if accompanied by massive efforts to extend intelligent, creative, tough-minded but loving help to other nations . . . is the ideal solution, the only one that could make our enemies no longer enemies.²⁶

---

24. "Renounce War!" in Hugh Nibley, *Brother Brigham Challenges the Saints*, 267.
25. *Church News*, December 19, 1981, 2. Matthew 5:44–45.
26. Eugene England, *Dialogues with Myself: Personal Essays on Mormon Experience*, 148.

This seems to be in accord with Jesus's call for a nonviolent but nevertheless assertive response to injustice. Biblical scholar Walter Wink calls this "Jesus's Third Way," which is neither passive acquiescence nor violent confrontation.[27]

What I imagine in the future is a Church of Jesus Christ of Latter-day Saints that deliberately, consistently, and systematically sues for peace, works for peace, and establishes peace. Think of what it would mean for preaching the gospel if Latter-day Saints were known all over the world for their anti-war, pro-peace ethic. That would clearly create a climate in which people might indeed say, "Let us go up to Zion."

Imagining a More Unified Political and Social Community

It is difficult to imagine a truly unified future for the Church considering the present political and social polarization dominant in the Latter-day Saint heartland. Since the mid-twentieth century, that culture has moved increasingly to the right. That is reflected in the fact that in the recent 2024 presidential election 64% of Latter-day Saint voters preferred Republican Donald Trump—twice as many as who voted for Democrat Kamala Harris. Trump's first weeks in office seem to promise not only significant strife and discord but increasing division and disunity. According to a February 13, 2025, opinion piece from the *New York Times*'s editorial board, "Only weeks into President Trump's second term, he and his top associates are stress-testing the Constitution, and the nation, to a degree not seen since the Civil War."[28]

When Utah was vying for statehood at the end of the nineteenth century, Church leaders, in an attempt to prevent the majority of Latter-day Saints from gravitating en masse to the Democratic Party—which at the time had been much more sympathetic to the saints than the Republicans—divided towns and congregations down the middle, with half going to the Republicans and half to the Democrats. That most Latter-day Saints identified with the Democratic Party can be seen by the fact that 82 percent of Utah citizens voted for Democratic candidate William Jennings Bryan in the 1896 presidential election. What we have today in the Intermountain West is almost a complete reversal, with Utah and Idaho in some years leading the nation in voting Republican. This is why Eugene England argued that some Utah Latter-day Saints should

---

27. Walter Wink, *The Powers That Be: Theology for a New Millennium*, 98–111.
28. *New York Times* Editorial Board, "Trump Dares the Courts to Stop Him."

consider becoming Democrats.[29] As a lifelong Republican, he was serious, because he knew that supermajorities inevitably infringe upon the rights of minorities. Lest one might think Gene was being unfair or unreasonable, he also proposed that more Latter-day Saints on the coasts should become Republican!

It is far too easy to confuse partisan political ideologies with gospel principles. Such confusion, I contend, is destructive to the Church's ultimate mission. The extent to which a right-of-center ideology is identified in the public mind with the Latter-day Saints likely undermines church growth and status, leading many outside the Church to regard Latter-day Saints as rigid and regressive, as anti-science and anti-intellectual, and as insular and narrow-minded. Such individuals are likely to hold negative stereotypes of Latter-day Saints, thus leaving them blind to the truly remarkable truths of the Restoration and the substantial gifts of Mormonism. Separating right-wing (or left-wing) politics from the gospel could aid us in a more expansive and reimagined Restoration.

The Value of a Liberal Education

Finally, I believe a key to imagining and then realizing the fullness of the Restoration is to encourage Latter-day Saints to obtain and then apply in their daily lives a truly balanced approach to education—one that includes and incorporates both conservative and liberal values, with an emphasis on open and informed hearts, minds, and spirits and on the freedom to choose. In such an educational environment, people do not flee from either faith or doubt, they honor both science and religion, and they rely on a diversity of cultural and social points of view and exploration. In such a system one does not surrender their own thinking or emotions to others nor do they rely on any authority that is not in accord with their own deepest sense of what is morally true and spiritually right.

The credo of such an education for Latter-day Saints is that of a 1969 address by President Hugh B. Brown to the students at BYU called "An Eternal Quest—Freedom of the Mind." Among other things, he said:

> One of the most important things in the world is freedom of the mind; from this all other freedoms spring. Such freedom is necessarily dangerous, for one cannot think right without running the risk of thinking wrong, but generally more thinking is required, and we [the First Presidency] call upon you

---

29. Eugene England, "On Saving the Constitution, Or Why Some Utah Mormons Should Become Democrats," 22–30.

students to exercise your God-given right to think through on every proposition that is submitted to you and be unafraid to express your opinions, with proper respect for those to whom you talk and proper acknowledgment of your own shortcomings.

He continued,

> Preserve . . . the freedom of your mind in education and in religion, and be unafraid to express your thoughts and to insist upon your right to examine every proposition.

And to this admonition he added these astonishing words:

> We are not so much concerned with whether your thoughts are orthodox or heterodox as we are that you shall have thoughts.

Essentially, President Brown was encouraging Latter-day Saints to open their minds to the expansive possibilities of the Restoration. In the same address, he said,

> While I believe all that God has revealed, I am not quite sure that I understand what he has revealed, and the fact that he has promised further revelation is to me a challenge to keep an open mind and be prepared to follow wherever my search for truth may lead.[30]

That promise and challenge of future revelation "remains one of the most exciting promises of the Restoration."

Conclusion

> *"Thy mind, O Man [and Woman], if thou wilt lead a soul unto salvation, must stretch as high as the utmost Heavens, and search into and contemplate the lowest considerations of the darkest abyss, and expand upon the broad considerations of eternal expanse."*
>
> —Joseph Smith[31]

Fifty years ago, Gene England invited me to participate in a BYU Humanities Forum he was moderating on Mormonism's contributions to the humanities and the imaginative arts. Gene spoke of the "real and the ideal, both doing 'the highest justice to the visible universe' . . . and also holding up models and visions of the highest good and possibilities

---

30. Hugh B. Brown, "An Eternal Quest—Freedom of the Mind."

31. Gaskill and Moore, *The Revised and Expanded Teachings of the Prophet Joseph Smith*, 174; see also Dean C. Jessee and John W. Welch, "Revelations in Context: Joseph Smith's Letter from Liberty Jail, March 20, 1839," 137.

for man."[32] That's one of the things the imagination does. In my remarks that day, titled "The Paradise of Meaning: Imagination and the Religious Experience," I argued that religion and the imagination "are fundamentally related and ... touch us at our deepest center; both reveal things to us that we can't know in other ways."[33] While each by itself is limited, together religion and the imagination create a paradise of meaning and possibility.

The focus of this book is the call for Latter-day Saints to forge a new future for Mormonism, one that imagines a religious way of life that builds on the best of the Restoration from the past, combines it with the most enlightened ideas of the present, and projects the dawning of a brighter day through the prism of a liberal ideology—liberal, as I have tried to resurrect its original meaning and intention—combined with the best conservative principles.

In imagining a fully realized Restoration, I am not suggesting that the Church change its essential mission or compromise its core values or principles. But history has shown that when religions have the courage to admit error—when they recognize their own fallibility and limitations—they look to the future and open themselves to new ideas, new growth, and new revelations. The Church needs disciples who are committed to improving it and helping it more fully realize the promises embedded in its enlightened scriptures and radical theology. As Christian Wiman argues, "Faith is not faith beyond some change. Faith is faith *in change*."[34]

As a church, we need to ask ourselves if there are present teachings and practices that we will look back on in the future with regret that we didn't challenge and change, just as we have been doing over the past half-century or more. The history of the Church suggests that social and spiritual evolution are not just inevitable but desirable. Society changes, innovative technologies emerge, new discoveries open wider vistas in many fields, and forces beyond our control dictate policy we can't even imagine (although that's exactly what I am urging us to do!). Add to all this the promise that God himself has made to reveal many great and glorious truths pertaining to His kingdom, and one has greater expectation for a dynamically evolving Church. I have always been struck by the fact that the Lord refers to His church as both "true and living." That organic metaphor is important for us to keep in mind as we participate in the continual unfolding of the Restoration.

---

32. Typescript of Gene England's notes in author's possession.
33. Manuscript in author's possession.
34. Christian Wiman, *My Bright Abyss: Meditation of a Modern Believer*, 104.

I imagine the Church of the future casting a broader net, building a wider tent, and teaching a more inclusive Christianity. I believe the Latter-day Saint tradition would attract far more people were we to remove the stumbling blocks to that attraction, as we recently have done by openly acknowledging past mistakes and changes in both doctrine and practice. Because we have at times not been more open and more willing to change, I feel we have lost many saints who might have stayed engaged. Unless we both change and adapt, we run the risk that more of our fellow saints, in the language of Jesus, will "go away" from us (John 6:67).

My heart breaks anew with each saint who leaves because I feel that each takes something vital with them and that anyone's leaving diminishes us as a community. I experience each departure of which I am aware as a loss, and I have a strong impulse to persuade all who leave to return. To that end, what I am calling for is a more expansive moral and religious imagination, one that more fully opens our hearts and minds to the profound treasures of the Restoration and then employs those treasures in blessing our own people as well as others in the wide world.

Finally, I contend that this reimagined Mormonism, which is a projection of the possibilities and promises embedded in the Restoration's seminal revelations, can be realized only through love. We need love—that of our heavenly parents, Jesus, one another, and ourselves—to fix the fissures in our faith community; we need love to bridge our seemingly unbridgeable differences; and we need love to heal one another's lonely and wounded hearts.

At present the community of believers that constitutes The Church of Jesus Christ of Latter-day Saints is not as unified as it could be; it is not as accepting and loving as it should be. I believe Christ calls all of us to unify, to harmonize our differences, to forgive one another, and to enlarge the capacities of our hearts to love. It is only through the lens of love that we can see the way things truly are and understand love's complexity and diversity as well as its enormous promises and blessings. These ways of seeing help us to understand that in every situation and context, and in every relationship, we are called to do one thing—the most loving thing of which we are capable.

A Final Word on the Imagination and Love

I would like to end with a story, a construction of the imagination, if you will. It is a story that illustrates the power of both the imagination and love's power in healing divisions. Raymond Carver's "A Small Good Thing" is a story about a couple, the Weisses, and the birthday celebration they are planning for their only son, Scotty. The mother orders a cake from the local bakery. On the day of the party, Scotty is hit by a car and lapses into a coma. The parents wait anxiously by the bedside day and night, but their son never awakens and, after a few days, dies. The baker, unaware of the accident, continues to call the parents to come and pick up their cake. Grieving, they do not return his calls. He continues to call and becomes abusive and threatening. Finally, one night they go to the bakery just at closing to express their outrage at the baker's behavior. When they tell him that their son is dead, he is embarrassed and ashamed. A simple man, he does the only thing he can think of to make amends—he offers them fresh-baked bread. As they sit in the darkened bakery eating, he reveals his own lonely life, childless, working sixteen hours a day baking thousands of wedding and birthday cakes and imagining the celebrations surrounding them, none of which ever touch him personally.

Carver describes that poignant moment when the baker takes a fresh loaf of dark bread from the oven, breaks it open, and offers some to them. "'Smell this,' he says, 'It's a heavy bread but rich.'" Carver writes,

> They smelled it, then he had them taste it. It had the taste of molasses and coarse grains. They listened to him. They ate what they could. They swallowed the dark bread. It was like daylight under the florescent trays of light. They talked on into the early morning, the high, pale cast of light in the windows, and they did not think of leaving.[1]

This is a powerful story of loss, grief, death, conflict, forgiveness, and redemption. It is also a story about empathy, sympathy, and compassion. The story's association of bread with light and the coming dawn reminds us of Christ who is both the bread of life and the light of the world, and

---

1. Raymond Carver, "A Small Good Thing," 376–405.

who is the world's greatest example of the virtues I have written about in this book and especially in the final chapter.

Partaking each week of the bread of life, we taste of his light and his love. It is a small, good thing we do every Sunday that is akin to all the other small gifts of kindness, grace, generosity, mercy, forgiveness, and love that we need both to give and receive from one another. Those acts of love, it seems to me, have their genesis in the light of Christ that is in each of us. But they also have their essential expressions in families, congregations, communities, churches, nations, and the world—all places in which we live and move and love and have our being. Marcel Proust said, "It is our imagination that is responsible for love, not the other way," suggesting that it is our subjective experiences and interpretations that are more influential in the development of love than the actual external qualities of the other person. But I think it works both ways: Love also lights, enlightens, and expands our imaginations and then, blessed realization, in turn, our imaginations magnify the mystery and magnifice of love, worlds without end. What a grand and loving design!

Acknowledgments

The following essays have been included or adapted in this volume with permission:

"A Holy Week of Celebration: An Easter Restoration." Wayfare. March 24, 2024. https://www.wayfaremagazine.org/p/a-holy-week-of-celebration.

"Earth Stewardship: Our Work for the Unborn." Sunstone Blog. June 15, 2023. https://sunstone.org/our-work-for-the-unborn/

"The Empty Tomb." Wayfare. December 13, 2024. https://www.wayfaremagazine.org/p/the-empty-tomb.

"Forgiving the Church and Loving the Saints: Spiritual Evolution and the Kingdom of God" *Sunstone* 16, no. 1 (February 1992): 18–27.

"Her." In *Dove Song: Heavenly Mother in Poetry*, edited by Tyler Chadwick, Dayna Patterson & Martin Pulido. Peculiar Pages, 2018.

"Imagining Peace: The Example of the Nephites Following Christ's Visit to the New World." In *War and Peace in Our Time: Mormon Perspectives*, edited by Patrick Q. Mason, J. David Pulsipher, and Richard L. Bushman. Greg Kofford Books, 2012.

"Mary and the Meaning of Christmas." Meridian Magazine. December 24, 2013. https://latterdaysaintmag.com/article-1-13718/.

"The Midrashic Imagination and the Book of Mormon." *Dialogue: A Journal of Mormon Thought* 44, no. 3 (Fall 2011): 44–66.

"Mother." In *Dove Song: Heavenly Mother in Poetry*, edited by Tyler Chadwick, Dayna Patterson & Martin Pulido. Peculiar Pages, 2018.

"The Prodigal Daughter." In *Parables for Today*. Alta Publishing, 2012.

"Reimagining the Restoration: Why Liberalism is the Ultimate Flowering of Mormonism." *Dialogue: A Journal of Mormon Thought* 50, no. 1 (Spring 2017): 3–30.

"Searching for Heavenly Mother: Toward an Imaginative Latter-day Saint Theology." Dialogue. Accessed July 8, 2025. https://www.dialoguejournal.com/articles/searching-for-heavenly-mother-toward-an-imaginative-latter-day-saint-theology/.

"Somewhere Near Palmyra." *Dialogue: A Journal of Mormon Thought* 13, no. 3 (Fall 1980): 105–6.

"*Tikkun K'nessiah*: Repairing the Church." *Dialogue: A Journal of Mormon Thought* 53, no. 4 (Winter 2021): 109–22.

"Toward a Mormon Feminist Midrash: Mormon Women and the Imaginative Reading of Scripture." *Sunstone* 166 (March 2012): 55–61.

Bibliography

"About the IPP Institute: Who We Are." Integral Polarity Practice Institute. Accessed April 10, 2025. https://theippinstitute.com/about/

Ackroyd, Peter. *Albion: The Origins of the English Imagination*. Anchor Books, 2002.

Allred, Janice. "Toward a Mormon Theology of God the Mother." *Dialogue: A Journal of Mormon Thought* 27, no. 2 (Summer 1994): 15–40. https://www.dialoguejournal.com/wp-content/uploads/sbi/articles/Dialogue_V27N02_27.pdf.

Anderson, Devery S. "A History of Dialogue, Part Two: Struggle toward Maturity, 1971–1982." *Dialogue: A Journal of Mormon Thought* 33, no. 2 (Summer 2000): 1–96.

Anderson, Lavina Fielding. "Joseph Smith's Sisters: Shadowy Women of the Restoration." In *Proving Contraries: A Collection of Writings in Honor of Eugene England*, edited by Robert A. Rees. Signature Books, 2005.

Anonymous. "Letters of Belief: An Exchange of Thoughts and Feelings about the Mormon Faith." *Dialogue: A Journal of Mormon Thought* 9, no. 3 (1973): 11–13.

"Anonymous." "Solus." *Dialogue: A Journal of Mormon Thought* 10, no. 2 (Autumn 1976): 94–99.

Ball, Terry B. "Nibley and the Environment." *Journal of the Book of Mormon and Other Restoration Scripture* 20, no. 2 (2011): 16–29.

Banta, Megan. "Utahns' opinions on same-sex marriage have shifted dramatically over the past decade." *The Salt Lake Tribune*. December 20, 2023. https://www.sltrib.com/news/2023/12/20/10-years-later-same-sex-marriage/.

Bates, Irene. "Another Kind of Faith." *Sunstone*. February 1989.

Bird, Phyllis. *Missing Persons and Mistaken Identities: Women and Gender in Ancient Israel*. Fortress, 1997.

Bloom, Harold. *The American Religion: The Emergence of the Post-Christian Nation*. Simon & Schuster, 1992.

Bolle, Kees. "The Buddhist Revolt Against Fixed Ideas." *History of Religions Newsletter* (published by the UCLA Department of History) 3, no. 2 (Fall 1975).

Bowen, Elizabeth. *The Heat of Day*. Jonathan Cape, 1948.

Bradshaw, William S. "The Biological Origin of Sexual Orientation." Manuscript in author's posession.

Bronner, Leila Leah. *From Eve to Esther: Rabbinic Reconstruction of Biblical Women*. Westminster John Knox Press, 1994.

Brown, Hugh B. "An Eternal Quest—Freedom of the Mind." May 13, 1969. https://speeches.byu.edu/talks/hugh-b-brown/eternal-quest/.

Burton, H. David. "The Sanctifying Work of Welfare." The Church of Jesus Christ of Latter-day Saints. April 2011. https://www.lds.org/general-conference/2011/04/the-sanctifying-work-of-welfare.

Bush Jr., Lester E. "Mormonism's Negro Doctrine: An Historical Overview." *Dialogue: A Journal of Mormon Thought* 8, no. 1 (Spring 1973): 11–68.

———. "Writing 'Mormonism's Negro Doctrine: An Historical Overview' (1973): Context and Reflections, 1998." *Journal of Mormon History* 25, no. 1 (Spring 1999): 229–71.

Capote, Truman. *The Complete Stories of Truman Capote*. Random House, 2004.

Card, Orson Scott. "The Book of Mormon - Artifact or Artifice?" Nauvoo. Accessed July 25, 2009. http://www.nauvoo.com/library/card-bookofmormon.html.

Carter, Jimmy. *A Call to Action: Women, Religion, Violence, and Power*. Simon & Schuster, 2014.

Carver, Raymond. "A Small Good Thing." In *Where I'm Calling From: New and Selected Stories*. Vintage Books, 2009.

Chadwick, Tyler, Dayna Patterson, and Martin Pulido, ed. *Dove Song: Heavenly Mother in Mormon Poetry*. Peculiar Pages, 2018.

"Charting the Book of Mormon." BYU Studies. http://byustudies.byu.edu/januarybomcharts/charts/108.html.

Children's Songbook. The Church of Jesus Christ of Latter-day Saints, 2011.

"Climate change." World Health Organization. October 12, 2023. https://www.who.int/news-room/fact-sheets/detail/climate-change-and-health.

Covington, Diane. "The Unseen Life that Dreams Us: John O'Donohue on the Secret Landscapes of Imagination and Spirit." *The Sun*. April 2007. https://www.thesunmagazine.org/issues/376/the-unseen-life-that-dreams-us.

"Cramer History, Family Crest & Coat of Arms." House of Names. https://www.houseofnames.com/cramer-family-crest.

Davidson, Gustav. *A Dictionary of Angels: Including the Fallen Angels*. Free Press, 1967.

Dickinson, Emily. *The Complete Poems of Emily Dickinson*, edited by Thomas H. Johnson. Little, Brown, 1960.

———. Letter to Thomas Wentworth Higginson, 1862–63. In *Letters of Emily Dickinson*, edited by Mabel Loomis Todd. Gosset and Dunlap, 1962.

Dillard, Annie. *Holy the Firm*. Harper & Row, 1977.

Dostoyevsky, Fyodor. *The Brothers Karamazov*. Macmillan, 1951. https://standardebooks.org/ebooks/fyodor-dostoevsky/the-brothers-karamazov/constance-garnett/text/chapter-2-6-3.

Ehrman, Bart. "Women Apostles in Early Christianity." The Bart Ehrman Blog: The History & Literature of Early Christianity. November 15, 2002. https://ehrmanblog.org/women-apostles-in-early-christianity/.

England, Eugene. *Dialogues with Myself: Personal Essays on Mormon Experience*. Orion Books, 1984.

———. *Making Peace*. Signature Books, 1995.

———. "The Mormon Cross." *Dialogue: A Journal of Mormon Thought* 8, no. 1 (Spring 1973): 78–86.

——— "On Saving the Constitution, Or Why Some Utah Mormons Should Become Democrats." *Sunstone* (May 1988): 22–30.

Errigo Isabella M., et al. "Human Health and Economic Costs of Air Pollution in Utah." Ben Abbott Lab. January 23, 2020. https://pws.byu.edu/ben-abbott-lab/human-health-and-economic-costs-of-air-pollution-in-utah.

Esplin, Martha Dickey. "Finding Our Bodies, Hearts, Voices—A Three-Part Invention." In *Women in Authority: Reemerging Mormon Feminism*, edited by Maxine Hanks. Signature Books, 1992.

First Presidency Letter to Waldo H. Anderson, president of the Northern States Mission. November 4, 1949. Permission to publish granted by Waldo Anderson's grandsons, James and Neil Anderson.

Flake, Kathleen. "Translating Time: The Nature and Function of Joseph Smith's Narrative Canon." *Journal of Religion* 87, no. 4 (October 2007): 497–527.

Flavelle, Christopher. "As the Great Salt Lake Dries Up, Utah Faces an 'Environmental Nuclear Bomb.'" *The New York Times*. June 7, 2022. https://www.nytimes.com/2022/06/07/climate/salt-lake-city-climate-disaster.html.

Foreman, Madeline, et al., "Genetic Link Between Gender Dysphoria and Sex Hormone Signaling." *The Journal of Clinical Endocrinology & Metabolism* 104, no. 2 (February 2019): 390–96, https://academic.oup.com/jcem/article/104/2/390/5104458.

Gaskill, Alonzo L., and Richard G. Moore, comp. *The Revised and Expanded Teachings of the Prophet Joseph Smith: Compared with the Earliest Known Manuscripts*. Greg Kofford Books, 2024.

Gilligan, Carol. *In a Different Voice: Psychological Theory and Women's Development*. Harvard University Press, 1982.

Givens, Terryl and Fiona Givens. *All Things New: Sin, Salvation, and Everything In Between*. Faith Matters, 2020.

Goldman, Francisco. "Introduction." In *The Gospel According to Matthew*. Grove Press, 1999.

Gordon, Rachael. "The Power of Imagination: A Kabbalistic Understanding." *Chabad* (blog). March 26, 2011. http://www.chabad.org/library/article_cdo/aid/1449301/jewish/The-Power-of-Imagination.htm.

Graham, Linda. *Bouncing Back: Rewiring Your Brain for Maximum Resilience and Well-being*. New World Library, 2013.

Greenberg, Robert. "Bach and the High Baroque." Teaching Company, 1998. Audiotape.

Hanks, Maxine. "Heavenly Mother's Day: Dreaming of the Divine Feminine." *Exponent* II. June 10, 2015. https://www.the-exponent.com/heavenly-mothers-day-dreaming-of-the-divine-feminine/.

———. *Women in Authority: Reemerging Mormon Feminism*. Signature Books, 1992.

Hassan, Ihab. "Fiction and Future: An Extravaganza for Voices and Tape." In *Liberations: New Essays on the Humanities in Revolution*, edited by Ihab Hassan. Wesleyan University Press, 1971.

———, ed. *Liberations: New Essays on the Humanities in Revolution*. Wesleyan University Press, 1971.

Heavey, Susan. "Study links 45,000 U.S. Deaths to Lack of Insurance." *Reuters*. September 17, 2009. http://www.reuters.com/article/2009/09/17/us-usa-healthcare-deaths-idUSTRE58G6W520090917.

"History, circa Summer 1832." The Joseph Smith Papers. https://www.josephsmithpapers.org/paper-summary/history-circa-summer-1832/1?p=1.

Hopkins, Gerard Manley. "As Kingfishers Catch Fire." Poetry Foundation. https://www.poetryfoundation.org/poems/44389/as-kingfishers-catch-fire.

Howard, Jane. "All Happy Clans Are Alike: In Search of the Good Family." *The Atlantic*. May 1, 1978.

Hyman, Naomi M. *Biblical Women in the Midrash: A Sourcebook*. Jason Aronson, 1998.

"Islam: Weekly Summary." Center for Action and Contemplation. September 29, 2018. https://cac.org/islam-weekly-summary-2018-09-29/.

Jessee, Dean C. and John W. Welch. "Revelations in Context: Joseph Smith's Letter from Liberty Jail, March 20, 1839." *BYU Studies* 39, no. 3 (2000): 125–45.

Jessee, Dean C. *The Personal Writings of Joseph Smith*. Deseret Book, 1984.

Kaiser, Jocelyn. "Genetics May Explain Up to 25% of Same-sex Behavior, Giant Analysis Reveals." Science. August 29, 2019. https://www.science.org/content/article/genetics-may-explain-25-same-sex-behavior-giant-analysis-reveals.

Katz, Brigit. "Pando, One of the World's Largest Organisms, Is Dying." *Smithsonian Magazine*. October 18, 2018. https://www.smithsonianmag.com/smart-news/pano-one-worlds-largest-organisms-dying-180970579/.

"KC." "Ten Women in the Book of Mormon." Book of Mormon Online. Accessed June 20, 2009. http://bookofmormononline.net/blog/ten-women-in-the-book-of-mormon/.

Kemsley, Tamarra. "Study shows shifting Latter-day Saint views on LGBTQ rights." *The Salt Lake Tribune*. March 19, 2024. https://www.sltrib.com/religion/2024/03/19/study-shows-shifting-lds-views/.

Kimball, Spencer W. "The False Gods We Worship." *Ensign*. June 1976.

Kohlberg, Lawrence, Charles Levine, and Alexandra Hewer. *Moral Stages: A Current Formulation and A Response to Critics*. Karger, 1983.

Kolbert, Elizabeth. *The Sixth Extinction: An Unnatural History*. Henry Holt, 2014.
Kramer, Stephanie. "U.S. Has World's Highest Rate of Children Living in Single-Parent Households." Pew Research Center. December 12, 2019. https://www.pewresearch.org/religion/2012/01/12/mormons-in-america-family-life/.
Kunst, Judith M. *The Burning Word: A Christian Encounter with Jewish Midrash*. Paraclete Press, 2006.
Leavitt, Chelom E. "Conversations about Intimacy and Sex That Can Prepare You for Marriage." *Ensign*. August 2020. https://www.churchofjesuschrist.org/study/ensign/2020/08/young-adults/conversations-about-intimacy-and-sex-that-can-prepare-you-for-marriage.
Lepore, Jill. "Richer and Poorer: Accounting for Inequality." *The New Yorker*. March 16, 2015.
Lewis, Thomas, et al. *A General Theory of Love*. Vintage Books, 2001.
Webster's Dictionary 1828—Online Edition. http://webstersdictionary1828.com/.
Lopez, Barry. *Crossing Open Ground*. Charles Scribner, 1988.
Madsen, Susan R., Tiffany Turley, and Robbyn T. Scribner. "Sexual Assault Among Utah Women." Utah Women Stats Research Snapshot, no. 15 (November 7, 2016), https://www.usu.edu/uwlp/files/snapshot/15.pdf.
Manning, Wendy D., Marshal Neal Fettro, and Esther Lamidi. "Child Well-Being in Same-Sex Parent Families: Review of Research Prepared for American Sociological Association Amicus Brief." *Population Research and Policy Review* 33 (May 11, 2014): 485–502.
McBaine, Neylan. *Women at Church: Magnifying LDS Women's Local Impact*. Greg Kofford Books, 2014.
Melville, Herman. *Moby Dick*. The Library of America, 1983.
Mitchell, Stephen. *The Gospel According to Jesus*. HarperPerennial, 1993.
Mooney, Chris. "The melting of Antarctica was already really bad. It just got worse." *The Washington Post*. March 16, 2015. http://www.washingtonpost.com/news/energy-environment/wp/2015/03/16/the-melting-of-antarctica-was-already-really-bad-it-just-got-worse/.
Nelson, Russell M. "A Plea to My Sisters." The Church of Jesus Christ of Latter-day Saints. October 2001. https://www.churchofjesuschrist.org/study/general-conference/2015/10/a-plea-to-my-sisters.
———. "Set In Order Thy House." The Church of Jesus Christ of Latter-day Saints. October 2015. https://www.churchofjesuschrist.org/study/general-conference/2001/10/set-in-order-thy-house.
Neruda, Pablo. *One Hundred Love Sonnets: XVII (I don't love you as if you were a rose)*. Poets.org. https://poets.org/poem/one-hundred-love-sonnets-xvii-i-dont-love-you-if-you-were-rose.

New York Times Editorial Board. "Trump Dares the Courts to Stop Him." *The New York Times*. February 13, 2025. https://www.nytimes.com/2025/02/13/opinion/trump-constitutional-crisis.html.

Nibley, Hugh W. *Brother Brigham Challenges the Saints*. FARMS/Deseret Book, 1994.

———. *Since Cumorah: The Book of Mormon in the Modern World*. Deseret Book, 1970.

———. "Subduing the Earth." In *Nibley on the Timely and the Timeless*. Brigham Young University, 1978.

Norton, Elizabeth. "Facial Recognition: Fusiform Gyrus Brain Region 'Solely Devoted' To Faces, Study Suggests." HuffPost. October 24, 2012. https://www.huffpost.com/entry/facial-recognition-brain-fusiform-gyrus_n_2010192.

Nye, Jeff. "Memo from a Mormon: In Which a Troubled Young Man Raises the Question of His Church's Attitude toward Negroes." *Look* 27 no. 21 (October 22, 1963): 74–78.

"Oxfam says wealth of richest 1% equal to other 99%." BBC. January 18, 2016. https://www.bbc.com/news/business-35339475.

Pearson, Carol Lynn. "Could Feminism Have Saved the Nephites?" *Sunstone* 19, no. 1 (1996): 32–40.

Peck, Scott. *The Road Less Travelled: A New Psychology of Love, Traditional Values and Spiritual Growth*. Simon & Schuster, 1978.

Poulsen, David L. and Martin Pulido. "'A Mother There': A Survey of Historical Teachings about Mother in Heaven." *BYU Studies Quarterly* 50, no. 1 (2011): 71–97.

Pray, Kerry. "To Dance in the Dim Light: Meditation on Joy pt. 1." In *The Book of Queer Mormon Joy*, edited by Kerry Pray. Signature Books, 2024.

Prescott, Marianne Holman. "Elder M. Russell Ballard tackles tough topics, shares timely advice with BYU students." Church News. November 14, 2017. https://www.thechurchnews.com/2017/11/14/23213097/elder-m-russell-ballard-tackles-tough-topics-shares-timely-advice-with-byu-students.

Prince, Gregory A. "A Tribute to Lester Bush on the Fiftieth Anniversary of the Article that Changed the Church." *Dialogue: A Journal of Mormon Thought* 57, no. 3 (Fall 2024): 66–82.

Prince, Gregory A., Lester E. Bush Jr., and Brent N. Rushforth. "Gerontocracy and the Future of Mormonism." *Dialogue: A Journal of Mormon Thought* 49, no. 3 (Fall 2016).

"Quaking Aspen." The National Wildlife Federation. https://www.nwf.org/Educational-Resources/Wildlife-Guide/Plants-and-Fungi/Quaking-Aspen.

Rabin, Roni Caryn. "Nearly 1 in 5 Women in U.S. Survey Say They Have Been Sexually Assaulted." *The New York Times*. December 14, 2011. http://www.nytimes.com/2011/12/15/health/nearly-1-in-5-women-in-us-survey-report-sexual-assault.html?_r=0.

"Race and the Priesthood." Gospel Topics Essays. The Church of Jesus Christ of Latter-day Saints. https://www.lds.org/topics/race-and-the-priesthood.

Rees, Robert A. "'Feed My Lambs': Jesus' Last Great Teaching." *Meridian Magazine*. December 15, 2014. http://ldsmag.com/feed-my-lambs-jesus-last-great-teaching/.

———. "Finding Christ at St. Paul the Apostle Church." *Sunstone*. April 28, 2015. https://sunstone.org/finding-christ-at-st-paul-the-apostle-church/.

———. "Monologues and Dialogues: Our Mother In Heaven." *Sunstone* 15 (April 1991): 49–51.

———. "Mother." In *Dove Song: Heavenly Mother in Mormon Poetry*, edited by Tyler Chadwick et al. Peculiar Pages, 2018.

———. "Our Mother in Heaven." *Sunstone* (April 1991): 49–51, https://sunstonemagazine.com/wp-content/uploads/sbi/articles/081-49-51.pdf.

———. "A Perfect Brightness of Hope." *Wayfare*. July 5, 2023. https://www.wayfaremagazine.org/p/a-perfect-brightness-of-hope.

———, ed. *Proving Contraries: A Collection of Writings in Honor of Eugene England*. Signature Books, 2005.

Richards, Stephen L. "Bringing Humanity to the Gospel." *Sunstone* (May–June 1979): 43–46.

Riess, Jana. "Jana Riess: A fifth of LDS college students in the U.S. don't identify as heterosexual." *The Salt Lake Tribune*. September 22, 2023. https://www.sltrib.com/religion/2023/09/22/jana-riess-fifth-lds-college/.

———. "Jana Riess: Who is leaving the LDS Church? Eight key survey findings." *The Salt Lake Tribune*. March 8, 2024. https://www.sltrib.com/religion/2024/03/08/jana-riess-who-is-leaving-lds/.

———. *The Next Mormons: How Millennials Are Changing the LDS Church*. Oxford University Press, 2019.

———. "Update — Jana Riess: There are more young lesbian, gay or bisexual Latter-day Saints than previously believed." *The Salt Lake Tribune*. June 21, 2021. https://www.sltrib.com/religion/2021/06/21/jana-riess-there-are-more/.

Roberts, B. H. *The Seventy's Course in Theology*. 1912.

———. "Two Kinds of Disciples." *The Improvement Era* 9, no. 9 (July 1, 1906): 707–13.

Robinson, Marilynn. *Gilead*. Farrar, Straus and Giroux, 2004.

Rohr, Richard. "Love Needs a Face." The Center for Action and Contemplation. January 15, 2018. https://cac.org/love-needs-face-2018-01-15/.

———. "The One Face and the Everything." The Center for Action and Contemplation. July 18, 2014. https://myemail.constantcontact.com/Richard-Rohr-s-Meditation--The-One-Face-and-the-Everything.html.

Sasso, Sandy Isenberg. *God's Echo: Exploring Scripture with Midrash*. Paraclete Press, 2007.

Semerad, Tony. "LDS Church on its way to becoming a trillion-dollar faith." *The Salt Lake Tribune.* July 16, 2023. https://www.sltrib.com/religion/2023/07/16/lds-church-its-way-becoming/.

Silesius, Angelus. "Angelus Silesius Quotes." AZ Quotes. https://www.azquotes.com/author/19709-Angelus_Silesius.

Smith, George A. "History of George Albert Smith by Himself." George Albert Smith, Papers, 1834–75, Church Archives.

Smith, Joseph F. "Message of the First Presidency." Report of the Annual Conference of The Church of Jesus Christ of Latter-day Saints. April 6, 1942. The Church of Jesus Christ of Latter-day Saints, 1942.

———. "Our Duty to Humanity, to God, and to Country." *Improvement Era* 20, no. 7 (May 1917): 645–56.

Sonntag, Kathryn Knight. *The Mother Tree: Discovering the Love and Wisdom of Our Divine.* Faith Matters, 2022.

Sorenson, John. "Mormon World View and American Culture." *Dialogue: A Journal of Mormon Thought* 8, no. 2 (Summer 1973): 17–29.

"Species Extinction." Environmental Issues. January 25, 2018. https://sites.psu.edu/sarahmarshcivicissues/2018/01/25/species-extinction/.

Stack, Peggy Fletcher. "LDS Church's newest apostle talks singles, women and LGBTQ members in sit-down interview." *The Salt Lake Tribune.* January 4, 2024. https://www.sltrib.com/religion/2024/01/23/tribune-interview-patrick-kearon/.

———. "A Mormon mystery returns: Who is Heavenly Mother?" *The Salt Lake Tribune.* May 16, 2013. https://archive.sltrib.com/article.php?id=56282764&itype=cmsid.

Stone, Ann Gardner. "Mother." In *Dove Song: Heavenly Mother in Mormon Poetry*, edited by Tyler Chadwick et al. Peculiar Pages, 2018.

Sullivan, John O. "Introduction." In *The United States Magazine and Democratic Review.* 1837.

Taylor, Barry. "Mary the Apocalypse." Sermon delivered at All Saint's Episcopal Church. December 23, 2012. Typescript in author's possession.

Thoreau, Henry David. "Civil Disobedience." 1849.

"Tikkun Olam: The Spiritual Purpose of Life." Inner Frontier. http://www.innerfrontier.org/Practices/TikkunOlam.htm.

Tippitt, Krista. "Transcript for Jaroslav Pelikan—The Need for Creeds." On Being. April 23, 2014. http://www.onbeing.org/program/jaroslav-pelikan-the-need-for-creeds/transcript/6285#main_content.

Todd, Mabel Loomis, ed. *Letters of Emily Dickinson.* New York: Gosset and Dunlap, 1962.

"Transcript for Arthur Zajonc and Michael McCullough—Mind and Morality: A Dialogue." On Being. Last updated March 12, 2015. https://onbeing.org/programs/arthur-zajonc-michael-mccullough-mind-and-morality-a-dialogue/.

Uchtdorf, Dieter F. "Are You Sleeping through the Restoration?" The Church of Jesus Christ of Latter-day Saints. April 2014. https://www.churchofjesuschrist.org/study/general-conference/2014/04/are-you-sleeping-through-the-restoration.
"UN Report: Nature's Dangerous Decline 'Unprecedented'; Species Extinction Rates 'Accelerating.'" Sustainable Development Goals. May 6, 2019. https://www.un.org/sustainabledevelopment/blog/2019/05/nature-decline-unprecedented-report/.
Ward, Ryan. *And There Was No Poor Among Them: Liberation, Salvation and the Meaning of the Restoration*. Greg Kofford Books, 2023.
Weaver, Sarah Jane. "First Presidency Discontinues One-Year Waiting Period for Temple Sealings after Civil Marriage." Church News. May 7, 2019. https://www.churchofjesuschrist.org/church/news/first-presidency-discontinues-one-year-waiting-period-for-temple-sealings-after-civil-marriage.
Webb, Stephen. *Mormon Christianity: What Other Christians Can Learn from the Latter-day Saints*. Oxford University Press, 2013.
Welch, J. Gregory and John W. Welch. *Charting the Book of Mormon*. FARMS/Maxwell Center, 1999.
Whitney, Orson F. "Bishop O. F. Whitney." *Woman's Exponent* 24, no. 2 (June 15, 1895): 9–10.
Williams, Camille. "Women in the Book of Mormon: Inclusion, Exclusion, and Interpretation." *Journal of Book of Mormon Studies* 11, no. 1 (2002). https://scholarsarchive.byu.edu/cgi/viewcontent.cgi?article=1346&context=jbms.
Williams, William Carlos. "The Gift." *The Collected Poems of William Carlos Williams, Volume 2: 1939–1962*. New Directions, 1991.
Wiman, Christian. *My Bright Abyss: Meditation of a Modern Believer*. Farrar, Straus and Giroux, 2013.
Wink, Walter. *The Powers That Be: Theology for a New Millennium*. Doubleday, 1999.
Wolpe, David. *The Healer of Shattered Hearts*. Henry Holt, 1990.
Wotherspoon, Daniel. "To Grow the Kingdom." In *Why I Stay: The Challenges of Discipleship for Contemporary Latter-day Saints*, edited by Robert A. Rees. Signature Books, 2021.
Wright, N. T. "The Bible and Christian Imagination," *Response* 28, no. 2 (Summer 2005). https://spu.edu/depts/uc/response/summer2k5/features/imagination.asp.
Zuckerman, Esther. "The Mormon Church Takes In $7 Billion a Year." *The Atlantic*. August 14, 2012. http://www.thewire.com/global/2012/08/mormon-church-gets-7-billion-year/55755/.

Index

Ackroyd, Peter, 7
Allred, Janice, 43
And There Was No Poor Among Them: Liberation, Salvation and the Meaning of the Restoration, 166
Anderson, Lavina Fielding, 91–92
angel, 8–9
  Gabriel, 7–8, 23, 53–55
  seraphim, 11
Ashment, Edward, 77

Bach, Johann Sebastian, 7, 25, 121–24
Ball, Terryl B., 133
Ballard, Russell M., 117
Bates, Irene, 110
Baxter, Nathan, 123–24
Bird, Phyllis, 89
Bloom, Harold, 2–3, 14
Book of Mormon prophets
  Alma, 12–13
  Alma the elder, 136
  Nephi, 8–9, 14
  Nephi (son of Nephi), 11–12
Book of Queer Mormon Joy, The, 109
Botticelli, Sandro, 58–59
Bradley, Raymond, 139
Bradshaw, William S., 110–11, 113
Brigham Young University, 76–77, 109
Bronner, Leila Leah, 83–85, 93
Brooks, Joanna, 43
Brothers Karamozov, The, 157
Brown, Hugh B., 169–70
Burton, H. David, 165
Bush, Lester Jr., 76–79

Capote, Truman, 14
Carlston, Jim, 109
Carver, Raymond, 173–74

Christ
  as advocate, 24
  as Messiah, 9, 53
  Atonement, 12–13, 15
  birth, 7–10, 14
  crucifixion, 127–28
  imagination of, 11–13, 15, 160
  in Americas, 11–12
  light of, 24, 173–74
  ministry, 60, 86, 164
  parables, 135–36, 139–40, 147
  resurrection, 129–31
Church, the
  as mirror, 141–42
  authority, 67–68, 70, 73, 119–20, 150–51
  brokenness of, 64–66
  bureaucracy, 67
  character of, 148–50
  conservatism, 68
  financial transparency, 69
  international, 68–69
  repairing, 63–66, 70–73
  patriarchy, 69, 82
  Plan of Salvation, 141
  polygamy, 35, 91, 115–16
  Proposition 8, 66
  purpose of, 156
  tolerance, 154–55
  unified, 168–69, 172
  Zion, 122
Clark, J. Reuben Jr., 75
creation, 4–5, 133
  God's, 1, 10, 23–24

Dickinson, Emily, 34–35, 39, 159
Dillard, Annie, 71
Durant, Will, 27

earth stewardship, 137–40
　climate change, 134–35
　extinction, 134
　Great Salt Lake, 137–38
　Pando, 138–39
Ehrman, Bart, 163–64
England, Eugene, 77, 167–71
Esplin, Martha Dickey, 40

face of God, 17–19, 22–23, 38
families, 105–8, 111–15
　connection, 112–12
feminism, 162–64
Flake, Kathleen, 2–3, 139
Frost, Robert, 49

Gardner, Neville, 10
Givens, Terryl and Fiona, 33
Goldman, Francisco, 135–36
Graetz, Naomi, 86
Graham, Linda, 20–21
Grant, Heber J., 165

Hanks, Marion D., 78
Hanks, Maxine, 39–40, 43
Hassan, Ihab, 1
Hawkins, Lisa Bolin, 43
Heavenly Mother, 91–92, 164
　co-creator, 36–37, 49–50, 61
　existence, 33–35, 45–48, 51
　hidden god, 36
　progression, 40–41
heavenly parents, 13, 21–25, 36, 42, 91, 114–15, 136, 164
Holy Week, 121–26
　Passover, 121
Hopkins, Gerard Manly, 24, 60
Howard, Jane, 105
Howe, Marie, 55
Howe, Susan Elizabeth, 44
Hyman, Naomi M., 81–85, 94

imagination, 1–5, 7, 10, 42, 159, 168–72

Jay, Emma, 44
Jeffers, Robinson, 133
Jewish midrash, 18, 23, 82–84
　Dinah, story of, 85–86
　gaps in, 87–88
Johnson, Melody Newly, 44

Kaiser, Jocelyn, 111
Kimball, Spencer W., 78–79, 166
Kearon, Patrick, 117
Kepler, Johannes, 1
Kelser, John, 149
Kohlberg, Lawrence, 144–52, 156
Kunst, Judith M., 81, 83, 93–94

Lens of Love, Eye of Universal Consciousness, The, 139
LGBTQ, 69, 105–20
　definition of marriage, 115–16
　myths, 108–10
　research, 108, 110–14, 116–17
liberal, 68, 159–60, 169
Lopez, Barry, 135, 139
Luria, Isaac, 63

Mary, 23, 87, 127–31
　annunciation, 53–55, 61
　mother of Jesus, 9, 12, 53, 56–57
　prophet, 56
　teacher, 57
Massai, the, 10
Matthew 25, 135–36
McBaine, Neylan, 163
McConkie, Bruce R., 77
McKay, David O., 75
Melville, Herman, 143–44
Moby Dick, 143–44
Mormon midrash, 89–91
　Abish, story of, 90, 101–4
　prodigal daughter, the, 87, 95–99
Mother's Milk: Poems in Search of Heavenly Mother, 42

Nelson, Russell M., 68, 79, 163
Neruda, Pablo, 112–13
Nibley, Hugh, 77, 133–34, 140, 166–67

O'Donohue, John, 5–6

Packer, Boyd K., 77
Page, S. E., 43
peacemakers, 166–68
Pearson, Carol Lynn, 42–43, 88–89
Peck, M. Scott, 155, 171
Penny, Jonathon, 43
Poulsen, David L., 36–37
Pray, Kerry, 109
Prince, Greg, 78–79
progressive, 4, 68, 161
Pulido, Martin, 36–37, 44

racism, 75–77, 151
    priesthood ban, 69–70, 75–79
Reger, Will, 43
Restoration, the, 2, 14, 18, 33, 35, 39, 72–73, 117, 126, 161–62, 169–72
revelation, 2–5, 9, 19, 94
Richards, Stephen L., 160
Riess, Jana, 108, 116
Rigdon, Sidney, 19–20
Robb, Charles, 123
Roberts, B. H., 3–4, 63, 94
Robinson, Marilynn, 13–14
Rohr, Richard, 18, 21
Rouanzion, Taylor, 43
Rumi, 49, 120, 147–48

Sasso, Sandy Eisenberg, 81, 83–85
Schaling, Martin, 25
Shakers, 105, 120
Shashaani, Avideh, 17
Silesius, Angelus, 14
Smith, Emma, 29–31, 91
Smith, Joseph, 2–4, 14, 33, 39, 79, 139, 159, 170
    death of, 22, 24–25, 31
    First Vision, 17–23, 27–29, 31, 126
    imagination of, 18
    visions, 19–20
Smith, Sophronia, 91
Snow, Eliza R., 92
Snow, Lorenzo, 40
Sonntag, Kathryn Knight, 44
spiritual matter, 23–24
Steenblick, Rachael Hunt, 42, 44
Stack, Peggy Fletcher, 35–36
Swing, William E., 125

Taylor, John, 24–25
Thomas, Lewis, 112–13
Thomas, Robert K., 77
Thomasson, Gordon, 77
Thoreau, Henry David, 150
Timpson, Tara, 44

Ward, Ryan, 166
Webb, Stephen, 19–20
Wellborn, Terresa, 43
Welty, Eudora, 11
Williams, Camille, 88–89
Williams, William Carlos, 7
Wiman, Christian, 171
Wolpe, David, 10, 23–24, 64
Women at Church: Magnifying LDS Women's Local Impact, 163
Wright, N. T., 14–15

Yeats, William Butler, 33
Young, Brigham, 78–79

Zajonc, Arthur, 140
Zen, 151–52
Zones, Jane Sprague, 93

Also available from
GREG KOFFORD BOOKS

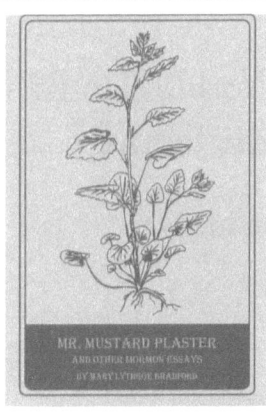

Mr. Mustard Plaster and Other Mormon Essays

Mary Lythgoe Bradford

ISBN: 978-1-58958-742-7

"Mary Bradford is the original literary 'Mormon Girl.' Long before anyone even imagined the bloggernacle, she believed that writing about everyday Mormon life—especially women's lives—could be beautiful and powerful. In her own essays, she brings unparalleled power of perception, generous humanity, and quiet humor to bear on even challenging Mormon subjects. This book is an incredible opportunity for a new generation of Mormon readers to get to know one of our faith's wise women elders. Don't miss it." — Joanna Brooks, author of *The Book of Mormon Girl: A Memoir of an American Faith*

"Mary Bradford believes that the distinctive nature of the personal essay originates from what she calls the three "I's" ("I's," eyes, ayes)—the authors' first-person perspective, their clear and rich vision, and their honest and affirming testimonies of life. Mary's own essays are true to form: her essays are vibrant portraits of a kind and loving soul, a rich and unique perspective, and a life well-lived and deeply loved." — Boyd Jay Petersen, author of *Dead Wood and Rushing Water: Essays on Mormon Faith, Culture, and Family*

"Mary Lythgoe Bradford offers her autobiography in personal essay—revealing a lifetime that bridged generations and pioneered the power of essay in Mormon literature. Since the first issue of Dialogue in 1966, Mary's wisdom and presence as an editor, writer, poet and biographer have linked us together, reaching back to women like Virginia Sorensen and moving us forward into feminism. Today at 84, Mary is still helping 'Mormon women speak.'" — Maxine Hanks, editor of *Women and Authority: Re-emerging Mormon Feminism*

The End of the World, Plan B: A Guide for the Future

Charles Shirō Inouye

Paperback, ISBN: 978-1-58958-755-7

Praise for *End of the World, Plan B*:

"Mormonism needs Inouye's voice. We need, in general, voices that are a bit less Ayn Rand and a bit more Siddhartha Gautama. Inouye reminds us that justice is not enough and that obedience is not the currency of salvation. He urges us to recognize the limits of the law, to see that, severed from a willingness to compassionately suffer with the world's imperfection and evanescence, our righteous hunger for balancing life's books will destroy us all."
— Adam S. Miller, author of *Rube Goldberg Machines: Essays in Mormon Theology* and *Letters to a Young Mormon*

"Drawing on Christian, Buddhist, Daoist, and other modes of thought, Charles Inouye shows how an attitude of hope can arise from a narrative of doom. The End of the World, Plan B is not simply a rethinking of the end of our world, but is a meditation on the possibility of compassionate self-transformation. In a world that looks to the just punishment of the wicked, Inouye shows how sorrow, which comes from the demands of justice, can create peace, forgiveness, and love."
— Michael D.K. Ing, Assistant Professor, Department of Religious Studies, Indiana University

"For years I've hoped to see a book that related Mormonism to the great spiritual traditions beyond Christianity and Judaism. Charles Inouye has done this in one of the best Mormon devotional books I've ever read. His Mormon reading of the fourfold path of the Bodhisattva offers a beautiful eschatology of the end/purpose of the world as the revelation of compassion. I hope the book is read widely."
— James M. McLachlan, co-editor of *Discourses in Mormon Theology: Philosophical and Theological Possibilities*

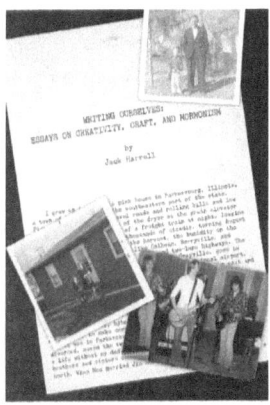

Writing Ourselves: Essays on Creativity, Craft, and Mormonism

Jack Harrell

Paperback, ISBN: 978-1-58958-754-0

Continuing a conversation as old as Mormonism itself, Jack Harrell explores the relationship between Mormonism and the writer. Mormons see the universe in mythic proportions. Their God is a creator, their devil a destroyer. This makes meaningful conflict fundamental to their worldview, and begs the terms for religious redemption, as well as the redemptive power of art. Harrell urges writers to be authentic as they embrace the difficulties inherent in the creative process. His essays blend faithful intellectual inquiry, personal narrative, research, and application to offer insights for anyone who cares about writing, creativity, and the human condition.

And There Was No Poor Among Them: Liberation, Salvation, and the Meaning of the Restoration

Ryan D. Ward

Paperback, ISBN: 978-1-58958-787-8

While The Church of Jesus Christ of Latter-day Saints has expanded many fundamental Christian doctrines, salvation is still understood as pertaining exclusively to the next life. How should we understand salvation and what does the timing of the Restoration reveal about God's vision of salvation for a suffering world?

To answer these questions, author Ryan Ward traces the theological evolution of salvation from the liberation of Israel from oppression to the Western Christian development of salvation as an individualistic, transactional atonement. This evolution corresponded with the shift of Christianity from a covenant community to an official state religion aligned with imperial power structures. Ward also explores the economic and social movements in the centuries leading up to the Industrial Revolution, which solidified the power of propertied elites at the expense of the poor, plundered entire continents, and killed millions.

Synthesizing these theological and historical threads, *And There Was No Poor Among Them: Liberation, Salvation, and the Meaning of the Restoration* asserts that the Restoration is God's explicit rejection of social and economic systems and ideologies that have led to the globalization of misery. Instead, Ward shows how the Restoration and the gospel of Christ is an invitation to a participatory salvation realized in Zion communities where "there are no poor among us."

Praise for *And There Was No Poor Among Them*:

"This a profound and profoundly important book, one of the most compelling in the history of modern Mormonism. . . . If I had the power, I would make *And There Was No Poor Among Them* required reading of every local, regional, and general leader of the Church." — Robert A. Rees, co-founder and vice-president of the Bountiful Children's Foundation

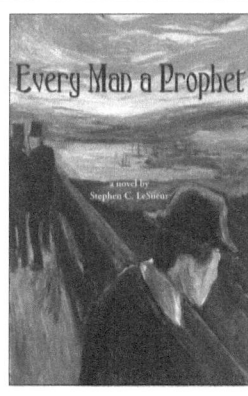

Every Man a Prophet

A Novel by
Stephen C. LeSueur

Paperback, ISBN: 978-1-58958-826-4

Every Man a Prophet by Stephen C. LeSueur is a powerful exploration of faith, love, and self-discovery set within the framework of missionary life in The Church of Jesus Christ of Latter-day Saints. Eddie Pedersen and Orrin Tanner, two missionaries serving in Norway, each grapple with the weight of expectation, personal desires, and the search for their true selves. Eddie struggles to reconcile his faith with feelings he has been taught to suppress, while Orrin's relentless pursuit of perfection masks a deep fear of failure. Together, they navigate a land of cold landscapes and colder hearts, striving to find meaning and connection in their spiritual calling.

Through Eddie and Orrin's intertwined journeys, LeSueur crafts a deeply human story of vulnerability and resilience. The novel delves into the complexities of identity, faith, and the universal longing to belong. As the two men confront the rigid doctrines of their religion and the unyielding truths of their own hearts, readers are drawn into an unforgettable narrative of courage and redemption. *Every Man a Prophet* is a profound tale of the sacrifices we make for faith and the truths we uncover about ourselves along the way..

Praise for *Every Man a Prophet*:

"In *Every Man a Prophet*, not only has Stephen C. LeSueur captured the lives, desires, trials, and struggles of young missionaries and their leaders better than in any other work I have encountered, **he has gifted the world with the best volume of Mormon fiction that I have read.** *Every Man a Prophet* touches hearts, opens minds, and changes lives. . . . It is a book that has the power to touch and change lives and maybe even wards, missions, and the Church." — Andrew Hamilton, Reviews Coordinator, Association for Mormon Letters

Shall I Have Pleasure?
An Answer for Sarah

Zachary McLeod Hutchins

Paperback, ISBN: 978-1-58958-819-6

Shall I Have Pleasure? An Answer for Sarah explores the complex relationship between faith, desire, and the pursuit of joy through a spiritual and philosophical lens. Drawing from religious narratives, scriptural analysis, and theological insights, the book delves into how pleasure is perceived within Christian traditions, particularly among members of The Church of Jesus Christ of Latter-day Saints. Through reflective anecdotes, historical context, and doctrinal interpretations, the author challenges the tension between spiritual duty and sensory enjoyment, encouraging readers to reconcile divine purpose with the pursuit of happiness.

Rooted in scripture and enriched by personal storytelling, this thought-provoking work invites readers to reconsider long-held beliefs about pleasure and self-denial. By examining biblical stories like Sarah's incredulous laughter at the promise of joy in old age, as well as Christ's compassionate acceptance of human love and generosity, the book offers a fresh perspective on living a life of spiritual fulfillment that embraces joy as an essential part of divine intent. Through this lens, *Shall I Have Pleasure?* becomes a call to rediscover pleasure as a God-given gift intertwined with human purpose and eternal potential.

Praise for *Shall I Have Pleasure?*:

"'Men are, that they might have joy.' But many Latter-day Saints are ambivalent towards—or even skeptical of— the role of pleasure in the joy God wants for us. In *Shall I Have Pleasure?* Zachary Hutchins responds to this confusion with a beautiful and profound affirmation of the divine goodness and gift of pleasure. He invites readers to see pleasure not as a temptation to avoid but an essential and cherished part of our embodied life." — Zachary Davis, Executive Director of Faith Matters and Editor of *Wayfare Magazine*

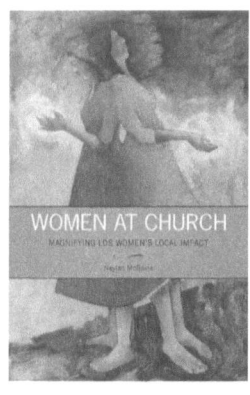

Women at Church: Magnifying LDS Women's Local Impact

Neylan McBaine

Paperback, ISBN: 978-1-58958-688-8

Women at Church is a practical and faithful guide to improving the way men and women work together at church. Looking at current administrative and cultural practices, the author explains why some women struggle with the gendered divisions of labor. She then examines ample real-life examples that are currently happening in local settings around the country that expand and reimagine gendered practices. Readers will understand how to evaluate possible pain points in current practices and propose solutions that continue to uphold all mandated church policies. Readers will be equipped with the tools they need to have respectful, empathetic and productive conversations about gendered practices in Church administration and culture.

Praise for *Women at Church*:

"Such a timely, faithful, and practical book! I suggest ordering this book in bulk to give to your bishopric, stake presidency, and all your local leadership to start a conversation on changing Church culture for women by letting our doctrine suggest creative local adaptations—Neylan McBaine shows the way!" — Valerie Hudson Cassler, author of *Women in Eternity, Women of Zion*

"A pivotal work replete with wisdom and insight. Neylan McBaine deftly outlines a workable programme for facilitating movement in the direction of the 'privileges and powers' promised the nascent Female Relief Society of Nauvoo." — Fiona Givens, co-author of *The God Who Weeps: How Mormonism Makes Sense of Life*

"In her timely and brilliant findings, Neylan McBaine issues a gracious invitation to rethink our assumptions about women's public Church service. Well researched, authentic, and respectful of the current Church administrative structure, McBaine shares exciting and practical ideas that address diverse needs and involve all members in the meaningful work of the Church." — Camille Fronk Olson, author of *Women of the Old Testament* and *Women of the New Testament*

Whom Say Ye That I Am? Lessons from the Jesus of Nazareth

James W. McConkie
and Judith E. McConkie

Paperback, ISBN: 978-1-58958-707-6

"This book is the most important Jesus study to date written by believing Mormons for an LDS audience. It opens the door for Mormons to come to know a Jesus most readers will know little about—the Jesus of history." — David Bokovoy, author of *Authoring the Old Testament: Genesis–Deuteronomy*

"Meticulously documented and researched, the authors have crafted an insightful and enlightening book that allows Jesus to speak by providing both wisdom and council. The McConkies masterfully weave in sources from the Gospels, ancient and modern scholars, along with Christian and non-Christian religious leaders." — *Deseret News*

The story of Jesus is frequently limited to the telling of the babe of Bethlehem who would die on the cross and three days later triumphantly exit his tomb in resurrected glory. Frequently skimmed over or left aside is the story of the Jesus of Nazareth who confronted systemic injustice, angered those in power, risked his life for the oppressed and suffering, and worked to preach and establish the Kingdom of God—all of which would lead to his execution on Calvary.

In this insightful and moving volume, authors James and Judith McConkie turn to the latest scholarship on the historical and cultural background of Jesus to discover lessons on what we can learn from his exemplary life. Whether it be his intimate interactions with the sick, the poor, women, and the outcast, or his public confrontations with oppressive religious, political, and economic institutions, Jesus of Nazareth—the son of a carpenter, Messiah, and Son of God—exemplified the way, the truth, and the life that we must follow to bring about the Kingdom of Heaven.

Future Mormon: Essays in Mormon Theology

Adam S. Miller

Paperback, ISBN: 978-1-58958-509-6

From the Introduction:

I have three children, a girl and two boys. Our worlds overlap but, already, these worlds are not the same. Their worlds, the worlds that they will grow to fill, are already taking leave of mine. Their futures are already wedged into our present. This is both heartening and frightening. So much of our world deserves to be left. So much of it deserves to be scrapped and recycled. But, too, this scares me. I worry that a lot of what has mattered most to me in this world—Mormonism in particular—may be largely unintelligible to them in theirs. This problem isn't new, but it is perpetually urgent. Every generation must start again. Every generation must work out their own salvation. Every generation must live its own lives and think its own thoughts and receive its own revelations. And, if Mormonism continues to matter, it will be because they, rather than leaving, were willing to be Mormon all over again. Like our grandparents, like our parents, and like us, they will have to rethink the whole tradition, from top to bottom, right from the beginning, and make it their own in order to embody Christ anew in this passing world. To the degree that we can help, our job is to model that work in love and then offer them the tools, the raw materials, and the room to do it themselves.

These essays are a modest contribution in this vein, a future tense apologetics meant for future Mormons. They model, I hope, a thoughtful and creative engagement with Mormon ideas while sketching, without obligation, possible directions for future thinking.

Rube Goldberg Machines: Essays in Mormon Theology

Adam S. Miller

Paperback, ISBN: 978-1-58958-193-7

"Adam Miller is the most original and provocative Latter-day Saint theologian practicing today."

—Richard Bushman, author of *Joseph Smith: Rough Stone Rolling*

"As a stylist, Miller gives Nietzsche a run for his money. As a believer, Miller is as submissive as Augustine hearing a child's voice in the garden. Miller is a theologian of the ordinary, thinking about our ordinary beliefs in very non-ordinary ways while never insisting that the ordinary become extra-ordinary."

—James Faulconer, Richard L. Evans Chair of Religious Understanding, Brigham Young University

"Miller's language is both recognizably Mormon and startlingly original. . . . The whole is an essay worthy of the name, inviting the reader to try ideas, following the philosopher pilgrim's intellectual progress through tangled brambles and into broad fields, fruitful orchards, and perhaps a sacred grove or two."

—Kristine Haglund, editor of *Dialogue: A Journal of Mormon Thought*

"Miller's Rube Goldberg theology is nothing like anything done in the Mormon tradition before."

—Blake Ostler, author of the Exploring Mormon Thought series

"The value of Miller's writings is in the modesty he both exhibits and projects onto the theological enterprise, even while showing its joyfully disruptive potential. Conventional Mormon minds may not resonate with every line of poetry and provocation—but Miller surely afflicts the comfortable, which is the theologian's highest end."

—Terryl Givens, author of *By the Hand of Mormon: The American Scripture that Launched a New World Religion*

Dead Wood and Rushing Water: Essays on Mormon Faith, Culture, and Family

Boyd Jay Petersen

Paperback, ISBN: 978-1-58958-658-1

For over a decade, Boyd Petersen has been an active voice in Mormon studies and thought. In essays that steer a course between apologetics and criticism, striving for the balance of what Eugene England once called the "radical middle," he explores various aspects of Mormon life and culture—from the Dream Mine near Salem, Utah, to the challenges that Latter-day Saints of the millennial generation face today.

Praise for *Dead Wood and Rushing Water*:

"*Dead Wood and Rushing Water* gives us a reflective, striving, wise soul ruminating on his world. In the tradition of Eugene England, Petersen examines everything in his Mormon life from the gold plates to missions to dream mines to doubt and on to Glenn Beck, Hugh Nibley, and gender. It is a book I had trouble putting down." — Richard L. Bushman, author of *Joseph Smith: Rough Stone Rolling*

"Boyd Petersen is correct when he says that Mormons have a deep hunger for personal stories—at least when they are as thoughtful and well-crafted as the ones he shares in this collection." — Jana Riess, author of *The Twible* and *Flunking Sainthood*

"Boyd Petersen invites us all to ponder anew the verities we hold, sharing in his humility, tentativeness, and cheerful confidence that our paths will converge in the end." — Terryl. L. Givens, author of *People of Paradox: A History of Mormon Culture*

For Zion:
A Mormon Theology of Hope

Joseph M. Spencer

Paperback, ISBN: 978-1-58958-568-3

What is hope? What is Zion? And what does it mean to hope for Zion? In this insightful book, Joseph Spencer explores these questions through the scriptures of two continents separated by nearly two millennia. In the first half, Spencer engages in a rich study of Paul's letter to the Roman to better understand how the apostle understood hope and what it means to have it. In the second half of the book, Spencer jumps to the early years of the Restoration and the various revelations on consecration to understand how Latter-day Saints are expected to strive for Zion. Between these halves is an interlude examining the hoped-for Zion that both thrived in the Book of Mormon and was hoped to be established again.

Praise for *For Zion*:

"Joseph Spencer is one of the most astute readers of sacred texts working in Mormon Studies. Blending theological savvy, historical grounding, and sensitive readings of scripture, he has produced an original and compelling case for consecration and the life of discipleship." — Terryl Givens, author, *Wrestling the Angel: The Foundations of Mormon Thought*

"*For Zion: A Mormon Theology of Hope* is more than a theological reflection. It also consists of able textual exegesis, historical contextualization, and philosophic exploration. Spencer's careful readings of Paul's focus on hope in Romans and on Joseph Smith's development of consecration in his early revelations, linking them as he does with the Book of Mormon, have provided an intriguing, intertextual avenue for understanding what true stewardship should be for us—now and in the future. As such he has set a new benchmark for solid, innovative Latter-day Saint scholarship that is at once provocative and challenging." — Eric D. Huntsman, author, *The Miracles of Jesus*

www.ingramcontent.com/pod-product-compliance
Lightning Source LLC
Chambersburg PA
CBHW030411170426
43202CB00010B/1575